Meditations on FARMING

Cataloging-in-Publication Data is available from the Library of Congress.

978-1-61249-996-3 (paperback)

978-1-61249-997-0 (epub)

978-1-61249-998-7 (epdf)

Cover image: Old abandoned silhouetted house and barn with beautiful sunset: nathan4847/iStock via Getty Images Plus.

The Agrarian Drive, Stress, and Mental Health

MICHAEL R. ROSMANN

Purdue University Press · West Lafayette, Indiana

CONTENTS

PREFACE

M editations on Farming: The Agrarian Drive, Stress, and Mental Health took twelve years to complete after my first book, Excellent Joy: Fishing, Farming, Hunting, and Psychology. Similar to Excellent Joy, I wanted to say everything just right in this book. It encapsulates much of my life's work since resigning as assistant professor of psychology at the University of Virginia to move to a family farm and to apply my skills as a psychologist in western Iowa. When I announced the decision to my research associates in January 1979, a third-year graduate student whose master's thesis I was supervising asked, "Why are you leaving the University of Virginia to work with farmers?"

At first unsure what to say, I drew on what I felt in my heart: "Somebody has to take care of the mental health of farmers." Five months later we arrived in Iowa, just as the farm crisis of the 1980s was ramping up. Over the next forty-five years, I tried to figure out why farming was so incredibly stressful and why so many farmers turned to suicide when foreclosure threatened or caused the loss of their family farm. In 2000, like-minded colleagues and I formed a seven-state, nonprofit corporation that undertook longitudinal research that drew on our past experiences serving the agricultural population. We tested models of assisting the agricultural population to determine the best practices that assisted distressed farm and ranch families, as well as farm workers and communities dependent mainly on agriculture for their economic livelihood. You will read about this difficult—and very rewarding—journey.

Many people have encouraged me to write this book because they have been drawn to its information and to my agrarian imperative theory as the most compelling explanation yet for why people farm, and why distressed farmers' mental health differs from the general population, including one of the highest—or the highest—rate of suicide, depending on the study cited. Meditations on Farming was a natural fit because it is through meditation that I developed an understanding of my purpose in life, figuring out what needs to be done to improve the behavioral well-being of farmers, ranchers, farm workers, and the agricultural community.

The subtitle, *The Agrarian Drive, Stress, and Mental Health*, required testing lots of ideas that seemed well-suited, at first. I rejected all of them eventually, because feedback from people whose opinions I value pointed out matters that I had not considered adequately. We had healthy debates about using the words "behavioral health" versus "mental health," and about the intriguing concept that all humans still today contain variations in our genomes, which include the survival characteristics that facilitated the development of farming. The subtitle's words, *The Agrarian Drive, Stress, and Mental Health*, seem right. Understanding how our behaviors affect our overall well-being is becoming recognized as a key to success as farmers and in other walks of life. I can proudly say that the book title passed "the Marilyn test," which is important for me, because my wife sees things that I sometimes miss. She criticizes my words and concepts honestly, and she can be very direct if I seem hardheaded when I ask her to review the articles I write for agricultural publications and newspapers. Marilyn never lost hope that I would refine the title until it was right.

You will read about many of my personal travails and what I learned from them. You also will learn some of the knowledge I accumulated from consulting with farmer organizations, as well as federal and state agencies, giving workshops around the country and abroad, answering tough questions during radio and television interviews, and contributing to many major newspapers and magazines respected for their thorough reporting.

As my experiences working with farmers accumulated, I probably learned more from them than they learned from me. I cannot call most of what I do work, because my actions are mostly undertaken out of love for what I do, which is taking care of farmers' mental health and overall well-being. Moreover, when I help others, I feel useful and appreciated. All of my efforts serve a passion that has been, and continues to be, incredibly meaningful. When I moved my office to my home in 2014, I continued to visit farmers at their homes when they asked me to meet with them. I consulted with five to ten other people weekly, mostly farmers who contacted me by email and telephone, but also students, reporters, and program administrators seeking information. I continued to write my syndicated columns about improving the well-being of agricultural producers for many farm newspapers and magazines. Some of the ideas expressed in the columns are included in this book.

Among some of the most informative travels was a trip to Italy in 2017 when our son and his wife joined Marilyn, me, and a few other travelers associated with Clarkson College in Omaha as we accompanied some twenty Clarkson students in nursing. The students were enrolled in my wife's course, "International Healthcare." We spent a day at a teaching hospital in Florence and visited an ancient-but-still-operating health spa, a farm vintner where we enjoyed home-produced wine with dinner, and many historic and cultural sites in Rome, Siena, and Venice, besides Florence, as well as the countryside. Marilyn and I spent a day at a typical southern Italian farm to learn about agrarian culture in that lovely country and to gather information for my *Farm and Ranch Life* columns and for an article that was invited for the *Journal of Biourbanism*. You will read more about the town of Artena and how concepts that are timeworn are being explored and applied in new, sustainable ways.

You also will read about perspectives I acquired from providing workshops about the stresses of farming to several Native American tribes, but truthfully, I learned more from them. The cultural trauma and associated historical depression that Native people experienced and continue to endure by removal from their sacred lands brings a whole new view to what happens when humans are stripped of their agrarian opportunities to farm, fish, and hunt. Slaves imported from Africa to America, and their successors, understand this cultural shock from the complete dispossession of their previous livelihoods, except for what they carried in their minds and genes.

This book involves becoming closer to our agrarian roots. As a farmer/psychologist, I explain how many modern advances by humans have their origins in agriculture. Our agrarian urges are necessarily tied with careful stewardship of the land and the resources gifted to all humans through nature. Undertaking agricultural endeavors that are respectful of natural processes helps us discover insights into whatever can be attributed only to a force that is higher than ourselves. Becoming better humans is entwined in the evolution of all life, which entails agriculture as a key to survival.

There are also many stories, all true, about what I have learned along my way through life. Most are about farming. A few of them involve fishing and hunting, which are passions for my son and me that fill our emotional fuel tanks and usually add to the family food supply. Every story has a message and a lesson I have learned, which I want to share with others because they illustrate key parts of the book's full title.

My first book, *Excellent Joy*, introduced the celebration of turning seemingly small nuances of fishing, farming, hunting, and practicing psychology into excellent joy. I appreciated Gabriela Worrell's assessment in *Foreword Reviews*, which selected *Excellent Joy* for the Silver Award in their nature category in 2012. Worrell wrote, "The book is without attempts to dazzle the readers, its beauty lies in straightforward story-telling." I tried to write *Meditations on Farming* in the same easy-reading style. My most useful inspirations came from the farm people I serve and from the experiences best described as the school of hard knocks.

If I am able to complete what I perceive as my purposes in life, another book, which is already underway, will follow. It will elucidate additional insights I acquired from many years of serving the farm population as a clinical psychologist and from four decades of mostly longitudinal research. *Meditations on Farming* pushes into these arenas in personal ways. This book is about developing an understanding of life's purposes to farmers and the "farmer in all of us." I hope it brings you closer to understanding your life's purposes as much as it did me.

ACKNOWLEDGMENTS

I n a sense, *Meditations on Farming: The Agrarian Drive, Stress, and Mental Health* should be dedicated to the people from whom I learned the most: the farmers, ranchers, farm workers, and their families whom I served over the past forty-five years. They were my best teachers. Some, who started out as clients, and I became good friends who shared our insights. It is likely I learned more from them than they learned from me, but let's just say it was a joint learning experience.

I thank Marilyn, my wife of fifty-two years, whom I mentioned in the preface, for her love and for being my best reviewer and encourager when it comes to writing. We take a few minutes every day for discussion and spiritual contemplation to try to keep our heads and hearts centered. She and I are good mates for each other; each of us has skills and aptitudes in areas where the other is less capable. Marilyn allowed me the necessary time, space, and freedom to focus on writing as much as I could. She provided an essential perspective and emotional sensitivity about some matters that I would have otherwise missed. She has an uncanny grasp of what strikes a positive chord with readers. Maybe that explains why Marilyn was much appreciated by her students and faculty colleagues during her forty-five-year career teaching and providing behavioral health nursing skills.

Our two children helped me with aspects of the book. Shelby, our daughter and a physician, answered my medical questions, even though she says I am a doctor's worst nightmare because too often I rely on my own judgment rather than a physician's advice when making health care decisions. Dr. Shale Dames, her husband, with expertise in bioinformatics and genetics, reviewed everything that had to do with genetics in my explanations of why people farm, and I followed all his advice.

Jon, our son, contributed to many of the stories in the book. He makes sure I still hunt and fish with him, despite my increasing physical limitations. We are very close; he is my best friend other than Marilyn. He never complains, even though now he must help me pull on my ice-fishing boots and crampons. Amanda, Jon's wife and a pharmacist, was a sounding board about several key concepts and stories.

I am grateful to our four grandchildren. They contributed to several of the stories in the book. Their honest observations lend humor—and wisdom.

With fondness, I think of Nugget and Hayden, whom I wrote about in this book, and who shared Jon and Amanda's family household until they passed away a few years ago. These canines treated Marilyn and me like family, too. We hunted pheasants, quail, prairie chickens, and waterfowl for many years.

Many people helped me with advice when I needed it. Dean Kuipers, the author of several popular books, strongly encouraged me to bring this book to completion.

I am grateful to Justin Race and the Purdue University Press for asking me to submit the manuscript for this book, and for conducting the review process, editing, and ultimately publishing it. Justin took a shine to the book from the very beginning and was a great motivator to me. The staff had significant roles in determining the title, the design of the cover, and finding my mistakes, so they could be corrected. Katherine Purple, in particular, was a highly skilled and thorough editor.

I appreciate the support and encouragement of the AgriWellness, Inc., board members, especially during the early years after we formed the seven-state, upper-midwestern, nonprofit organization. Our regional collaborative was comprised of Wisconsin, Minnesota, North Dakota, South Dakota, Nebraska, Kansas, and Iowa. Our partners brought knowledge and experiences from the 1980s Farm Crisis and from their ongoing efforts thereafter to serve their respective state's farmers while also contributing to the knowledge about how to assist farmers everywhere. I especially thank Susan Helgeland and Charlie Griffin, board officers and the longest serving president and past president, respectively; we are close friends. All past and present board members deserve a share of the credit. Many thanks also are due to Jim Meek, Shari Stucker, and Carol McHugh, core staff at AgriWellness, who, like me, worked overtime regularly and helped find solutions during eras of financial uncertainty. I thank Dr. Pat Hart, a competent evaluator of several key grants that assisted our state partners with projects. I could not have had more supportive colleagues.

Dr. Bob Fetsch, a Colorado State University professor emeritus, encouraged our work for more than two decades. He grew up on a Texas farm, still conducts research about counseling farmers and ranchers, and administers the Colorado AgrAbility project. We have known each other for over fifty years, going back to attending the same college for three years.

I also thank Dr. Stefano Serafini and Sara Bissen, who think and write creatively about biourbanism. I appreciate James Barrat, the producer of superlative televised documentaries, one of which was about suicide and included considerable analysis of why farmers sometimes end their lives prematurely. I appreciate my close friend, Darla Tyler McSherry, who grew up on a wheat/barley farm in northern Montana, and someday should be writing her own books.

Finally, I must acknowledge the many respected news reporters, several authors of important articles about farmers, various radio and television interviewers and producers, and the hundreds of people who invited me to provide workshops or speeches. They had a positive impact on me, which has helped me to write this book. Along the way to completing this book, I owe thanks to many friends and colleagues. I apologize for not mentioning them by name, but they know in their hearts that I appreciate our relationships and their knowledge of their crafts.

1

OPENING DAY

Opening day of fishing season! My University of Virginia colleague, Darren, and I were on our way to our intended destination. Darren and I had made plans during the preceding week to join the spring ritual by fishing a lively creek flowing eastward out of the Shenandoah Mountain. We suspected the stretch of creek we hoped to fish would be crowded because we saw the fish hatchery truck unload a glob of rainbow trout into the stream when we scouted it late the afternoon prior. While in one sense both of us abhorred fishing for stocked trout, in another sense we felt we deserved the same opportunity as everyone else.

It was my first full academic year, 1975, as an assistant professor in the Psychology Department of the University of Virginia. I was a greenhorn in many ways. I finished graduate school at the University of Utah less than a year earlier. I hardly knew how to handle myself in an historic setting that was regarded as a leading institution of higher learning. I originated on a farm in western Iowa and had limited previous exposure to such lofty social and educated circles.

I also was a greenhorn at fly-fishing. Married to Marilyn for three years and having had only the seasoning her expert fly-fisherman father gave me as he quietly took me under his wing, I knew just a bit about tying my own flies, casting them into rivers and lakes, and capturing trout that were attracted to these imitations of their dinner entrées. Thoughts of broadening my fly-fishing skills and my career aspirations percolated through my mind during the quiet moments of our sojourn to open the fishing season. I stepped on the gas pedal of my International Scout to hurry along.

From my first week on campus, Darren and I had hit it off together well. He already was tenured faculty. Darren, a social psychologist, and I, a clinical psychologist, had a lot of common ground, not just in an academic sense, but in the way we viewed life. Both of us liked the outdoors. We often talked when we worked late into the night in our Gilmer Hall offices to prepare lectures, conduct research, and carry out the many necessary tasks to advance the education of University of Virginia students and our careers. Marilyn thought Darren, a graduate of the University of Wisconsin, and I were motivated by the same Midwestern work ethic.

When I took on the role of contractor for the construction of our new home in the foothills of the Shenandoah Mountain, even though I had not built a house previously, Darren teased, "An ancient proverb says to be a complete man, one must build a house, father a son, and write a book."

It took me sixty-five years to complete the three requirements. In addition to overseeing and helping to build our first family home in the foothills of the Blue Ridge Mountains when we lived in Virginia, I designed and built our Iowa house in 1988, and many farm buildings along the way. Becoming dad to Jon in 1978 was the second requirement I fulfilled, but now I think the proverb should be amended to say that the gender of the child isn't important, and that fatherhood can be accomplished through adoption or procreation. Writing an entire book by myself took the longest. Although I had written chapters for scholarly books and for fiction and nonfiction literary books, my first complete book was published in 2011; the awards it received were unexpected.

Darren helped me construct the only canoe I have ever owned or needed. When I had questions about the construction process, I phoned Darren. He came to my back-porch-turned-shop and showed me how to fix various problems. He was on hand when I poured fiberglass resin onto the mesh that gave the wooden strips a firm structure. Darren and I christened the canoe that I had built with his assistance and *Popular Mechanics* diagrams. We took it to nearby Rivanna Reservoir for a jaunt. I thought it maneuvered even more dexterously than Darren's similarly hand-constructed canoe. Mine was longer, by eighteen inches, and faster, in my biased opinion. On that baptismal voyage each of us caught several largemouth bass and bluegills. I felt assured this wonderful craft would be more than suitable to explore many rivers and lakes and to catch fish of all types.

As Darren and I cruised over the gravel road to the creek we had chosen to enjoy the opening day of trout-fishing season, we gulped hot coffee and waved at people who passed ahead of us and those who were following us to this hot spot. Apparently, others also had read in the Charlottesville *Daily Progress* that the brook to which we were heading was one of those into which many eight- to ten-inch rainbow trout had been planted.

When we arrived at a grassy pasture next to the stream and about a quarter mile below the section we had checked the previous day, some sixty vehicles were already parked there. We strung our fly-fishing poles and tied on flies. We hastened to the creekside where we knew many trout had been dumped for catching. It was still a few minutes before sunrise and the opening of fishing season.

Darren and I watched various fishers of all ages congregate around us. Glancing at him affirmed second thoughts we both apparently were having about whether this was what we really wanted to do. Some of the eager fishers were adolescent and younger boys and girls with their fathers, none of whom wore waders or hip boots. Others were "veterans," with Eddie Bauer waders and vests, expensive fly rods, khaki hats, and all the expected accoutrements. Darren and I wore hip boots—this was a small stream, only ten to twelve feet wide, and three feet deep in the darkest pools. Fishers lined up a few feet apart along both creek banks. A conservation officer, with a referee's whistle in his mouth, waited patiently on our side of the creek.

As the sun rose over the hills of the surrounding pasture on this fifth day of April, the game warden blew his whistle. Everybody simultaneously cast their lines into the stream, some 150 to 200 people. Darren and I mechanically tossed our flies into the stream below a couple large rocks we had selected from among the remaining choice locations. Within seconds, kids and adults shouted excitedly, "I got one!"

Darren and I captured flaccid, nine-inch, greenish rainbow trout on our first casts. As we were removing the fish from our hooks, the pressure of our fingers pushed the contents of their digestive tracts out their anuses. I noticed a whitish deposit dripping from my insipid trout. Darren and I looked at each other and our catches. Darren said, "I don't want to keep this."

I was thinking the same thing, and Darren's pronouncement confirmed my decision. We tossed our fish back into the stream. For a few minutes Darren and I watched the menagerie. People jostled each other to get into favored spots. Kids, parents, grandparents, and enthusiastic fishers of all types pushed, shoved, and shouted excitedly as they reeled wriggling trout into their nets and outstretched hands.

Starting to feel chagrined, and even a little sickened, Darren and I looked at each other and backed away from the streamside. Darren said, "I think I don't want to do this."

"I'm beginning to feel the same way," I replied.

I was less certain of my feelings than Darren was of his feelings. Part of me wanted to enjoy more tugs at the end of my fishing line, but another part of me was thinking, "This isn't right." A definition of fishing I had read somewhere crossed my mind: "A jerk at one end of a line waiting for a jerk at the other end."

Darren and I backed farther away from the conglomeration of people along the stream and stood together for a while, gazing and thinking. I pulled my pipe out of my shirt pocket, filled it with my favorite tobacco brand, and struck a match. As I puffed on my pipe, a variety of thoughts crossed my mind about how to salvage the day. I wanted to show Darren that his invitation to join him for the opening day of fishing in Albemarle County was much appreciated, but I also wanted to be true to my instincts and ethical inclinations. Maybe Darren felt the same way, as we both stood some thirty feet behind the eager fishers and silently pondered the situation for a while.

Darren broke the spell: "How about if we head up the stream to where it comes out of the mountains?"

That seemed like a good idea, so I followed Darren as we trekked along the stream a good mile to where the creek flowed under a barbed wire fence. It was easy to discern that this would be more challenging than it was fishing downstream. The crystal clear water loudly tumbled in two- to three-foot falls over rocks and through crevasses. I could see no planted trout in the water here. Apparently, no hatchery fish had migrated this far upstream overnight. Darren and I noticed a half dozen other fishers also trailing on either side of the stream toward where we were studying the creek. All were men without anyone accompanying them, and all but one had fly rods. Only a couple of them dabbled flies into the stream. Darren and I decided that if we were going to catch any fish, we had better try fishing here.

Over the next couple hours, Darren and I experimented with nearly our entire collections of artificial flies, without catching a fish. We noticed that none of the other fishers were catching anything either. All the other anglers seemed like experienced fly-fishers, for they were dressed in the appropriate attire—well-worn vests, tattered hats or caps, hip-boots or waders, and they seemed to know their way around a stream. By 9:30 a.m., Darren and I retreated to a large protruding rock a few feet from the side of the creek. I lit a new bowl of tobacco in my pipe and Darren put a chunk of "chew" into his left jaw. We both gazed into the stream, not sure what to say next, if anything.

Quite a few moments passed. Suddenly Darren blurted, "Do you see that fish under the rock there?" He pointed to a dinner-plate-sized flat rock in the streambed ahead of us. "Move slowly or you'll scare it."

I struggled to keep myself calm as I squinted to locate the fish Darren was pointing out. "Right there," he pronounced, as he maneuvered his fly rod in front of my eyes, aiming it at a spot in the stream ahead of the flat rock he had described.

"I still can't see it," I responded. I already knew that I was partially red-green color-blind.

"All you can see is its head and its eye—the rest of its body is under the rock." I strained to follow the line of vision along his fly rod. "I see it," I announced excitedly. "I wonder if it will take anything," I whispered.

"We have to move very carefully," Darren suggested in a hushed voice. "I'll use a little fly I haven't tried yet, a Royal Coachman," I whispered. Excitedly, I attached onto my tippet this well-known enticement that I had learned to tie from a fly-tying guidebook. Moving very cautiously, I slid forward from the boulder on which we were sitting, extended my rod above the flat rock, and floated the Royal Coachman fly over the trout hiding in its lair. No take. I offered the fly again, with the same result. I tried a Light Cahill, with the same outcome.

Darren offered the reluctant trout a Pautzke salmon egg at the end of his leader. When the fish didn't budge, he put half a garden worm onto his hook, but again, the fish showed no interest.

Meanwhile, I had tied on a small artificial nymph. I tumbled it over the rocks. It fell directly ahead of the trout hiding under the flagstone. No success!

"I don't think it's a rainbow trout," I suggested. "It looks like a brown or brook trout."

"Let's see if we can catch it in my net," Darren ventured.

We didn't know what else to try, for we weren't catching any fish and it seemed like fun. We were two playful boys as we surreptitiously crept next to the rocks behind the trout and as Darren slowly stepped into the water, over his knees. He cautiously extended his net above the trout's lair and gradually lowered it directly in front of the trout. When he gave me a signal, I poked the end of my fly rod below the back of the flagstone, touching the tail of the trout.

A twelve-inch trout surged directly into Darren's fishing net. He raised his net triumphantly, announcing, "Got it!"

It wasn't a planted rainbow trout. It was a native brook trout, bigger than any of the stocked trout we had observed earlier.

"Do you think we should keep it?" Darren asked.

Thinking for a moment, I responded, "This fish deserves to live."

"I think you're right," Darren agreed. Gently, he lowered his net into the stream and allowed this fish, native to all of eastern North America, to freely pursue its destiny. It deserved the opportunity to pass along its survival capacities to future generations.

When Darren and I rose from our stooped positions, we both felt better and closer to what we wanted for our lives. Looking at each other knowingly, we nodded and began sauntering toward our vehicle. We had both learned something important.

Opening day truly was an "opening day!"

2

WHY PEOPLE FARM

What led us to practice agriculture? The answer is not as simple as "We need food to survive."

A rapidly growing body of findings from anthropology, archaeology, and paleontology suggests that agriculture extends back only about 13,000 to 15,000 years. Jared Diamond, the noted University of California at Los Angeles professor of geography and physiology, and the author of *Guns, Germs, and Steel*, contends that the earliest agriculture traces to the Fertile Crescent of southwest Asia, where strains of barley, wheat, and protein-rich pulse legumes were domesticated through selection for their most desired characteristics, such as production yields, taste, nutritional value, tolerance for adverse growing conditions, and other features that modern humans deemed useful. Receding glacial ice across northern Europe, Asia, and North America from the most recent ice age—which began about 100,000 years previously and mostly melted by some 10,000 years ago, except for ever fewer remaining glaciers—drastically changed the geography, animal life, plants, and the humans that capitalized on the warming conditions. As grasses and other cold-tolerant plants invaded the receding ice fields, mammoths and other flourishing species of animals were hunted to extinction.

It was in this environment that people initially farmed, first in the warmer climes of southwest Asia. Waves of ever more sophisticated Africans who had outstripped the capacity of their territories on which to live in Africa migrated regularly into new areas, such as Asia Minor, then gradually spread into Europe, across Asia and into the Pacific Islands, Australia, and eventually, the Western Hemisphere.

Was agriculture a major factor that influenced the places to which our ancestors spread, or did farming just happen to develop?

In an article in the April 2010 issue of the *Journal of Agromedicine*, I proposed a theory, *the agrarian imperative*, as an explanation for why people engage in agriculture. The agrarian imperative is a basic human instinct to acquire sufficient territory and the necessary other resources to produce the food and shelter required by families and communities. The agrarian imperative instills in farmers an ethic to work incredibly hard, to endure unusual pain and hardship, to rely on personal judgments, and to take uncommon risks. There are several lines of recently uncovered scientific evidence that validate the agrarian imperative: anthropological, historical, genetic, and psychological findings.

Anthropologists have established that walking upright, grasping tools, and developing ever larger brains to store more information and communicate in an increasingly complex manner contributed survival advantages to the forerunners of humans over their competitor species some six million years ago in Africa. Characteristics that proved a survival advantage became encoded in their DNA, which regularly changed due to feedback from their environments. All of us possess useful proclivities from our earlier primate relatives—along with subsequent changes that facilitated human survival—in our inherited genetic material.

Our ancestors, *Homo erectus,* developed in Africa about two million years ago, and were preceded by *Australopithecus afarensis* for a couple million years and *Ardipithecus ramidus* for a couple million years more before that. The earliest *Homo erectus* humans were scavengers who lived off plants and their seeds or fruits, tubers, insects, eggs, and whatever sources of carnivorous protein and nutrients they could find, such as the carcasses of animals slain by more powerful predators or capture themselves, like small animals, birds, crustaceans, and fish. When our ancestors banded together in groups that mainly were formed by kinship, they could hunt larger prey and protect themselves more effectively. They established territories, which they marked by cairns or announced by shouting and loudly banging rocks and sticks together. The most powerful clans occupied the most desirable terrains and waters with the greatest opportunities to obtain food, shelter, and other important resources, such as medicinal herbs. Often their claimed territories were temporary because they exhausted the available food sources and were forced to migrate in order to follow the movements of animal herds and the seasonal production of plants.

Gradually, the clans outgrew the carrying capacity of the territories they inhabited, including those to which they migrated as nomads. Many had little choice but to seek new, more favorable terrain and bodies of water for the food they needed. Life remained uncertain for these aboriginals, as the plants and animals on which they subsisted varied in their availability. Several early subspecies of humans, such as Neanderthals, were hunter-gatherers who became extinct as more intellectually sophisticated clans superseded them.

Ever more modern nomadic people migrated out of Africa along the Nile Valley northward and eventually crossed into Asia Minor. Our most recent ancestors, *Homo sapiens*, emerged from Africa only about 300,000 years ago. Like their predecessors, they were searching for sustainable food, shelter, clothing, and tools that enhanced their likelihood of surviving and reproducing. In all likelihood, some of these most observant hunter-gatherers noticed that seeds they had collected and inadvertently dropped around their temporary living quarters sprang up into the plant species they were exploiting, or, more likely, when they returned to a previous living site. They figured out several next steps, such as how to tuck seeds into moist ground, to scrape away competing plants, to use organic detritus for fertilizer, and to select the most nutritious items from among those they grew. They learned how to store the food items that had inadvertently or purposefully flourished. Storing their food enabled them to survive winter and other times of shortage, such as droughts, which gave agrarian clans a powerful advantage over hunter-gatherers. These were the first farmers.

Historical evidence suggests that cultivating land and domesticating animals to produce food, clothing, and shelter some 150 centuries ago allowed modern humans to survive lean times and to proliferate faster than our hunter-gatherer ancestors during preceding eras. Clans that earlier had to relocate frequently could now remain in one place. Many formed communities that allowed for greater safety in numbers, as well as specialization in crafts and industries, if sufficient food and other necessities for life were available to them. Agriculture gave tremendous advantages to these congregations and allowed them to rapidly enhance their culture, power, knowledge, and overall well-being.

Additional historical evidence suggests their successors from Africa spread from Mesopotamia westward, northward, and eastward throughout Europe and Asia. Mostly within the past 40,000 or so years, these human bands mastered fishing from watercraft and the building of boats enabled them to cross seas to Australia and many islands around the world. Others crossed ice or land bridges to North America and traversed down the Isthmus of Panama to South America. Likely, some of the African immigrants into Asia and elsewhere brought with them knowledge of how to refine metals to make tools, or independently developed their own methods of obtaining metals from ore and shaping them into useful items. The earliest farmers have been traced as crop producers in the Fertile Crescent of what is modern-day Iran, Iraq, and Syria, only about 13,000 to 15,000 years ago; they took their methods of subsistence with them to wherever they moved northward in Europe and Asia. Raising crops may have begun independently in eastern Asia, experts think, and several centuries later in the South Pacific isles. Some agricultural techniques probably developed independently. For instance, in the Americas, teosinte seeds were first cultivated around 7,000 years ago and carefully selected to result in maize, and its successor, corn. Agriculture clearly gave survival advantages to agrarian humans over other modern humans who didn't farm, and over all other species.

Selecting and raising animals for food, clothing, and tools came a couple thousand years later than crop farming. However, dogs and humans have longer mutually beneficial relationships, for dogs were domesticated as much as 45,000 years ago. Genetic analyses indicate all canines descend from wolves. Wolves hung around hunter-gatherers, such as Neanderthals, to scavenge food scraps or to eat their human neighbors when need and feasibility allowed.

In his 2011 book, *How the Dog Became the Dog: From Wolves to Our Best Friends*, Mark Derr explained that humans probably took care of orphaned wolf pups and kept them for food when little else was available, and if the wolves didn't eat the humans first. The animals that were most docile were allowed to breed. Through selection, over successive generations ever-tamer pet wolves were produced until they diverged enough to be considered dogs.

With their keen olfactory sense, dogs provided assistance by tracking prey and guarding their human associates. Some scientists speculate humans' need for an acute olfactory sense diminished as they came to rely on the sensitive noses of dogs, and because upright-walking humans no longer had their noses close to the ground, as did their earlier quadruped ancestors in Africa.

Eventually, domesticated dogs with sufficient strength and endurance were harnessed to pull travois (two long sticks strapped to the beasts onto which packs of belongings could be fastened and drug behind the animals) on the ground or on sleds in snowy terrain. Dogs also helped their human associates capture animals of all sizes, varying from birds and small mammals, such as hares, to large ungulates, such as mammoths and aurochs. Besides providing assistance to humans, and as food during lean times, dogs provided skins and bones for use by humans. Canines benefited by having a steadier food supply than if they depended only on themselves, and they experienced protection when proximate to human groups who had weapons and could start fires.

What about cats, the second most popular pets these days? Cats probably adopted humans, rather than vice versa. Cat owners might say kitties are more interested in satisfying their own needs than the needs of their humans. As modern man began to harvest and store the grains and legumes they raised some 13,000 to 15,000 years ago, rodents invaded grain containers and chowed down on spillage around the human camps. These rodents were a ready source of nourishment for some of the small felines. Cats that hung around humans gradually developed ever shorter flight distances and eventually let humans pet them. Through selection by their human caretakers, contemporary breeds like the Persian and Abyssinian emerged over time.

Available historical and genetic evidence suggests domesticating available types of ungulates began as recently as 10,000 years ago, although humans hunted them long before they were tamed. Like crop farming, raising livestock for food was initiated in Asia Minor. Sheep and goats were good choices for domestication, probably because they thrived on the increasing availability of grass plants, legumes, and shrubs that sprang forth as the most recent glaciers receded northward. Wild goats and sheep roamed the nearby Zagros Mountains. Moreover, that they possessed few defenses, such as sharp teeth and claws, and relied for safety on a natural grouping tendency, made them all the more favorable for domestication. Once again, dogs showed their adaptability as they became herders of sheep and goats. The sheep and goats were small enough that people could handle them physically.

Most of the animals became more docile over successive generations, which made them readily available sources of meat, skins, bladders, and stomachs for storing things. The animals also had sinews, horns, and bones that could be made into tools. Use of these animals' hair for clothing developed later and was enhanced when herders selectively chose and raised sheep for wool, which differed from their stiffer hair fibers, and was more useful for producing yarn that could be sewed into garments. Raising these animals for milk likely developed through selection, too.

Domestication of cattle occurred a couple thousand years after sheep and goats, again in southern Asia first, and then later in other parts of Asia and Europe. Cattle served several useful purposes: they furnished larger amounts of meat and hides than sheep and goats, had longer lactation periods after giving birth, and could be trained to pull carts and plows.

Chickens were domesticated around the same time as cattle, initially in southeast Asia, where they were sought after for their tasty meat and eggs. Wherever they were introduced, such as in Europe and Polynesia, they were quickly adopted into households. Pigs followed, probably about 7,500 years ago, and also in southeastern Asia. They, like chickens, had desirable advantages, such as consuming leftovers of many sorts (including human waste), while furnishing meat and the fat needed for human brain development. It should be expected that today's influenzas often developed strains that used humans, pigs, and chickens as vectors in China and other parts of southeastern Asia, because all three species lived together in the same abodes, although usually in different parts. Similarly, ducks and geese were tamed first in China, but probably only about 3,000 years ago. They furnished protein from their eggs and meat, while joining the ranks of birds sequestered close to humans and pigs that could generate flu and respiratory viruses.

Horses came onto the domestication scene around the same time as chickens and pigs. Horses made traveling faster and pulling things easier than tamed cattle. They also had useful purposes in battle, for which they were probably exploited first in East Asia, and thereafter in West Asia, North Africa, and Europe.

Fewer prospects of indigenous animals for domestication were available in the Western Hemisphere, although dogs probably accompanied Asians across the Bering Sea land bridge between what is now Alaska and Russia when the oceans weren't as deep as they are now. The first human presence in the Western Hemisphere likely occurred some 20,000 to 45,000 years ago, although there is disagreement about the first date of human habitation and the method of reaching the Americas. Besides possibly crossing the Bering Sea by land, ice, or boats, some archaeological experts suggest that Pacific Islanders may have reached the coast of what is now Chile by utilizing their sailing crafts and expertise. Regardless, an ice age was likely in full effect when the ancestors of the first humans in the Western Hemisphere crossed continents, without knowing the significance of their ventures. Whatever their method of arrival in the Americas, they dispersed quickly across both continents. They probably didn't bring knowledge about agriculture with them; they learned on their own.

The natives of the Western Hemisphere who were most successful in taming animals congregated in the temperate regions of northern South America. The Incas and other tribes in the general area found llamas to be the only indigenous beasts that could transport goods, starting about 4,000 years ago, scientific authorities say. As llamas were domesticated and trained to carry items on their backs, their soft undercoat hair, which could be spun like wool, was used to make clothing, along with alpaca fleece, which was especially workable for sewing garments. The Incas and other advanced tribes nearby also raised guinea pigs for meat.

The indigenous natives of Central America established their own cultures, which emphasized growing crops, such as maize. Wild turkeys are known to have been domesticated, mainly for their meat and possibly for a few eggs during the spring nesting season. Turkeys, and a few other tethered birds kept as pets and for food, were raised by the inhabitants of Central America northward to the Anasazi tribes that inhabited what is now the southwestern United States, up to a couple thousand years ago.

Raising livestock for their meat, milk, eggs, materials for clothing and tools, and to assist with traveling and farming greatly facilitated the advancement of agriculture. People with animals had a steadier supply of protein and beneficial fat than when they were hunter-gatherers and even when they raised only crops. The advantages of communities that raised both crops and livestock persist today. The crops furnish food for humans and livestock, which in turn furnish excrement to nourish crops and grazing fields in a regenerative ecosystem. Humans seem to flourish best when they have omnivorous diets, although vegetarians contend mostly plant-based diets are superior, and vegans contend that diets without any animal-based foods, such as eggs and milk, are best. Consumption of moderate amounts of practically all foods and drinks are likely to remain fundamental to human diets.

The well-known author Victor Davis Hanson described how he thought agrarianism shaped early human civilizations. He suggested that farming parcels of land and the struggle for control/ownership of these territories necessitated the formation of governments. Laws were formulated to manage territories. Instead of wars that resulted in deaths, courts and imperial edicts settled disputes.

Numerical systems were developed in the Middle East, where farming crops and domestication of livestock first took place, approximately around 3100 BC. Increasingly innovative humans needed methods of counting to keep track of agricultural production and other matters. When counting by using fingers and toes was insufficient, tallying with marks became one of the first methods of recording numerical information, but it became outmoded as tabulations became larger and more complex. Numerical systems, such as counting by tens, became favored, but the concept of zero took longer to grasp. Addition and subtraction were invented first, but multiplication, division, and ever more sophisticated calculations were required, such as how to figure out the number of baked clay shingles were needed to cover the roof of a building. The foundations of geometry, algebra, calculus, and theoretical mathematics emerged and were refined, chiefly among Middle Easterners, but also as sophistication in thinking and exchange of information by land and sea advanced in Greece, Egypt, and among other populations.

Increasingly, modern humans, including farmers, found it necessary to record information. To be useful to successors, oral histories were passed along, but as is now well-known, human memories change and are inferior in their accuracy to recorded information, which also can be transmitted to others. Initially, hieroglyphics enabled different groups to share information, but the interpretation of hieroglyphic pictures varied from one culture to another. Cuneiform writing was developed next in the Middle East as a method of communication by means of a complex system of symbols. Eventually, the symbols were simplified to represent specific language sounds, thereby becoming a method of written communication among other cultural groups that learned the associated meanings of vowels and consonants in written languages. The alphabet that was inspired in southwest Asia was modified to transmit Latin languages, which became the major forerunner to today's most widely adopted international written language, English. English is also the chosen international language for sharing scientific information today.

A strong case can be made that even the scientific method owes its inception to the keen observations of farmers. As farming methods advanced, farmers compared the results of innovative methods, such as applying fertilizer in the forms of fish and human wastes to food plots, versus no fertilizer. Other agricultural lessons abounded around 5,000 to 6,000 years ago, which involved systematic selections of grain seeds in Europe and Asia, and maize in Central and South America. When maize plants mutated to furnish ears of their grain on the stalk, instead of the tassel, observant farmers quickly replicated the mutated maize. Farmers also selected varieties of maize for their tastefulness, yield, capacity to be ground into flour, tolerance for drought, and many other beneficial traits. The same approach was applied by farmers everywhere to determine the most beneficial characteristics of various crops. Agriculture and availability of a multitude of grains, fruits, vegetables, fish, and animal species have come to be part of life today.

How did the agrarian imperative develop in agricultural producers, and abide still in people today?

Anthropological and genetic evidence indicates the drive to acquire and use territories for agricultural purposes has an inherited basis. Underpinnings for the concept of the agrarian imperative can be traced to Konrad Lorenz, who with Nikolaas Tinbergen and Karl von Frisch, won the Nobel Prize in Physiology or Medicine in 1973 for their methods of observing animals, fish, and other species in their natural environments, as well as Robert Ardrey for describing territoriality in humans. These animal ethologists described how most species establish territories with sufficient resources to enable the maintenance and reproduction of additional members. They establish a dominance hierarchy, or pecking order, with the best territories usually going to the fittest individuals within a group of competitors. Contemporary livestock farmers are aware of the dominance hierarchy within a pen of cattle, pigs, or chickens. I've observed boss cows regularly shove others away from favored positions at the feed bunk.

Animals mark the boundaries of their territories in prominent ways. Dogs and cats spray urine on tree trunks, plants, and sometimes furniture. Birds fly from tree to tree singing loudly to proclaim, "This area belongs to me." Personal objects that signify ownership are the modern human pheromones. We mark our territories with fences, signs, sidewalks, and legal descriptions. We decorate our office cubicles—if we work in such confined spaces—with nameplates, and carefully chosen artifacts and photographs that advertise, "This space is mine." Territoriality and dominance behaviors have become encoded into the genetic makeup of most species, and particularly in humans.

Humans are carrying around in our DNA the remnants of genetic codes that influenced our earlier ancestors. *Ardipithecus ramidus* provided us with modifications in the pelvic attachment of hip bones, which allowed for upright walking and freed our hands for grasping and other functions besides climbing. *Australopithecus afarensis* gave us larger skulls to accommodate more brain matter to store a growing fund of information and increasingly complex language. *Homo sapiens*, our most recent ancestors, developed sophisticated social, artistic, religious, and occupational behaviors necessary to make tools and organize groups of humans to function together efficiently. The inherited capacities and acquired mutations that afforded our earlier predecessors with survival advantages are included in our gene pools today. Those who lacked these adaptations succumbed in the competition for life.

All species carry the history of successful adaptations of their ancestors in their genetic material; the stored information is available when needed. When pigs become feral, their hair becomes thicker, longer, and coarser; their tusks elongate and their behavior becomes wary. They know instinctively which plants are harmful to consume. Dogs that are left to fend for themselves form packs and pool their resources to capture food and protect their puppies.

It is interesting how the human body changes and the behaviors associated with farming wash out of people within a few successive generations of removal from the land. But their agrarian tendencies rekindle in just a few years of working the land. Urban residents who marry farm people or who move to rural areas to establish, or join, farming operations usually acquire closeness to their land within a few years. They pass along to their children their hardy work ethic and the psychological commitment to make the land produce. This rapid reversion taps into strands of our genetic code that are dormant until agricultural activities stimulate the emergence of survival capacities that are included in our DNA. How quickly our bodies harden and toughen when we leave an urban lifestyle and become immersed in nature. Our fingers thicken and our hands enlarge; our movements, such as scooping grain or digging a trench, become efficient, and our manners become geared toward accomplishing tasks with a minimum of energy and physical wear and tear. We become competitive about acquiring suitable farmland and develop an emotional—and often spiritual—attachment to the land we work. We take great pride in our crops and livestock. Bonds of mutual dependency develop between humans and farm animals. Farmers experience fulfillment in producing essentials for life—food, fiber, and fuel for families, neighborhoods, and the larger human community. We are exhibiting the agrarian imperative as a way of life.

Henry Cole, a respected professor of preventive medicine and environmental health at the University of Kentucky, and also a farmer like me, offered an alternative explanation to why people farm in the same issue of the *Journal of Agromedicine*. He reasoned that people farm because they choose to do so, and only if they have access to the necessary economic, cultural, and social capital resources. I think the agrarian imperative is a better argument in this nature versus nurture debate. As Steven Kirkhorn, then the editor of the *Journal of Agromedicine*, suggested, "the love of the land and the skills and ability to succeed in this endeavor may be expressed in both the genotype and phenotype of those engaged in farming." In other words, genes influence our basic urge to farm. We can detect genetic selection in the personalities of those who farm.

Psychological evidence, particularly personality research, suggests behavioral traits that are characteristic of persons who engage in agriculture. Joyce Willock and her colleagues at the University of Edinburgh evaluated the attitudes, objectives, behaviors, and personality traits of 242 male and 10 female farmers in Scotland. Personality traits most predictive of success in farming included conscientiousness, risk-taking, and self-reliance. These personality traits have survival value in the competition for farmland and working the land as a way of life.

Marilyn Shrapnel and Jim Davie at the University of Queensland identified five personality factors that motivated the 60 farmers they studied: conscientiousness and willingness to work hard; confidence in taking risks and making their own decisions; great capacity to cope with adversity; self-reliance and diminished need for companionship; and low ability to acknowledge or express mental health problems and to seek help. Similar to Willock's findings, these factors seem to be essential characteristics of the agrarian imperative.

The same traits that motivate farmers to be successful also are associated with depression and suicide when the objectives of farming are not met. Fiona Judd and her Australian colleagues conducted a number of studies during the past couple decades to explore why Australian farmers have a significantly higher rate of suicide than nonfarmers. In comparison to nonfarming rural Australians, farmers exhibited significantly higher levels of conscientiousness and lower levels of neuroticism. The authors described neuroticism as the ability to acknowledge or express mental health problems and to seek help for these problems, which they said are deficient in the otherwise successful farmers. Other traits that contributed to their success as farmers, namely, perseverance in the face of adversity and a tendency to keep problems to themselves, also appeared to work against them when times were tough, such as an era of low market prices, when they could have benefited from taking breaks from stress to restore their energy and perspective, and consulting with trustworthy advisors in areas for which they lacked sufficient expertise, such as experts who specialized in marketing of farm commodities.

The rate of suicide among male farmers is much higher than that of their nonfarming counterparts in most studies undertaken in agricultural areas around the world. Farm women also have a higher suicide rate than nonfarm women, but their overall rate of suicide is about a quarter that of farm men. The incidence of suicide is tied mainly to episodes of severe economic stress, although exposure to certain classes of insecticides, such as organophosphates, can also be a factor. The suicide rate among farmers is higher in nearly every country, from India to Japan, the United Kingdom, Australia, and the United States. In Great Britain the suicide rate of livestock and dairy producers rose to as much as ten times the usual rate for several months in 2001 when their sheep and cattle were killed and burned to prevent the spread of foot-and-mouth disease and mad cow disease (bovine spongiform encephalopathy). These hard-pressed farmers could not bear to see their beloved animals—the means to their economic livelihood—slaughtered. The same traits that helped them be good farmers also contributed to their demise in this instance. In the overall course of life, however, great capacity to deal with adversity, conscientiousness,

Successful
farmer traits [handwritten annotation]

risk-taking, and self-reliance contribute more to survival than incapacitation.

Does the agrarian imperative imply that we have little or no control over the behaviors entailed with farming? Clearly not, for instincts incorporate patterns of behavior but don't dictate responses to individual events and circumstances. Living and working on the land influences what is learned and absorbed into our genetic material; however, genetic inclinations toward an agrarian imperative are only one influence—the most important, I think—that explain why people farm. The more we advance as a species, the more likely we are to incorporate mutations, the expression of which enhances the likelihood of survival.

Farmers have little control over the climate, agricultural policies, global food production, and consumer demand, but farmers have a great deal of control over how they farm, whether they manage their available resources responsibly or not, and how they govern their time and energy. Farmers choose whether or not to get adequate sleep, recreation, and to install rollover bars on their tractors. Farmers are in charge of how they deal with frustrations, whether they share their concerns with people who can help them, such as counselors who understand agriculture and behavioral health. Choices are behaviors. They don't automatically become encoded into our DNA; however, beneficial behaviors contribute to their likelihood of becoming incorporated into our genome when mutations occur that favor the expression of such beneficial genetic inclinations that enhance their survival. It took a long time for the agrarian imperative to develop, essentially, thousands of generations of ever more successful farmers, all of whom followed territorial inclinations inherited from people in Africa and those who had already populated other continents.

Their inherited agrarian imperative drives agricultural producers to be useful to their families, communities, and to some extent, almost everyone, except enemies. People engaged in agriculture find their meaning in producing essentials for life: food, fibers for clothing and shelter, and such renewable fuels for energy as firewood, soy diesel, and wind.

Farmers protect their land and strive to preserve other resources necessary for agriculture, including but not necessarily limited to water, clean air, farm equipment, livestock, facilities for raising crops and animals and storing agricultural products, human capital (e.g., employees, family, advisors), and the financial capital needed for operating the farm. The land is the most important, for it is the essential beginning to farming productively. That's why possible loss of farmland is the greatest threat to the well-being of farmers, according to polls of farmers commissioned by the American Farm Bureau Federation in early 2019, late 2020, and several times since. Research undertaken by AgriWellness a dozen years earlier drew similar conclusions. Threatened loss of land was ranked highest and tied with the death of a child in a farming event as the greatest stressor. Respondents ranked the loss of a person essential to the farm operation (e.g., spouse, parent, a trusted employee, etc.) second; a major health issue that encumbers the main producer in the farming operation was third. Divorce and other breakdowns in significant relationships followed; weather-related disasters, disease outbreaks in crops and/or livestock, and machinery breakdowns were next in the rankings.

There is an agrarian imperative in everyone. People who don't farm carry genetic proclivities associated with the agrarian imperative, even if they aren't farmers. Despite genetic variations in our overall genome, the urge to produce necessities for life is so central that it resides in our DNA. The urge to acquire territories may be expressed differently, such as urban residents marking the boundaries of their homes with sidewalks, hedges, the display of a name on a mailbox or their address in a prominent place, and legal descriptions, all of which are not very different than the fences, signs, and legal titles that farmers use to signal ownership and occupation of farmsteads. People who work away from home identify their workspaces and businesses with nameplates, photographs of loved ones, artwork, sometimes with favorite sayings, and with carefully chosen objects as the pheromones that signal their workstations. Even persons who are disposed of property, such as refugees in camps, lay claim to their small spaces as soon as possible upon settlement into safe quarters with boundaries that may consist of nothing more than a blanket stretched over their few possessions. Moreover, users of social media proclaim their spaces on the Internet with photos, brief biographies, and their written words or videos. In short, the agrarian imperative is fundamental to human existence.

Unique, genetically inclined traits that are found in successful farmers include tendencies to react to threats of the agricultural operation with heightened anxiety initially, and subsequently with depression when coping capacities became exhausted. Dr. Christian Montag and his colleagues at the Giessen Gene Brain Behavior Project in Bonn, Germany, confirmed the long-held suspicion that the homozygous change in the *COMT* gene from valine to methionine is linked with the development of alarm in response to being startled. People with this variant, based on genomic-wide allele frequencies, are more prone than those without it to react to stress with a flood of neurotransmitter chemicals, including adrenaline, which gear up these persons to deal with a perceived threat. Sometimes incorrectly called the Teutonic gene, this variant has been postulated to be more common in successful European farmers, but it also sets them up to experience excessive anxiety when they become alarmed. Severe and repeated threats ultimately lead to the depletion of beneficial bodily chemicals, such as serotonin, norepinephrine, and oxytocin. Depression usually results, and may lead to suicidal behavior.

This genetically linked variant occurs more commonly among people who trace their ancestry to medieval Germanic Europeans than most other ethnicities. These Central Europeans, who were required to feed the Roman armies that resided among them, ended the control of their territories by the Romans by purposefully producing insufficient food for the Roman occupiers of their land. Overpowering the Romans who controlled them for multiple previous centuries wasn't easy, because the Teutons were more skilled in agriculture than warfare. When Roman soldiers demanded that the Teutons cease their rebellion and threatened them with death, adult male defenders sometimes undertook suicide rather than to experience the humility of surrender or slaughter. The women sacrificed their children and killed themselves as well.

Roman conquerors who required total submission of the Teutonic inhabitants initiated a diaspora of Teutonic people in Central Europe to lands they deemed safer at the time. Moreover, successive waves of mostly invasive western Asians accelerated the dispersion of Teutons for several centuries. Teutons, who were accustomed to being subjugated, chose to move to other areas rather than to resist intrusions from invaders who employed powerful military tactics. The new invaders are sometimes labeled as barbarians still today, even though they brought with them useful knowledge that included how to construct Gothic architecture that became the hallmark of northern European culture, and agricultural techniques, such as crossing strains of bovines to produce better draft animals and producers of milk and meat. They also learned methods of farming from the Teutons they overpowered.

The Teutons fled their homelands to settle into such regions as Scandinavia, Eastern Europe, and eventually the British Isles and other parts of the settled world. Some Teutons intermixed with native Scandinavians and became Vikings. They found power in seamanship and military conquests, but they also instilled advances into the agriculture of the inhabitants they subdued.

A key consequence of the Teutonic diaspora is that their descendants became the bulk of Europeans who settled in North America, Australia, and South America, where they sought land to farm, mainly during the nineteenth and twentieth centuries. They carried the Teutonic variation of the *COMT* gene with them. When conditions threatened their success as farmers in newly settled lands, many were forced into alternative ways of life. Through selection of the best farmers over many generations, hanging onto their land became a prime motive for the farmers who survive yet today.

Do farmers around the world who do not contain Teutonic tendencies in their genetic makeup also experience excessive apprehension, followed by depression, and do they have high rates of suicide? The answer is yes, because threats to the possession of their farmland is commonly associated with self-sacrifice among farmers in India, Japan, and elsewhere. The number of farmers examined within these various ethnicities is small, however, making this finding in need of additional scientific investigations.

A stronger case can be made that all farmers share the common characteristic of attachment to their land. It's likely that a farmer in Kansas has more in common with a farmer in Africa or China than with an attorney in Kansas City who has no background in farming.

Successful farmers also have a proclivity for attention deficit hyperactivity disorder. Dr. Dan Eisenberg, now at the University of Washington, was affiliated with Northwestern University when he found that successful, nomadic, Kenyan cattle herders were four times more likely to exhibit a specific gene mutation associated with ADHD than Kenyans who were no longer involved in pastoral pursuits. The ADHD farmers had higher activity levels, were more alert for danger, and were more likely to locate ample forage for their herds than those without this genetic mutation. This finding has subsequently been replicated in research on other farm populations. These are some of the upsides to ADHD. The findings make sense, because successful farmers are more likely than less successful farmers to look out for threats to their livelihood, to not require as much sleep, and to take risks in an effort to succeed as farmers. Sometimes, however, the ADHD gene is also associated with a propensity to cut corners concerning safety when pursuing their dreams of agrarian success, which likely contributes to farming as the most dangerous occupation, as reflected by occupation-related injuries and fatalities (as noted in "Injury Facts," as reported by the National Safety Council; and in Rosmann's 2001 *Agricultural Behavioral Health: In Critical Need*, which is a chapter in a textbook that was published by the Wisconsin Office of Rural Health).

Inherited personality traits most predictive of success in farming are becoming clearer, as confirmed by Shrapnel and Davie, 2001; Willock,

Deary, McGregor et al., 1998; and Judd, Jackson, Fraser et al., 2006. As noted earlier, these traits include conscientiousness and willingness to work hard, confidence in taking risks and making one's own decisions, self-reliance and diminished need for companionship, great capacity to cope with adversity, and low ability to acknowledge or express mental health problems and to seek help. Obviously, these traits can work against successful farmers as well, leading to overload with anxiety, followed by depletion of coping capacities that result in depression, and a heightened tendency to blame themselves for failures, which I have observed in psychological autopsies in the suicides of farmers after they occurred.

Overall, however, acquiring land and the other resources needed to farm brings hope to agricultural producers. For agricultural producers, farming is a noble calling, a highly spiritual way of life. Farmers detect a higher force that instills the seeds they plant to pop out of the ground and their animals to give birth to offspring. For farmers, God is all around them. The outdoors is their spiritual environment that teaches them faith, hope, humility, and respect. Perhaps this inclination explains why so many people who don't farm seek adventures, solitude, and contentment in the outdoors for vacations or by owning small parcels of land on which to raise gardens and perhaps a few animals. Mostly everyone wishes to inhabit or visit environments similar to when all people made their way of life off the land and seas, and just simply to appreciate the goodness of nature.

During a conference I attended with economically distressed farmers from around the United States and Canada, I listened to a television reporter, who interviewed me and also asked a male farmer who was standing next to me: "Why do you farm if you keep losing money?" The farmer answered, "It's in my genes. I have to keep trying to do what I feel is right." His response encapsulates the agrarian imperative. That's why people farm.

3

LIFE-SHAPING ENCOUNTERS

The experiences that shake our physical, psychological, and spiritual foundations can be blunt, like a life-threatening medical issue, or subtle, such as false accusations in one's workplace or community. They hit us so hard that sometimes we question our basic purposes for existence. These experiences may bring us closer to what is most important in our lives, but only if we learn from them. I've learned mostly through tribulations that I must pay attention to these indicators to assess what I am doing wrong and to become better grounded, or else the nudges become ever stronger, even to the point of jeopardy to my earthly well-being.

For my first forty-four years I never felt so vulnerable that my total well-being was thrown into complete upheaval. An experience on July 24, 1990, changed everything. I wasn't prepared for it, because I felt I could accomplish almost anything I aimed for, if I tried hard enough.

I acquired a perspective toward accomplishment partially from my upbringing on a farm, which emphasized working harder than everyone else. I didn't realize my trouble paying attention in elementary and high school were partly due to ADHD until attention deficit hyperactivity disorder was formally defined by the American Psychiatric Association in its second edition of the *Diagnostic and Statistical Manual of Mental Disorders* during the late 1960s. Professors at the University of Colorado, where I finished my senior year of college after spending three years at a Catholic seminary until the summer of 1967, recognized my latent abilities and encouraged me to join others whom I recognized as the top undergraduates in the most popular major, psychology. One of my professors invited me to join the psychology honors

program, to conduct my own research projects and to deliver conference presentations, and to represent the University of Colorado (CU)
students at some public forums. I learned to manage moderate ADHD
and test anxiety by developing a method of studying intensely when
completely alone for several hours at a time, but taking frequent short
breaks to dissipate energy, for two to three days prior to a test, mostly
relaxing the night before an exam. When I realized my undergraduate
grades and various competitive test scores at the University of Colorado were superior to those of most other students, I gained a type of
confidence I didn't have earlier during my parochial life. I had felt inferior because I was an average athlete and not as "cool" as many peers
in my Catholic school. Teased for wearing glasses, I purchased contact
lens as soon as they were affordable after my sophomore year at Conception Seminary College. I was a farm boy who hailed from a sheltered life and was entering larger arenas.

Graduate school at the University of Utah, volunteering for two
years of alternative service as a conscientious objector during the Vietnam War, while also working toward further academic degrees that
took me an extra year, marrying Marilyn, and assuming appointment
as an assistant professor in the University of Virginia's Department of
Psychology in 1974 all felt right. I also felt very lucky.

When my family left our newly constructed home near Charlottesville, Virginia, and academic positions at the University of Virginia in May 1979 to begin new endeavors in Iowa, Marilyn and I were
thirty-three years old and our children, Shelby and Jon, were four years
and 16 months, respectively. Even before I could secure an Iowa license
to provide psychological services, people began calling me at home to request appointments. After receiving licensure, I met them at their homes
or at the Methodist Church offices in Harlan, which graciously offered
me space without charging a rental fee. The secretaries sometimes set
up appointments with callers, as word of my availability got out. I handled the record-keeping and billing for services from my home. Besides
my almost full-time professional psychology occupation, over the next

few years I became the primary operator of 405 acres of land farmed organically in western Iowa with a competent part-time employee, Dan, who had his own farming operation as well. Our family farm operation was registered as Rosa Blanda Farms, Ltd., drawing on the taxonomic name of Iowa's state flower, the wild rose. We raised registered Simmental cattle mostly as breeding stock for other producers, and sold the rest as organic beef to customers and on the open market. Most years we produced 50,000 bushels of corn, 10,000 bushels of soybeans, 16,000 small square bales, and 650 large round bales of alfalfa-orchard grass hay. Marilyn and our two children helped with farmwork, when their busy schedules allowed, by walking beans, hoeing our garden, caring for chickens and turkeys, and occasionally helping me deliver a calf when necessary. Jon ran our tractor and hay baler, hauled and unloaded harvested grain, and assisted with livestock chores. Neighbors offered me opportunities to rent more farmland, but I turned them down because Dan, Marilyn, and I couldn't handle any more responsibilities.

It was fun to review the Simmental journals and cattle sale catalogs that I kept, along with fly-fishing literature, as reading material under my side of the bed that Marilyn and I shared. The literature helped me to choose cattle shows and sales to attend and to select sires for artificially inseminating cows and fertilizing embryos from superior cows we had purchased or raised for transplant into properly prepared recipients. We took pelvic measurements of heifers in order to eliminate those that might have birthing problems, and regularly weighed the animals we raised, so that I knew which animals grew the fastest. I handled the artificial insemination work and the preparation of donors and recipients for embryo transplant procedures, as well as most of the calving checks during nights and on weekends. I didn't mind the routine of rising nightly every two hours during spring and fall calving seasons for about two months each; in fact, I enjoyed it. While riding a horse or an ATV around the calving pasture, I could listen for coyotes, owls, and other sounds, also greet my cows, and I could help an expectant mother if she was having difficulty calving.

Our cattle won prizes at the Shelby County Fair when our children were in 4-H, partly because there were only a few competitors in their classes, such as cow/calf pairs. We seldom entered state or regional cattle shows and fairs because the entries at these events were judged more on their appearance than on their ability to convert feed into meat and other consumable products. Instead, we routinely entered steers into state and regional cattle-feeding futurities. The production futurities enabled us to compare our cattle with a couple hundred steers that were fed similarly until they were ready for market, which was the purpose of the futurities: producers could select breeding lines with heritable traits that yielded the highest retail value per day of age and other desirable characteristics, such as choice meat cuts. USDA evaluators graded all the carcasses of the processed animals, and futurity officials calculated their total value as products for retail sale.

When futurity officials reported their findings from the many different cattle that were fed and cared for similarly, Rosa Blanda Farms' cattle nearly always ranked at the top. We won all but one of the dozen or so beef futurities we entered, with either the top individual or the top group of three to five steers. Our entrants into the production futurities weren't our best beeves because we kept our superior male animals as bulls to sell to other cattle producers at sales and to customers who visited our farm, or for our own use as herd sires. We selected our entrants for the feeding futurities from among the steers we raised for meat after the animals were weaned around six months of age.

In May 1990, I accepted the job of establishing and directing a new community mental health center in Shelby County, as requested by the county supervisors and the local hospital board. Prairie Rose Mental Health Center would become an integral part of the Shelby County health system, along with the established hospital and newly constructed outpatient medical clinic. I aimed for our mental health center to become the best outpatient behavioral health program in Iowa and devoted fifty to sixty hours weekly to its development. With only two licensed professionals during the startup, I covered half of the "on-call" emergency visits during off-hours its first summer.

Meanwhile, Marilyn and I also managed a rental home and farm we had purchased from my aging grandmother a decade earlier when times were good for farmers. We were paying for our own new house that I designed and built in 1987–1988 with the help of local craftsmen. Marilyn had "set her foot down" and proclaimed, "No more new barns, because our cattle live better than we do, and we need a decent home." This was the decade of the worst farm economic crisis since the Great Depression. After my first proposal and a professional architect's plans proved too expensive, we proceeded with additions to our century-old farmhouse that I drew up. We used lumber, flooring, and wooden trim from an old house on one of our farms that a neighbor high school lad and I tore down, as well as heavy planks and bridge stringers that I purchased from Shelby County's annual sales of used bridge timbers.

Moreover, Marilyn and I were musicians at her Seventh-day Adventist church and my Catholic church. Shelby, fifteen, and Jon, twelve, were highly involved in school class positions to which they were elected; they liked their 4-H club, and Marilyn served as one of their club's leaders. They participated avidly in the school marching and jazz bands, took piano lessons, flute lessons (Shelby), and drum lessons (Jon), and they were involved in academic honors programs and Faith Sound, a touring musical group. Marilyn and I attended as many of their events as time allowed; our kids understood when we couldn't always be there. We all pitched in with the garden where we raised most of our vegetables and fruit and canned or froze the ample produce for ourselves, and some for my widowed mother and as gifts for others. We worked late into the night and enjoyed our light-hearted camaraderie canning and freezing food together.

Marilyn left the University of Nebraska Medical Center Nursing School in the late 1980s, where she had begun teaching for six years, to become employed full-time by the same Shelby County health system that later hired me. She became the behavioral health nurse consultant in the public school system to help our community deal with an epidemic of suicides, substance misuse, and other behavioral health issues of the students. I served on the Harlan Community School Board and belonged to the Regional Economic Development Council, two national boards, the Iowa Psychological Association Executive Council, and I was involved in state and national politics. I took care of my mother as her designated business and health care agent after Dad died of a heart attack in 1980 and as Mom became unable to manage her affairs by herself some ten years later until she passed in 2010.

We were too busy! Yet, we usually found several occasions each summer to take our truck camper for overnight stays at county and state parks, and on family vacations to visit Marilyn's parents in Idaho and to explore national parks and places to fish. Shelby took it upon herself to clean and stock the camper for our excursions. Sometimes we also traveled by car or airplane to conferences when I had a speaking event; the kids ran the slideshow and distributed the papers I had written to the attendees. Jon and I fished when we could. He was an adept fisher by age five. After he completed a gun safety course around age ten, we hunted pheasants, rabbits, squirrels, and other game when time allowed.

Depending on the season, I habitually rose daily between 4:00 and 5:30 a.m. and completed the morning livestock chores and one or two farming tasks by 7:00 a.m., so I would have enough time to shower, shave, and get to the office by 7:30. I didn't need much sleep, four to six hours was sufficient. My modest degree of ADHD probably facilitated my high activity level and diminished my need for sleep from childhood on. At the time I thought I could do most anything if I put my mind to it; I was wrong. I had no warning that my life as I knew it was coming to a turning point. In retrospect, I had overlooked indicators that were apparent.

A few hours after July 24, 1990, began, I hustled to the office while the morning dew dried off the oat fields so Dan and I could begin harvesting oats early in the afternoon. I fed the livestock, greased the equipment, and fueled the International Harvester combine before I left home for Prairie Rose Mental Health Center. Dan was ready to head to the nearest oat field at 1:00 p.m., when I arrived home for the remainder of the day.

Marilyn had gone shopping in Omaha with her mother, Michi. Her parents were visiting us from Idaho for two weeks. Grandpa Walt was planning to transport Jon to his baseball game that afternoon.

I towed a wagon with my farm truck into the field across the road from our home as Dan drove the combine to cut a short test swath, just enough to glean a few bushels of oats into the machine's hopper. He parked next to the wagon to unload the tad bit of grain so as to push out the few soybeans in the mechanical implement's inner workings from its previous use last fall, along with enough oats to test their weight and percent of moisture. As Dan unloaded the few bushels of oats, I jumped into the hopper to sweep any remaining grain into the unloading auger.

Foregoing a broom that we kept on the combine to sweep out the hopper, I used my right foot to push the oats into the auger because it was a quicker way to clear out the hopper. My foot got too close to the whirling auger blade. Instantaneously, my heavy work shoe was caught and dragged under the auger.

Reflexively, I jerked my foot out of the auger. The front part of my shoe was missing. *No big deal*, I thought immediately.

Milliseconds later I saw blood stain the opened front-third of my shoe. *A few stitches should suffice and I will be good to go again*, I rationalized momentarily.

Then I saw the inch-thick Vibram lug sole was torn from my shoe, as blood spurted from my right foot. *Oh no*, I speculated, *This is worse than I thought*. I yelled to Dan to shut down the combine.

I gathered my senses, jumped out of the hopper, and climbed down to the ground. A glimmer of a prayer entered my mind, *Oh, God, what does this mean?* As I unlaced and pulled off the remainder of my shoe, the steel toe protector fell out. My big toe was still connected and my little toe was dangling by scant tissue, but most of the front of my foot was missing.

When Dan saw my foot he said, "You need to go to the hospital right away."

We jumped into the pickup truck parked nearby and Dan drove us to my home, where I called the hospital to advise the emergency room staff that I was on my way. After wrapping my foot in a towel and checking with Walt, who had not yet taken Jon to his baseball game, Dan hurriedly ferried me in our pickup truck to the ER some six miles distant.

When we arrived at the ER, a nurse was there to scurry me into a wheelchair. I insisted on walking into the hospital myself. I was not in shock or pain. My right foot felt numb. My personal physician, a native of Taiwan, was waiting inside the ER. He had also taken care of my father for years. When my father had his heart attack ten years earlier, he let me see Dad's limp body with its bruises from unsuccessful attempts to resuscitate his heart. We liked and respected each other.

"We send you to Omaha," my physician said after briefly examining me. "I call them."

The doctor tried to explain my condition in his somewhat broken English. It was clear from what I could hear that the receiving nurse at the Clarkson Hospital in Omaha didn't understand all he was saying, so he transferred the phone to me when I offered to speak. I told the Clarkson nurse, "I'm the patient; my second, third, and fourth toes on my right foot have been severed, and my little toe is barely hanging on. Can they be reattached if we bring them to the surgeon?"

"Yes," the nurse responded. "Bring your toes and the surgeon can decide if they can be reattached."

I telephoned Walt from the ER, who said he would ask Shelby and Jon to search for my toes in the combine's hopper and put them on ice. I called two large indoor retail malls where I figured Marilyn and Michi might be shopping to ask for a message to be broadcast (we didn't have cell phone service yet) so they could meet me at Clarkson Hospital.

The local ER staff loaded me into an ambulance. We headed to Clarkson Hospital some sixty miles away. My three missing toes, wrapped in dry ice and placed in a cooler by Shelby, followed an hour later in another vehicle, but I don't know exactly how. How did she know to store them with dry ice? I never found out and I don't know who transported them, but I am grateful. Shelby said years afterward that finding my toes in the combine hopper was a determining factor in her desire to become a medical doctor. Jon didn't faint like he usually did when he saw blood; he located my toes, the steel toe protector, and the sole of my shoe and handed them to Shelby.

As the ambulance approached a steep incline in the Loess Hill formation a few miles east of Omaha, l told its driver I could smell radiator fluid and recommended pulling off the highway before the engine was ruined. "No," the driver responded. "We need to get you to the hospital ASAP."

"The engine will seize up," I remonstrated. Shortly, I saw white puffs of smoke and steam blowing past the window I could view from my gurney. The engine ground to a halt as the driver pulled the rig onto the highway shoulder.

It took ninety minutes for another ambulance to finish the route; I finally arrived at Clarkson Hospital at 4:30 p.m. Marilyn and Michi were waiting for me at Clarkson Hospital, having heard the emergency intercom request at the Omaha Crossroads Shopping Center. I told them how sorry I was to cause them this burden. My severed toes had arrived before I arrived at the hospital. My pain was not severe.

While waiting at the Clarkson ER I called my office administrator. Gloria said she already knew I had been injured. She had advised the other mental health provider, an MS psychiatric nurse practitioner who also had a PhD in family studies and human development. The two of them would do their best to keep the center running. Gloria was busily informing patients who had scheduled appointments with me of options to see my capable but overworked colleague or wait until I returned to work.

Around 6:00 p.m. an orthopedic surgeon and a plastic surgeon arrived at Clarkson Hospital to inspect my damaged foot. They said they would try to reattach my toes but they were uncertain until the torn tissue could be examined in surgery. They doubted they could repair my little toe. Minutes later an orderly arrived to move me to surgery. My foot hurt to the point that I could hardly bear the pain that had set in gradually. I was writhing because I had refused painkillers so as to think clearly enough to help the surgeons decide if it was worth trying to salvage my severed toes. I remember that the orderly who wheeled my gurney to the surgery wing apologized profusely when an elevator door squeezed my injured foot while closing. Surgery preparation was perfunctory; I prayed for a successful outcome as I drifted off when anesthesia was administered.

The next three hours are blank until I remember awakening around 9:30 p.m. in the recovery room. A patient of mine who learned of my injury was talking to me. I remember not making much sense, except to try to say I would see her in the office as soon as possible. She laughed and said, "You're out of it." I never learned how she managed to get into the recovery room; this person was always very resourceful, despite her many other issues.

Seven years later the patient accused me and other previous mental health care providers of not providing her good care; she sued us. That's another story.

The next morning the orthopedic and plastic surgeons told me they weren't able to attach my toes and that I would be hospitalized for at least two weeks. The front third of my foot and parts of three metatarsal bones were ground off. They had grafted skin from my hip to close the wound. It was fortunate the steel shield in my shoe saved my big toe. They thought they had salvaged my little toe, which they said would help with balance as I grew older. (I am older now and I often wish I didn't have my little toe. It froze at least twice during cold weather. I can't feel it much and I have arthritis in the toe, and spurs under its phalange. Whether it is an asset or detriment is still undetermined.) I told the surgeons I was surprised I hadn't developed an infection, for mice had scrounged around in the combine while it was parked in a machine shed during the previous winter. They immediately contacted hospital infection control to request several consults, but I didn't develop an infection, and only God knows why.

Over the next two weeks in the hospital, I became vulnerable and wept twice when alone. *What does this mean?* I asked. I prayed for understanding of what I was feeling. My physical life didn't seem in jeopardy, but my psychological and spiritual adjustments were in upheaval. They were more important to me in the whole scheme of things than my physical life. I felt the presence of a higher force observing me. Gradually, I realized my motives for going about life were misguided. I wanted to be in charge and too often felt I was right. I had thought I could accomplish practically anything if I put my mind to it. I was giving directions instead of asking for directions. While I liked the impact that I was creating locally and in larger realms, I felt lucky, but little did I know I was losing touch with what is more important in life: giving rather than acquiring or achieving, accepting input rather than assuming control, and caring for others first, as my life's aims.

Painfully, I realized that financial success, political and social power, and praise for accomplishments can easily become selfish and empty. My life as I had known it had fallen apart in less than a second. But adjustment took me weeks, and is still an ongoing process to figure out "Not my will, but thine be done."

The burial of my severed toes was a particularly telling event. The hospital returned my toes to me, which we kept in the chest freezer in our basement. Marilyn, Shelby, Jon, and I gathered outside after our crops were planted in May 1991 on the prairie flower and grass berm shielding the north side of our new home and diverting cold winter winds upward and over our house. I cried as we said "Good-bye" to the severed parts of my body. Amid a prayer together, we buried my toes under a rock next to a prairie yucca. I determined at that time to have the rest of my body cremated when I die and after any useful parts are removed. My survivors can spread my ashes on the berm and in a fishing stream. I dedicated myself to purposes other than for personal gain. As I considered these life-changing realizations, I became calmer.

I modified my intense disposition and altered my motives, daily activities, and approach to work and play. Over the next year I resigned two board positions, while retaining those that could most help others. We sold the farm we had purchased from my grandmother in 1981 when land prices were still high before the Farm Crisis took hold; we had to absorb a loss. We sold another eighty acres to my brother, who wanted the land. We quit taking our turns leading music at the Catholic Church, and I joined the choir instead so as to not compete with others involved in leading the music for church services after the music director said some musicians complained that Marilyn was not Catholic. Over the next few years, Marilyn continued her affiliation with the Seventh-day Adventist religion; I gradually withdrew from public religious activities except for special occasions like weddings and funerals. I focused on contemplative spiritual meditation. I also focused on not competing as a general approach to life. Marilyn and I established a habit of prayer and talk sessions each morning before going to work. It helped us get a grasp on our daily lives and purposes. I learned to park the farm machinery even during busy planting and harvesting seasons. It sunk in that recreation and time to meditate were important for maintaining perspective and that vacations help maintain personal dispositions and family relations. It might have seemed odd to our neighbors to see my farm equipment parked, instead of me finishing important farming activities while I, or Jon and I together, headed on our country road in our truck with a canoe on its rack. These changes probably saved my life.

Gradually, and with increasing inner peace, I began to ascertain answers to the question I had surmised as I pulled my foot from the combine auger earlier, *Oh, God, what does this mean?* I began to implement, "Not my will, but thine be done." I wasn't in charge anymore. My life was in the hands of a higher power. I felt closer to understanding my purpose in life.

The lawsuit I mentioned earlier also shaped what is most important. The patient who visited me in the surgery recovery room during the evening of July 24, 1990, called me at my home in mid-1995 to threaten a lawsuit. Her threat didn't come to fruition until March 1997, when the administrator of Shelby County Medical Center, of which Prairie Rose Mental Health Center was a part, showed me her notice of a court filing. The patient was suing the hospitals and doctors that had provided her mental health services, except the psychologist in the community to which she had moved a few months earlier.

The former patient alleged in her court filing that she was misdiagnosed with multiple personality disorder (now called dissociative identity disorder) and that false memories of childhood sexual abuse had been placed in her mind by those of us who were her professional caregivers. She did not contest an additional diagnosis of borderline personality disorder.

I had kept very thorough clinical notes, which became public record during the court proceedings. Early entries showed that after the patient and I met in 1983, she claimed her husband was often emotionally—and sometimes physically—abusive. Her behavior was alternately frantic, explosive, thoughtful, uncooperative, or productive to therapeutic progress. Over the ensuing next few years, she occasionally became suicidal, especially around the anniversaries of reported sexual abuse when she was a child and teenager. Eventually the woman divorced her husband. She undertook suicidal behavior several times by overdosing on prescribed medications and self-inflicted cutting, which were usually followed by hospitalizations until she was again stable behaviorally and physically. If her self-inflicted injuries were superficial, physicians who evaluated her allowed her to go home but requested that someone was needed to monitor her as needed. With my prompting, the patient chose a team of several supporters in 1990 who included a coworker at the children's shelter in Council Bluffs where they were employed and who became a faithful caregiver when no licensed professional was available. With the patient's agreement, this person joined her in therapy sessions thereafter to witness whatever occurred and to assist the patient with carrying out what were determined as next steps.

When I changed employers twice over the years of assisting this lady professionally, she chose to follow me to both new settings. The circumstances that troubled her gradually came to light. The patient told me, with her supportive friend present, about severe sexual abuse and possible involvement in a cult as a child. She gave me the names of persons she said were past perpetrators, and a well-used "satanic bible" she had kept. She reported such extensive details of specific events that I doubted they could have been fabricated. I documented allegations, and with her permission, I consulted with other health care professionals, law enforcement officials, and with family members, to consider other possible interpretations and therapeutic interventions. With her agreement, I arranged for evaluation of her claims of two pregnancies and a former pelvic fracture from the rituals she claimed to have endured as a young teenager. The University of Iowa Hospitals and Clinics, to whom I had referred her, verified her broken pelvis and uterus scars from radiologic images and other procedures that suggested that these two pregnancies and a fractured pelvis in the pubic area likely occurred during her youth.

The patient displayed drastic measures she had developed to cope with her alleged childhood mistreatment, such as compartmentalizing horrendous sexual abuse experiences. Initially, she denied memories of sexual abuse until one day during a session she abruptly spoke, screamed, cried, and acted like a frightened child during the latter part of a counseling session. When I asked her to write her name, she printed her name as a first grader might print it. Occasionally, she signed checks with this printed name thereafter. She requested that I verify with her bank that this signature was acceptable. She slipped into different dissociative states of mind, but she couldn't remember what had occurred in other mind-states than the one she exhibited at the time. Only one mind-state had the memories of severe sexual abuse and bizarre rituals she had endured, and which she could recite with great detail. Other dissociative states of mind were devoted to her children, employment, and a few other aspects of her ongoing life. Her

psychiatrist, who also became a key defendant in the lawsuit, diagnosed
her as exhibiting multiple personality disorder and borderline personality disorder. I agreed with these diagnoses. Multiple personality disorder is currently called dissociative identity disorder by the American Psychiatric Association, which has published updated versions of
the *Diagnostic and Statistical Manual of Mental Disorders*, as research
findings have accrued.

Additional evidence validated these diagnoses. In one instance a
personality (i.e., mind-state) developed an allergic reaction, which was
displayed when her face became so swollen that she was having difficulty breathing. When her main support person contacted me by telephone, I directed them to go immediately to the ER of the medical center in Harlan. By the time they arrived at the ER, the patient appeared
mostly normal, having switched to her commonplace daily personality. Several alternative personalities that the patient had developed occasionally emerged during various situations. One was very competent, such as when she was dealing with problematic interactions at
her job and in situations she perceived as threatening. Mostly this complex woman slowly became ever more competent in all aspects of her
life. She no longer switched identities about a year before she reached a
point at which she was ready to terminate counseling. Following several
months of preparation, therapy ended on a positive note in early 1995.

During her years of mental health therapy, the patient attended college and completed a bachelor's degree. She became employed full-
time, working in a restaurant and as a trainer for adoptive parents, turning her gains in self-awareness into information she could teach others.
She took in foster children and was a protective but generally reasonable and stable mother. She was financially independent.

The former patient decided to move to another community to assume a new job. A few months after relocating, she called me several
times for reassurance and to report how she was doing. During one of
the last of these calls she said she had begun counseling with a therapist in her new community. She said her new therapist told her that her

memories of abuse were not real. She seemed to have regressed, for she was accumulating charges of unpaid bills and was having trouble with her employer. She demanded that I acknowledge what she had revealed about her past abuse was false.

I didn't agree with my former patient that her memories of abuse were false, and I told her so on the phone. I explained why I didn't agree with her or her current therapist, and I pointed to her many accomplishments since coming to terms with what had happened to her, until just recently. She threatened a lawsuit nonetheless, and nothing I said satisfied her. Eventually, I learned this was the first post-degree job for her new therapist, a psychologist. I recognized his name, for I had helped his employer recruit him when his employer asked for my help finding a PhD psychologist. This psychologist and his supervisor did not seek records of any of her extensive previous treatments that I knew of.

In early 1997 I received notice of a lawsuit, which I shared with the new administrator of the health system that included Prairie Rose Mental Health Center. It was filed by a law firm with a Des Moines address, but it appeared an out-of-state group was involved that supported many lawsuits alleging false memory syndrome, which was a hot topic for litigation at the time. Since I had served as this former patient's main therapist from 1983 to early 1995, I was at the top of the list of defendants in her civil suit; three health care systems and two psychiatrists were also named as defendants. The local Harlan newspapers ran a front-page story about the accusations, mostly citing the plaintiff's allegations and a brief statement that I provided when the newspaper contacted me and that my attorney advised me to make available. I had previously contacted my professional malpractice insurer, who assigned the Des Moines-based attorney to my case.

My attorney and I undertook several in-person meetings and telephone conferences. I could tell early on that he was capable, objective, and dedicated to establishing truth. As he quizzed me in preparation for my deposition and the trial, he said he wanted me to be fully honest, which I had already intended, but this gave me additional reason to trust him.

During the two years from the filing of the lawsuit to the trial, I participated in a several-day deposition myself and I reviewed transcripts of many depositions by witnesses. I told relatives, trusted friends, and my licensing boards what was happening. I had no doubts about the truth and my motives, but I worried increasingly about the outcome as the trial date of early February 1999 drew nearer. There was a risk that my family and I could lose our farm and home, our reputations, and our livelihoods if the jury decided in favor of the plaintiff.

I didn't like it but I had no choice when the various defendants' insurance companies attempted a settlement with the plaintiff. The plaintiff rejected the insurance companies' offers and demanded many millions of dollars in claimed damages. Her civil suit asked for much more than what my malpractice insurance and homeowners' liability insurance policies allowed.

When I couldn't sleep well, I meditated, but my restlessness also kept Marilyn from sleeping well, so I tried sleeping on the couch in our den. One January night in 1999, I was so distraught that in utter desperation I said while praying, *It's in your hands; I'll do what you want.* Immediately I felt great relief and peace. I sensed a higher power with me that was like a comforting hand on my shoulder. After that night I felt I could endure anything as long as I was able to turn everything over to God.

As the court date approached in mid-February 1999, the local newspaper ran another front-page article about the impending trial that seemed like an indictment. In a gesture that sustained Marilyn and me, six friends took us to a restaurant for dinner that evening. I also received a letter without a return address which listed the names of about forty persons who were praying for me. I knew most of the persons who were Shelby County residents.

The proceedings were sensational for a small locality that had never witnessed a five-week trial. Some defendants were dropped, which left me, the Shelby County Health System with its affiliated Prairie Rose Mental Health Center, one other hospital, and the psychiatrist who helped uncover the patient's abuse as the remaining defendants who would have to bear any damages that could be awarded by the jury.

The plaintiff and her personal witnesses asserted I was the most responsible for planting false memories in the plaintiff's mind. Her psychologist/therapist was present nearly every day of the trial. Guided by the plaintiff's attorney, their hired expert witnesses from around the country testified about false memory syndrome, claiming that memories of abuse were often encouraged by mental health providers, and the memories were later proven false. The plaintiff's attorneys cited a well-known researcher who had devoted much professional work to investigating false memory syndrome. Years later, this researcher's conclusions were disputed as additional evidence accumulated that memories deemed as false were valid in many cases.

Around 7:30 each morning of the court proceedings the psychiatrist, and occasionally his wife, met me at my new office two blocks from the courthouse; we walked together to the courthouse. At noon we ate lunch in my office and briefly prayed together: he—a Mormon bishop—and I—not a traditional Catholic, but a spiritual man. We were not rattled, although we didn't know what the outcome of the trial would be.

When the defendants had our turn, we told the truth as we knew it. I had twelve years of extensive, methodical, medical records of every session I was involved in and information from outside health care providers throughout this patient's life to substantiate the abuse she had experienced, the memories she had revealed, and her personal improvements until she left our care. I pointed out how the patient had called me at any hour of the day or night and found ways to get past the answering service that assessed a caller's need for professional assistance. I had made sure another person approved by the patient was present to witness what took place whenever we met. These people testified at the trial. The psychiatrist gave his testimony accurately and succinctly. The Prairie Rose Mental Health Center administrative assistant verified how case notes were kept. Even Marilyn was called to testify regarding allegations of the plaintiff. To address a claim by the plaintiff that my inappropriate affection for her included keeping her pictures and handwritten notes under my bedside, Marilyn testified, "Mike only keeps his cattle journals and fly-fishing magazines under our bed; I change the bedding."

All the defendants' attorneys offered rebuttal evidence that debunked the claims of mistreatment alleged by the plaintiff; my attorney skillfully took the lead. When the closing arguments were heard and the judge declared the trial over after five weeks, except for the verdict, we headed to our homes on a late Friday afternoon in mid-March 1999.

Hardly had I arrived home around 5:30 p.m. when the telephone rang. It was the psychiatrist. He said, "My attorney just called me to say the jury ruled unanimously in favor of the defendants. The jurors felt we had done our best to help a troubled lady and that she benefited from our assistance. Their decision took fifteen minutes, but the jury members decided to stay together another fifteen minutes to say good-bye to each other. It's over."

The local newspaper published a couple-paragraph article in an inside page of the next edition. Legal appeals followed but were denied by the Iowa Supreme Court as having merit.

Shortly after the trial, I accepted the offer of a position as assistant director of Iowa's Center for Agricultural Safety and Health and to become a staff member of the Department of Occupational and Environmental Health at the University of Iowa. I had not applied for these positions, but I gladly accepted them because I believed in the causes espoused by these Iowa entities. My family needed the income because Jon was an undergraduate student at the University of Iowa, and we paid his tuition and most of his expenses. Furthermore, Shelby was in medical school there and I could stay overnight with Shelby and her husband in Iowa City. Although Marilyn and I didn't pay for Shelby's medical schooling, I could defray some of her expenses by paying rent when I stayed with them overnight two or three times each week.

About a year earlier and after I resigned from the Shelby County health system, I rented an office in Harlan to provide counseling services to farm people, mainly from Iowa. I entered a new phase devoted almost entirely to understanding the motivations and mental health vulnerabilities of people involved in agriculture. With help from dedicated supporters of the same purposes, we founded AgriWellness, Inc., a nonprofit corporation that sought to improve the behavioral welfare of all agricultural people. Universities, organizations, and companies began asking AgriWellness and me to help them respond to the mental health concerns of agricultural people, including farmers, ranchers, farmworkers, and anyone else whose livelihood depended on producing food and fiber, which included occupational fishers, professional hunters, and lumber harvesters. Combining my professional services with my appointment at the University of Iowa worked well to accomplish goals I was forming, but I had to sell my beloved cattle. That was one of the hardest things I had to do, ever. I still dream about my cattle and remember some of their names and ear tag numbers. I wasn't home enough to run our farm on a daily basis, and I didn't have enough time to do things right in our farming operation, even with a helpful hired hand. I turned over the crop farming to the neighbor who had rented our farm prior to us moving from Virginia to Iowa. However, I continued to manage our farm, including its thirty-five acres of land enrolled in the Conservation Reserve Program. By the early 2000s, additional health issues were creeping up. I knew God had control of my life.

And still, more than twenty years later, I say prayers of thanks, not for the outcome of the civil trial or for the outcomes of any of my health scares, but for helping me understand what is most important in life: service to others, while fully implementing "Not my will, but thine be done."

Losing three of my toes and enduring the lawsuit were shaping events. They helped prepare me for what was ahead.

In 2002, I experienced prostate cancer, the first of multiple serious medical events. The surgeon who removed my prostate found that the cancer was kept inside the gland by a membrane the thickness of a sheet of newspaper. What does this say about protection by a higher power? Prostate cancer changed me a lot physically. My hair became white. After my prostatectomy my hyperactivity subsided considerably. I began to sleep longer and to no longer crave caffeine. Even my desire for smoking a good cigar diminished, except when fishing. The urologist made the surgical cut into my abdomen too long; I soon developed an umbilical hernia while lifting something heavy, but I don't recall what it was I lifted. The hernia didn't hurt, it just looked funny.

In 2004, I experienced my first major cardiovascular event during a warm mid-May Sunday morning while fishing at a favorite farm pond that was owned by an AgriWellness staff member and her husband. After catching all the bass, bluegills, and perch that I wanted, I was having difficulty slogging through suctioning mud that cattle in the surrounding pasture had created when they wallowed into the pond to drink water, cool off, and to avoid flies. Struggling to reach the shore, I found myself gasping for air and my limbs feeling very heavy as I finally crawled onto the bank.

After gathering myself and carefully driving home, I apprised Marilyn that I might be having a coronary event of some kind. Worriedly, she drove me to the local hospital emergency room, where after examination, I was forwarded by ambulance to the Nebraska Medical Center in Omaha for further evaluation. A cardiovascular surgeon was contacted to make an angioplasty assessment. He found my left anterior descending artery (LAD) was completely occluded and had probably been blocked for many years. The surgeon placed stents into two other coronary arteries that showed partial occlusions; he wanted to reopen the LAD with another stent. I was awake during the cardiovascular procedures. The surgeon announced that my LAD had a troubling ninety-degree bend at one location, which might make it difficult to move the stent properly into place.

I asked for a consultation from another cardiovascular surgeon to determine what was the risk of perforation of the blood vessel wall during this type of stent placement procedure. The consulting surgeon, who arrived on the scene shortly, said there was a 20 percent chance of perforation. When I asked if there was sufficient time to open my chest and to stop the bleeding before I died in case of a perforation, he said, "Probably not." I stated my preference to not go ahead with the LAD stent. Additional procedures were terminated and I was sent to my hospital room.

The cardiology stent specialist came to see me in my room that evening. He was livid as he pronounced that I could die within a year if I didn't have the LAD stent. I asked for a second opinion, and I had already called my daughter, Shelby, who was finishing her four-year internal medicine residency and starting a rheumatology fellowship next month at the University of Utah. My stent specialist also talked to her on the phone. Shelby's cardiovascular physician acquaintances recommended open heart surgery to replace the LAD. Yet, I wondered and prayed for an answer. Was coronary bypass surgery necessary, given that I had not suffered a typical heart attack, and had developed collateral arteries in my heart to move blood around? Moreover, medications had been developed to reduce blood platelets from sticking together and new blood thinners were becoming available. I mentioned this.

"Okay, I'll get you a second opinion," my surgeon ranted as he strode out of my hospital room. A few minutes later the doctor came into my room with a second-year cardiology resident following him.

"Here's your second opinion," my cardiovascular surgeon huffed as he left my hospital room.

I asked the resident a couple questions. "Are you ready to make this kind of determination? Doesn't this put you in an awkward position, because he's your supervisor?" I asked as I explained that my surgeon had called my daughter, who gave him the recommendation of her physician colleagues for coronary bypass surgery.

The resident shrugged and said, "I'm not ready for this kind of recommendation. Sorry."

I asked for my angioplasty surgeon to return to my room. I requested an opinion from an experienced department colleague; he brusquely said he would arrange it.

An hour later a gray-haired man entered my room, well past 10:00 p.m. He said he was the cardiologist who was requested to look at the angiogram data and the cardiovascular surgeon's report and comments. He noted the development of alternative arterial routes in my heart. He thought blood-thinning medications, combined with annual checkups that included stress electrocardiograms to determine if my heart was functioning adequately, would suffice. I thanked him and thanked the higher power in my life for helping me reach a decision.

The next morning my cardiologist visited my room. I told him my decision to not go ahead with the LAD stent. He apologized for his temper outburst the evening before and explained how he cared a great deal about his patients. I didn't doubt that a bit; we shook hands. He said I could go home, but I had to see him in two weeks and at least once every year thereafter, which I did. We became friends. Newer research literature that I looked up suggested that diet, exercise, taking blood-thinning medications, and keeping blood pressure down through behavior management, such as controlling anger episodes, could yield better outcomes than reopening a blocked LAD with a stent or coronary bypass surgery to implant another artery. I didn't know how much longer my heart would function adequately, but I felt good, backed up by regular medical evaluations that agreed until 2019; that's later in this sequence of events.

In 2005, a round of retinal detachments occurred during that summer. The first detachment occurred in my right eye while I was flying to Jackson Hole, Wyoming, in late May to participate in the National Rural Mental Health Summit. I could see well with my left eye, but it seemed like a blackout shade had been drawn down to cover my right eye, leaving only a tiny sliver of light at the bottom.

The federal program organizers had asked three people to provide the opening plenary address: the president of the National Association for Rural Mental Health, a division leader of the Federal Office of Rural Health Policy, and me, a farmer and psychologist. Many federal and state officials attended this strategic planning meeting, which convened every five years.

Our task was to set the tone for the conference by identifying the needs of the rural and agricultural populations for mental health assistance. When the moderator introduced me as the last keynote speaker, he told the conference attendees about my vision problem. I detected concern from many in the audience, so I opened my talk with the line, "My vision to the left is fine," which generated a laugh and put most people at ease. I went on to say, "Farmers, ranchers, and agricultural laborers view mental health as something they don't talk about. Even when they, or family members, realize that treatment is absolutely necessary for a serious mental illness, they avoid talking about their problems except with caregivers, a few family members, and highly trusted persons. To them, needing mental health care is a sign of weakness. We need to understand the cultures of the people we serve."

It felt right to recommend not using the term *mental health*, and instead use the term *behavioral health* whenever possible. "Everyone," I said, "understands what behavior is. The word *behavioral* doesn't have the same negative stigma as the word *mental*." I went on to make a case to the summit attendees that "Services must be culturally acceptable to agricultural people, and to all people, for that matter." Federal officials at the conference must have been listening.

Within weeks after the conference, U.S. Department of Health and Human Services officials formed a national task force of about three dozen representatives from many walks of life, including me, to formulate a national plan, and to debate federal-level adoption of the term *behavioral health* instead of *mental health*, when appropriate. I suggested that the task force include Department of Agriculture-funded participants. We met in person and via telephone conference calls several times. The debate was heated. Some task force members said mental illness isn't under our control. A few others, and I, indicated we are mostly able to manage our behaviors. We choose to seek behavioral health care, which may include taking medications, learning skills from counseling, and considering advice from others we value. "Some persons," I said, "might assert in a derogatory fashion that so-and-so is 'mental,' when they describe a person who is suffering serious mental illness, and sometimes only to 'put down on' a person they dislike, but no one can credibly label so-and-so as 'behavioral,' in the same fashion." I added, "Seeking behavioral health care is a sign of strength, not weakness."

The task force recommended a carefully thought-out strategic plan to address the needs of rural people for behavioral health care and to use the term *behavioral health care* whenever possible. Both recommendations were adopted. Use of *behavioral health* helped to bring understanding and respect for persons coping with psychological problems. The term is part of common nomenclature. Prairie Rose Mental Health Center is now called Shelby County Behavioral Health Services. Educational training programs have been changed to such titles as Behavioral Health and Psychiatry, or something similar.

When the next national planning conference convened in 2010, it was called the National Rural Behavioral Health Summit. The conference organizers asked me to give the keynote address at the Glendale, Arizona, event. I thanked the federal officials for adopting "behavioral health" as a positive and non-stigmatized term.

The dozen years after 2005 were very busy. An increasing number of farm people, mainly in the Midwest, contacted AgriWellness or me at my home. I fulfilled as many speaking requests, and participated in radio, television, and online media programs as much I could, but it became necessary to add thoughtful and efficient coworkers at AgriWellness, when grant funds allowed. We were highly productive; we elected a staff member to receive a monthly award, which we called the King or Queen of Parsimony for writing the most succinctly; we wrote many research and magazine articles, and held biennial conferences called "The Clock is Ticking for Rural America: A Behavioral Health and Safety Conference," that regularly attracted 120 to 230 participants from around the United States. AgriWellness board members from our seven states (Wisconsin, Minnesota, North Dakota, South Dakota, Nebraska, Kansas, and Iowa) met in person a couple times each year, and monthly or more often as needed by telephone.

Eventually, however, grant funds became increasingly difficult to obtain. The building that housed AgriWellness and my consulting offices was sold in March 2014 to a prominent local corporation that chose to make it their headquarters. One AgriWellness staff member succumbed to cancer and another began to experience incapacitating health issues. While the remaining AgriWellness staff moved on to other opportunities, I maintained the AgriWellness activities and my agricultural behavioral health care practice from my home after April 2014. I had begun in 2012 to write a weekly column, called *Farm and Ranch Life*, for agricultural weeklies, some monthly, and for several daily newspapers in the Midwest. Readers of the syndicated column contacted me increasingly. Requests for assistance with personal problems of people engaged in agriculture, as well as for interviews by the media, speaking events at farm organization conferences, and workshops at educational institutions burgeoned. I responded to every request, except a few whom I referred to other professionals for follow-up.

My health remained mostly trouble-free until 2018. During the last two days of February, my hearing became severely limited by otitis media, which broke one eardrum just prior to traveling by airplane, and the other while in-flight to give an invited address to state and federal leaders of USDA extension programs, as well as to other federal administrators and some elected federal officials. I relied on visual cues to navigate my way through airports and to take the Washington Metro from Reagan National Airport to my reserved room at the hotel where I was scheduled to speak at the noon luncheon the next day. I asked the program planners to place three-by-five-inch cards on the approximate hundred guest tables so that participants in the meeting could ask me written questions. My talk was about why our country needed a national system of behavioral health supports for agricultural producers. I took and answered all the questions that were submitted. I left the podium while receiving an unexpected standing ovation and eventually arrived back home okay, except for my hearing loss. Medication subsequently quelled my ear infections; my hearing improved.

What I didn't know was going on behind the scenes was that officials who were appointed to major positions of the Department of Agriculture and the Department of Health and Human Services, along with congressional elected officials, were considering how to better address the behavioral health care issues of distressed agricultural producers, including suicide. A legislative provision that AgriWellness board officers and I had drafted, called the Farm and Ranch Stress Assistance Network, was originally proposed in 2008 and authorized by Congress, but when the federal budget was considered, some of its previous supporters chose not to fund the program. Why was Congress reconsidering the Farm and Ranch Stress Assistance Network?

In December 2017, Debbie Weingarten, a highly competent and perceptive writer who had lost her farming operation in Arizona several years previously, and Audra Mulkern, a photographer and vegetable producer in the Seattle area, visited our home and the homes of several other midwestern farmers to develop an article about the extraordinarily high rate of farmer suicide, which was published in the *Guardian* in December 2017. Additional articles followed in the *Wall Street Journal*, the *Washington Post, Forbes* magazine, and many more publications. Interviews were requested by most of the major U.S. news networks, the BBC, NPR, PBS, and other media. Debbie's articles and Audra's photos were distributed widely, including to elected leaders in the U.S. Congress. I'm sure they contributed to a momentum that was building to assist the agricultural population with behavioral health issues.

What followed in 2018 was unexpected, as Congress formulated the next Farm Bill. Federal administrators, two senators—Joni Ernst (R-IA) and Tammy Baldwin (D-WI)—and several members of the House of Representatives on both sides of the political aisle—chiefly Congressmen Tom Emmer (R-MN) and Collin Peterson (D-MN)—strategized how to incorporate behavioral health care of stressed farmers into the 2018 Farm Bill. Congress reconsidered the 2008 Farm and Ranch Stress Network proposal and included behavioral health care services as part of the bill that was passed on December 30, 2018, and signed into law a day later by President Trump. The legislation authorized $50 million to be spent over the next five years to establish four regional centers at agricultural land-grant universities around the country, and to provide a range of farm crisis services that AgriWellness had determined to be best practices. The Farm and Ranch Stress Assistance Network funded crisis telephone and email hotlines in all agricultural states or regions, covered the costs of counseling to distressed farmers (like many employers provide employee assistance programs confidentially to their employees), trained licensed counselors in agricultural behavioral health, and sought to advance research concerning the behavioral health of the agricultural population.

The year 2019 was consumed with more writing, workshops, speaking events, and assisting agricultural producers and/or their families with personal issues, as well as responding to the inquiries of researchers, educators, media representatives, and anyone interested in improving the behavioral well-being of the agricultural population. The American Psychological Association invited me to the 2019 Farm Aid Concert events, where I addressed the media about the stresses of farming. During the first week of December 2019, it occurred to me that, once again, I had exceeded my capacities. I developed Type A flu, even though I had a flu shot, while delivering a workshop at Colorado State University and arrived home exhausted. Marilyn did all the driving. Although medication successfully eliminated the flu, three days later I asked her to take me to the local ER because I didn't feel right. The

ER physician assistant and my personal physician diagnosed my condition as cardiovascular insufficiency. I was transferred by ambulance to a Des Moines hospital of my choice that specialized in treatment of cardiovascular issues.

Possibly serendipitously, but I prefer by higher design as more accurate, I underwent two major medical procedures: triple coronary bypass surgery and a thirty-one-day stay in two hospitals during December 2019 and January 2020, followed by repairs to an aortic aneurysm in July 2020 and five days of hospitalization. The surgeons and hospitals provided expert care. My caregivers and I became friends as I learned from them and follow-up care providers more than I had figured out on my own. The surgeon who repaired my aneurysm also fixed my umbilical hernia. COVID-19 halted most live speaking events in 2020 and during part of 2021, but not virtual events or my writing. Gradually, I resumed an almost full-time schedule of work during 2020 and up to the present. I can't call what I do "work," because it brings me the excellent joy of feeling useful to the people who reach out to me and benefit from my efforts. I still don't bill anyone who requests my services, but I ask for reimbursement from the publishers that print my *Farm and Ranch Life* columns, organizations and institutions that seek my professional consultation, and those that ask me to provide workshops and major speeches.

In spite of many medical procedures since July 1990, I have never felt in danger of death. When I awakened from sedation by anesthesia after my surgeries, the first thing I noticed was that I could think, hear, feel, see, and move all my body parts. I uttered a prayer of thanks.

Even if I wasn't going through a health problem, neighbors and friends showed up at our house to move snow when needed, to fell dead trees and haul them to a burn pile, and to fix our farmstead outbuildings, without Marilyn or me asking them. They refused to accept payment. I didn't suffer any significant damage to my heart during all my coronary events. My most obvious physical limitations currently are worn-out knees and hips, which I attribute mostly to aging and to jumping on and off farming equipment, as well as stacking hay bales—a task I particularly enjoyed all my life. Most of the time I don't pay attention to my difficulties walking and bending; they are a part of life. I'm thankful for being "able" in other ways.

The aim of taking care of the behavioral health of farmers now sustains other persons' efforts of caring for the behavioral health of agricultural people. Much of this work is being undertaken by younger colleagues, many of whom I communicate with regularly. All of us are surprised that an avenue to move forward always develops, such as the Farm and Ranch Stress Assistance Network. Research and programmatic efforts are being pursued by the next generation of behavioral health care professionals who are devoting their lives to caring for the agricultural population. It wasn't luck that these circumstances occurred—it had to be divine intervention.

It feels now like a higher power is always watching over me. I regularly ask during meditation to become closer to understanding and carrying out God's purpose for my life. I know my purpose is helping others. I also know that I easily fall into self-deception. *Am I progressing in serving God's purpose?* is always a valid question, and one that I am still trying to answer.

4

MY WIFE'S GARDENS

Like many farm couples, my wife plants the flower gardens and I take care of the vegetable gardens, now that the kids are on their own. Anyhow, that's how she sees it. I can the tomatoes, salsa, and beets; I freeze the beans, okra, asparagus, and give away the excess fresh veggies to our adult children and my office staff. It's fun for both of us.

We both have enjoyable off-farm employment and obligations as well, but our farm brings me a different type of fulfillment than Marilyn obtains from her flowers, even though we now rent our cropland to a capable farmer. I manage the overall operation of our farm and the several tracts of our conservation habitat for prairie plants, pollinators, and wildlife, as well as our vegetable gardens.

It's fun to be the first in the neighborhood during the spring to harvest fresh spinach because I mulched the August-planted spinach late last fall just after picking our last salad greens of the year; it overwintered fine. When I uncovered it in mid-March, it was already growing nicely; two weeks later we had our first garden produce. And it's fun when my office staff appreciatively praises my fresh tomatoes, peppers, beans, and assorted surprises.

But this is about my wife's gardens. Midafternoon, for the second time in as many hours, my phone rang at my office. "Hi, it's me again. Can you stop at the Garden Supply and pick up six more bags of red cedar mulch? Get the same stuff that we bought yesterday. Can you pay for it? I didn't have my credit card when I called to see if they still had mulch. And, oh, pick up four more Japanese lilies, and get some rooting hormone."

How could I resist such a cheery voice? And, of course, I wasn't one to stand in the way of home improvement projects. So, two hours later, I unloaded the mulch and various items next to her plots of tulips, daffodils, lilies, irises, gladioli, asters, and assorted native prairie plants. As I finished the unloading chores, my wife pleasantly asked, "Can you haul these branches for me? And can you bring me a couple buckets of water for the new plants? Would you make sure the lawn tractor starts okay, because we haven't used it yet this spring? And where is the spade? Is there any fertilizer left from last year?"

"How about if I change clothes first so I don't get my clean pants dirty," I intoned. Nonetheless, I cranked up the lawn tractor and hooked it to the cart, tossed in the spade, loaded two buckets of water and a partial bag of fertilizer, and then drove to where my wife was working in her gardens before entering the house to change clothes.

While I was changing clothes, I could hear the lawn tractor rev up. The motor droned outside the bedroom windows, and I was glad it seemed to be working okay. For the next hour I could hear the tractor surge as Marilyn clipped dandelions with the belly mower instead of hauling the trash for which she had requested the tractor and garden cart. She trailed the cart the entire time. I went ahead with watering her newly planted flowers and carried away the trash she had raked into piles next to her flower beds with my arms because the garden cart was unavailable.

Not wanting to interfere with progress, I said nothing until the tractor sputtered to a stop in the farthest corner of our farmstead. I went about tilling my gardens and planting a few beets, lettuce, radishes, and broccoli seeds in the rich soil. "Can you see what's wrong, the tractor won't run," my wife pronounced.

"Did you check the gas?" I asked.

"There was about a quarter tank left when I started," she responded. "It just won't start now. Can you see what's wrong with it?"

I started to feel the blood collect in my neck and head. Certain words that husbands should keep to themselves collected on my tongue. I slammed my hoe to the ground and stalked to the lawn tractor and cart. I immediately raised the hood and saw the gas tank was bone dry. My blood pressure simmered as I galumphed to the shop to get the gas can.

Marilyn had gone into the house. When the tractor started, I drove it to the shed and parked it. As I collected garden tools, I saw the spade lying where she had last used it. Not wanting it to rust, I shined it up and smeared a thin coating of petroleum jelly on the metal surfaces. I washed up and entered the kitchen.

"Don't you think my gardens look good!" my wife joyfully professed. "Julie stopped by and said my gardens always look so nice."

I started to say something, but instead I sat down and penned "My Wife's Gardens."

5

I DO SOME OF MY BEST THINKING IN THE RASPBERRY PATCH

At the end of a mind-numbing day that has frazzled me, from late June until the first hard frost, I often end up picking red raspberries from our ever-bearing canes. For every four or five that I deposit in the bowl to take to the house later, I stuff a luscious plump berry in my mouth and think, *Marilyn won't realize I ate a bunch, will she? She will probably say only how nice the raspberries look.*

Most gardeners, farmers, and others whose occupations allow them to spend time in the outdoors will attest they do some of their best thinking in their "raspberry patches." For me it's not only the raspberry patch where I can sequester myself from telephone calls and the traffic that goes by on our gravel road. By early July the rows of pole beans that were planted in May have now climbed the cattle panels I attached to steel posts in one or two of my raised bed gardens; they also provide another good place for solitude. I can pick beans and meditate at the same time.

The barns and the thick groves of pines and cotoneaster bushes that surround our farmstead also are welcome places to think and meditate. If Marilyn calls from the back door to say, "Mike, there's a phone call for you," I can choose if I want to let her know my whereabouts. I answer unless I definitely feel I have not allotted myself sufficient time to become grounded. But if she follows up with a comment such as "A patient is on the phone and needs to talk to you right away," or voices some other urgent request, I answer back.

"Okay, I'm coming."

I usually ask Marilyn to field the calls on our landline phone when I am out of our house, because I know she can make a sage determination of whether the call requires an imminent response. She has good judgment. Marilyn was a behavioral health nursing professor until three years ago. As my mate for fifty-plus years, she also knows enough of the basics about my personal circumstances to determine if a rapid response is necessary, and sometimes better than I know myself.

I purposefully don't take my cell phone with me into the garden, or wherever I retreat to, unless I'm expecting an important call. I let my mind sail to wherever it wants to go. It always sails to the things that most need to be attended to. My gut tells me what is important to review in my life. Maybe I said something hurtful to Marilyn or wrongly offended someone else, or maybe I was treated unfairly by other persons and now I feel angry.

Metaphorically speaking, picking pole beans, whether lima or green beans, is a lot like life. If I head to the garden thinking there won't be many beans to harvest, I usually can't find enough for a meal. I pay the price for this outlook the next time I pick beans, for I usually discover overly mature beans that I had previously overlooked. Now they are beyond their peak of delicious flavor and tenderness. If I proceed to pick beans with an attitude that I will find enough for a meal, I always can find enough for supper. My outlook largely determines how many beans I find.

Some of the best beans are at the bottoms of the plants and hidden among the stems and leaves. And that's the way life can be too—some of my most teachable moments occur when I am at my bottom. When I learn, I become buoyed up. Some of the best people I encounter are those at the bottom of the human pecking order. They know humility and acceptance better than me. I can learn much from them.

I have a friend, Brian, who spent several months during the 1970s working with Mother Teresa, the Catholic nun who devoted her life to caring for the most destitute in Calcutta, India. Brian, a Buddhist, asked Mother Teresa the day he began his sojourn if she would teach him compassion. For several weeks Brian lived and worked in the hospital operated by the Missionaries of Charity. Periodically, he repeated his request to Mother Teresa; she did not answer him. Just as Brian was about to give up and move on to the next phase of his life, that evening Mother Teresa told Brian to meet her at 4:00 a.m. the next morning by the hearse the sisters used to haul the sick and dying to the hospital. She asked Brian to drive the vehicle.

As they coursed the streets of Calcutta, Mother Teresa directed Brian to pull next to a leprous man lying on the street. She gathered the gravely ill man in her arms and told him, "My brother, you are saved." Together, she and Brian maneuvered the dying man onto a gurney and lifted him into the hearse. After unloading the sick man at the hospital, the two set out to find other indigents in great need of care. They spotted an emaciated man lying in his own vomit on the side of the road and covered with flies and feces.

Mother Teresa directed Brian to pick up the man. He approached the deathly ill man but was so put off by his odor and filth that Brian halted and began to cry. After several minutes Brian regained his composure. Brian cradled the sick man in his arms and easily lifted him into the hearse by himself, gently voicing, "Be comforted my brother!" Brian thanked Mother Teresa for teaching him, but she said, "No, thank the man you just cared for."

My experiences of insight usually aren't as powerful as Brian's, but in their own way they help me remake my outlook. They bypass me if I don't discipline myself to meditate. If I neglect meditation on a regular basis, God always nudges me. Sometimes I have to be "just plain knocked off my horse" to see what I have been neglecting. My "opening up" experiences can be intense as they bring me closer to discovery.

For example, a number of years ago my urologist called me at home in the early evening to tell me I had prostate cancer. I had hoped and prayed through the days before my diagnostic tests that I didn't have this dreaded disease. When the biopsy results indicated significant cancer cells and that complete body scans were necessary to learn if the cancer had spread, I didn't want to accept the prognosis. I wanted things my way.

I regularly have to ask for help to accept the course that lies ahead rather than the path I wish to take. It's always been hard for me to accept whatever comes; I am my own biggest obstacle. The experience of cancer was good for me.

I chose surgical removal as the method of cancer treatment and was fortunate. The cancer had not spread outside the prostate, although it was contained by a membrane with the thinness of a sheet of newspaper. What does that say about being cared for by a higher power! Cancer gave me an opportunity to remake myself into a better person. It provided an opportunity to practice "Not my will, but thine be done."

Meditation is cleansing and "opening up." Sometimes I don't find answers right away and I have to work on the issue repeatedly to figure out if I am doing things right. I can feel when I have attained peace.

Over the years of combining farming with psychology, sometimes my "raspberry patch" was the Honda all-terrain vehicle that I used to check cattle in various pastures or simply to motor over hills and valleys on nearby dirt roads. At other times it was the Ford 1900 tractor we affectionately called "the little blue Ford" that I used to rake hay. This was such a simple job that I could meditate while rolling the hay into neat windrows. Other farm chores, such as disking cornstalks while riding in a tractor cab, afforded opportunities to contemplate if they didn't require much attention or complex decision making.

At other times it was—and still is—posting a weedy, pheasant-filled draw at one end while the other guys and their bird dogs flush the gamebirds from their haunts and blast at them or spook them to run through thick undercover toward me. Still other times, my moments of solitude and meditation find me in my float tube, paddling on a healthy farm pond and periodically pulling in a nice crappie, bluegill, or bass. These fly-fishing episodes aren't always calm when a husky bass strips line from my reel, or when a yard-long snapping turtle eyes my bulging fish bag, or when a violent gale shoves me around on a white-capped body of water. But when the conditions are calm, whether with an empty or heavily laden fish bag, there are few indulgences as pleasant as casting for fish from a float tube while meditating nearly the entire time.

I have figured out how to meditate even while driving, as long as the roadway conditions are favorable. I can contemplate for hours of discovery and "cleaning up my act." These are highly restorative and spiritual occasions. Few moments are as beneficial as these contemplative experiences that bring us closer to what is most important.

6

FISHING FOR CRUISERS

Few experiences excite anglers more than a conglomeration of fish trolling the surface of a lake or any water habitat, usually just beyond the reach of our casts as they madly pursue some kind of milling prey. Our adrenaline surges; we focus singularly on figuring out how to pick off the coursing predators as they attack a swarming buffet of appetizers. We get so caught up in the pursuit of the cruisers that sometimes we abandon our good sense to stay far enough away so we don't disrupt the party.

Repetitive slashing of eager cruisers is obviously advantageous for them when they surround and exploit a food source. The prey must also experience some benefit for their survival or these scenarios wouldn't occur regularly in a world where most humans give credence to the Darwinian theory of survival of the fittest. The many cruisers and their prey, such as small fish, insects, or other delicacies, furnish a multitude of eyes that can spot those higher up on the food chain, such as humans, eagles, or bigger fish. Maybe the milling prey are seeking food for themselves or mates for their procreation. Perhaps the prey are victims of well-executed maneuvers by predators to corral a food supply into easier apprehension, while escapees pass along acquired survival tactics that become encoded into the DNA of their progeny. I don't know enough to explain the phenomenon fully, but I know that fishing for cruisers can take place on creeks, rivers, ponds, and oceans, and that the experience is captivating, fun, and can be funny.

My first experience trying to catch cruising fish was on a less-than-foot-deep-and-two-foot-wide pristine Wasatch Mountain rivulet in July 1970. I had read an article in the Salt Lake City *Tribune* about a tiny mountainside creek that was only a dozen miles from the University of Utah where I was enrolled in graduate studies in clinical psychology. While hiking a mile alongside thick creek-side willows, I found several ten-inch cutthroat trout and a few larger whitefish periodically pouncing on small lavender butterflies fluttering just above a two-yard-long mudflat submerged under two inches of water on the side of the rippling stream opposite me. Many butterflies rested on the muddy shoreline as well, but rose in a flurry when a nearby catapulting fish disturbed their serenity. From my crouching position twenty-five feet upstream from my quarry, I cautiously floated worms, salmon eggs, and tiny spinners over the mudflat but generated no strikes from the trout or whitefish. As surreptitiously as possible, I crept to the cruising site and captured a few of the lepidopteran insects with my fishing net. I had to wait a while for the scene to return to normal before I floated a violet-winged insect I had threaded onto a size 24 hook attached to a nine-foot leader and three feet of tippet down to the reassembling melee. When the dead butterfly drifted near the mudflat a cutthroat trout seized it immediately. Every few minutes that afternoon I captured a trout or whitefish each time until I used up my supply of butterflies. Each time I hooked and played a fish, I had to allow the remaining pack members several minutes to settle back into their schooling routines; the length of recovery time between catches gradually increased. I kept a limit of trout and a couple whitefish. They made tasty dinners for a week, and all the more pleasant as I replayed my experiences catching them.

My second trip a week later to this remote fishing spot yielded two cutthroat trout and three whitefish, enough for four meals. During my third successive weekend trip to the same fishing hot spot I gave up after I spent four hours landing just two fish, even though there were several more fish manning the site. The small lavender butterflies were fewer and the predatory fish were "onto me," but it had been fun while it lasted. I decided to leave any congregations farther upstream to themselves, or to fellow fishers, so as to maintain this precious native area.

Surprisingly, however, I didn't encounter anyone else on my enjoyable foraging trips.

After I met Marilyn in January 1971 when we were both graduate students at the University of Utah and I had learned from her father how to tie flies, I constructed my own artificial lavender butterflies. When I experimented with my hand-tied flies on the same Wasatch Mountain stream that summer, they worked fairly well but not as regularly as live-caught butterflies threaded onto a tiny hook. Nonetheless, I was glad to have figured out how to construct my own imitations of insects that attracted the fish I wanted to catch and to leave the butterflies for the fish.

Another occasion when I witnessed a congregation of fish swarming together in a body of water was in the Pacific Ocean off the western Mexico coast while pursuing sailfish and marlin with my roommate, Ken, during spring break in 1971. Carlos, the captain of our chartered boat, excitedly pointed to several of our prey as they followed a school of some kind of small baitfish near the surface. Only Ken hooked and caught a sailfish during the first day of our excursion. Carlos was obviously frustrated because he couldn't maneuver us close enough to the top-water ruckus to figure out what the predators were pursuing before they all fled the scene.

We regrouped the following day for another try. Carlos solved the mystery of what our sport fish were feeding on. We drifted cautiously onto the outskirts of a feeding frenzy and caught six sailfish, which we released, and a marlin over the next several hours, using the same bait as the billfish were pursuing. Ken and I had so much fun together that we downed a half-dozen cervezas during our ninety-minute return trip to the harbor. Ken had his picture taken next to the nine-foot-long blue marlin he caught while onlookers watched, and later we cut backstrap steaks from his trophy fish.

Formative learning experiences with freshwater cruisers also took place on Beaver Creek Reservoir in Virginia when I fished there from a homemade canoe in the latter half of the 1970s. My family lived just a few miles east of the reservoir, which was about equidistant but in the opposite direction from my first postgraduate job as a psychology professor at the University of Virginia.

One Sunday afternoon in August, Marilyn paddled our canoe with our two-year-old daughter next to her and with me in the back to steer and occasionally to help maneuver as we sought bass, crappie, and bluegills. Marilyn left the fishing up to me, but we all liked canoeing and eating dinners of any fish I managed to catch. I noticed several predatory fish of some kind encircling a swirling top water gathering of some sort.

Periodically, one of the dining fish on the outskirts of the swarm charged into the hors d'oeuvres to grab a treat, then quickly retreated. The assemblage reminded me of the gatherings of teenage boys on weekend evenings in my western Iowa hometown when I was one of them, driving hotrods around the main drag—usually a school parking lot or the courthouse square—looking to impress girls, or to talk with other guys, and sometimes to enjoy a soda or maybe a beer if feeling brave. Occasionally, the local studs pressed on their accelerators to make their mufflers roar and tires squeal as they raced among the other cars and departed briefly, only to rejoin the herd a few minutes later. Dad wouldn't allow my older brother and me to own a hotrod, so I had to ride with someone else. Like cruising fish, everyone kept a keen eye out for the local police so we wouldn't be apprehended for speeding, excessive noise, or an open container of beer.

The first few times I spotted cruisers on the Beaver Creek impoundment enjoying a revelry, I searched for any prey, such as insects, at their coursing site. I couldn't land any fish although I tried my entire arsenal of flies, which my father-in-law or I had tied. Another time later when I was fishing alone, I found a small, floating, obviously dead minnow when I paddled my canoe into the scattering throng. I let the throng calm down and move to quiet water while I threaded the minnow onto a fishhook. When I located another gathering spot, I cast the minnow a couple feet short of the throng of predators and prey. *Bingo!* When I reeled in my catch, I learned that the town studs in

Beaver Creek Reservoir were adolescent largemouth bass having fun together. It figures!

Over my fishing years I've noticed occasional accumulations of adolescent largemouth bass, bluegills, and many trout roiling the water surface just beyond reach of my casts from a canoe or float tube. Usually, I barely saw the tops of their heads, dorsal fins, and tails as they circled around their town drag. Eventually, I ascertained that the source of the fish merriment was almost always a swarm of tiny shiners or minnows of some sort just under a dimpled water surface where I couldn't see them. The closer I drew, the more likely the predators and the prey were to retreat. I enjoyed these pivotal lessons. Any unusual sound they heard through the water also scattered them, like noisily placing a paddle in the canoe. Landing a spinner bait among the fish triggered an immediate dispersal when it plopped onto the water. The noises were like a town cop switching on a patrol car siren: the culprits and the objects of their attention quickly scattered.

I switched entirely to a fly rod for its softer delivery of bait. I discovered that silently paddling a float tube was less alarming to the fish than approaching them in a canoe. To avoid disrupting the cruisers' fun, I began to work on casting long. I learned to accurately cast a fly over seventy feet with a single vigorous backward thrust of my retrieved fly and a stronger, well-timed, forward fling. No matter how softly my fly landed in the middle of the horde, their enthusiastic activity quickly diminished but did not cease entirely; a few partygoers usually hung around to finish the remaining hors d'oeuvres. After a second successful or unsuccessful cast, the fish left the scene as quickly as underage drinkers scattering from police busts. If the fish had been having a really fine time, sometimes the festivities recurred fifty to one hundred yards away and the party gradually resumed rock-and-roll status until I disrupted their merriment again.

In the process of disrupting their revelries I usually picked off two or three cruisers as I learned to lightly deliver my fly into the outskirts of the milling carousers. A fish would usually attack it as I started my retrieve. I quickly stripped in line to segregate it from the rest of the bunch so as to minimize alarm to other partiers. But after two or three tussles with fish on my fly line, their fellow partygoers became apprehensive and dispersed for a half hour or the entire assembly moved several hundred yards away.

While my catches were mostly adolescent largemouth bass in Virginia, in Iowa, where I now live and fish the most, there are a few hard-to-find smallmouth bass hangouts. Smallmouth bass, and Iowa's predominant bass, the largemouth species, tend to not throng readily. If any fish are cruising, it's almost always crappies, bluegills, and less frequently, twelve- to fourteen-inch largemouth bass. These big-mouthed teenage bass become indignant when hooked. They scatter and sulk for longer periods of time than most other cruisers.

Regardless of the species, cruisers are always enjoyable to watch and exciting to catch. It's fun to figure out the situation I am dealing with and what the partygoers are dining on, because it isn't always a species of minnows or tiny fry. Now I cast only my handtied flies that imitate bait I have figured out the predators are seeking. It can be a hatch of emerging mayflies, other insect congregations, a species of minnows in the throes of courtship, even grasshoppers thrust into the same locale on a windy day. I have constructed lures that resemble all these. I refrain from chumming with artificial and unnatural bait, such as canned corn, or using worms, except when ice fishing. When ice fishing, I've noticed nearly all the fish species form schools that move around regularly. They aren't partying, for they are trying to stay alive in oxygen-deprived water unless there is active inflow from oxygenated streams or thawed surface areas where wind whips air into the water. The schools of fish eat at odd times of the day under the ice, and when feeding requires the least effort, so as to conserve oxygen, which is also why they usually keep swimming to maintain water flowing through their gills. I have to thank a new friend, a retired conservation officer named Steve, for explaining what is going on in winter when ice freezes over bodies of water.

I figured out that rapid retrieves on surface water work best, regard-less of what I toss toward the cruisers. Slow-sinking flies don't work any better than floating flies. The retrieve is key. The faster I retrieve the fly as soon as it lands near the marauders, and if I keep retrieving it sev-eral more feet with very brief pauses when stripping the line, the more likely I can expect an attack on my fly.

Eventually, I determined that the little black fly I invented to resem-ble fish fry and minnows is often the optimal party favor, and it has to be retrieved fast too, as if desperately fleeing from attackers. Retrieved quickly, it can appear at first glance to its predators as a minnow or as an insect emerging from its birthplace to join a copulation party. Op-timal hook sizes range from 14 to 8, and medium shank lengths work best. The fly should stay near the surface when retrieved, so floating lines and slow-sinking lines with long leaders and fine tippets are ideal.

During my over fifty years of fishing I've enjoyed many parties thrown by cruisers on western trout lakes and rivers, ocean and sea-shore fishing excursions, and big Canadian lakes. As I developed a preference for fishing a pond or lake in my float tube, I've observed many species of fish, including cutthroat, brown, and rainbow trout hold a feeding celebration in the middle of a reservoir I was fishing or near the shorelines. The trout often made a mad dash toward what-ever was whetting their appetites, and they fought to see who would get the entrée.

Sometimes the invitation to trout frolicking was a hatch of emerg-ing insects or a congregation of fish fry of some kind in a partially sub-merged weed bed. Happily, I remember a late September day about fif-teen years ago. My son, my only living brother-in-law, and I fished from float tubes on a southern Idaho reservoir during cold cloudy weather. Over a the span of a couple of hours the three of us connected on few hits while casting nymphs into mostly submerged weed beds that usu-ally harbored fine trout in many parts of the reservoir during summer weather. Eventually, my brother-in-law noticed the surface water stir-ring along the rocky shoreline among cockleburs and other weeds that had been killed by frosts earlier and were gradually becoming inundated by the ever-so-slowly rising level of water being stored for irrigation during the next farming year.

When we cast the same size 14, dark brown, artificial nymph flies that we had been tossing elsewhere into the half-submerged shoreline weeds, we hooked cutthroat trout sixteen to twenty inches long on every first or second cast. The cutthroats were patrolling the clusters of dead weeds that apparently harbored really cold insects that lost their perches and fell into the surrounding water. Our slow-sinking flies resembled the banquet the trout were dining on. If we approached too closely—less than forty feet—or if the fly landed awkwardly as it hit the water, their dining activities ended abruptly. Sometimes the banquet ceased until we moved to a different site.

One of my all-time great experiences experimenting with cruising fish occurred on Peterson Lake in the Selway–Bitterroot Wilderness of western Montana when Marilyn and I were on our honeymoon in early September 1972. The Selway–Bitterroot Wilderness area was our first stopover during a two-week camping sojourn through the Montana and Canadian Rocky Mountains. With friends Bob and Carol from Missoula, we backpacked about ten miles into the wilderness area. We hiked mostly uphill the entire way and were wearing out by mid-afternoon. Finally, as we topped a ridge, we spotted Peterson Lake a half mile downslope. When we drew nearer to the several-acre lake we could see the surface was dimpled with fish rising everywhere, especially along its eastern shore. Many fish were trolling near the surface, for their fins often stuck out of the water. Peterson Lake was surrounded on all sides by thick stands of conifers except at its marshy inlet and for about twenty-five feet from its rocky shore. The close proximity of the timber to the shoreline would make fly-fishing difficult because backcasts could easily snag the trees.

Eager to go after the hordes of fish cruising in the alpine lake, Bob found a level lakeside spot on which we set up our tents. While Carol and Marilyn finished camp preparations, Bob and I unpacked our fly-fishing equipment. We had noticed many small, dusty-white moths fluttering everywhere in the gentle west breeze. Bob identified them as spruce moths. When a moth flitted close to the lake surface, trout raced toward the insect and often hurled themselves out of the water in attempts to seize the moth. Any unfortunate spruce moth that touched water or floated on its surface was snatched quickly. The dining party was taking place everywhere on the lake and particularly along the eastern shore where the westerly wind caused drowning moths to congregate.

Being fairly new to fly-fishing, for I had been introduced to the art by Marilyn's father only during the previous two years, I had one artificial fly, a renegade pattern with enough white hackle that it might resemble a moth's outstretched wings. However, the handtied fly had some brown hackle and a brown body. I attached the renegade fly that Walt had given me onto my leader. When I flipped it into the water, trout raced toward it, but none swallowed it. Trout would repeatedly swarm to wherever I tossed the fly, but after inspecting it, they went about other business. I tried the few other flies I possessed that had some white on them, such as a royal coachman, and I even tried my lavender butterfly imitations, but I didn't succeed in attracting a hit. I used roll casts to get the flies to land into the water as distant from shore as possible, but the distance from me wasn't important to the hungry fish.

Bob had no close matches to the spruce moths either. After trying unsuccessfully to catch the moths with his net, Bob found a few small, whitish-colored flowers in the nearby woods. He pressed two petals and a short pale-green stem onto a bare hook, which he gently tossed a few feet into the water's edge. Immediately, a hungry ten-inch rainbow trout hooked itself and Bob reeled it in. The fish's head was disproportionately large for its skinny body. Thinking it might not be healthy, Bob tossed it back into the lake. Using similar flower petals and stem parts, Bob caught a second trout. It was longer but also had a large head and slender body.

"These trout aren't sick," I exclaimed, "they're emaciated." We decided that although their bodies were relatively thin, a dozen twelve- to thirteen-inch trout could furnish supper for the four of us. I tied a size 16 Mustad hook to the end of my tippet and slipped several flower petals and a bit of stem over the hook shaft. Emulating Bob, I gently tossed the hook a few feet into the dwindling sunlit water. A foot-long rainbow trout grabbed my offering within seconds.

Soon we had enough trout for supper, but our wives weren't ready yet with our evening meal, so Bob and I caught enough fish for breakfast. We experimented with other possible attractants besides the ivory-colored flower petals and a bit of stem to represent a thorax. We tried small pieces of toilet paper that we tore into shapes to resemble moth wings on bare hooks. They occasionally worked, but not as well as when lightly smeared with dirt. I found a smudged white feather sticking out of a seam of my goose-down sleeping bag that Marilyn had sewn during earlier summer months. Using a bit of thread, I tied the feather onto a bare hook. It also caught a couple fish. Bob and I laughed like two kids playing video games as we reeled in and released trout.

We didn't go hungry that evening or the next day. Bob and I experimented most of the next morning with concoctions of all sorts: pieces of a paper towel, bits of a linen handkerchief, aluminum foil (which didn't work), and various types of flower petals, as we toyed with the hungry fish to figure out how far we could diverge from the shape and color of a spruce moth before the trout would not accept our offerings. The best offerings had to be approximately the same size as the moths, with off-white wings and a body that resembled a spruce moth's thorax. That's why my renegade fly with its bright white and brown hackle and dark body didn't work. Yellow flower petals or pieces of green leaves torn to resemble moth wings didn't yield success either. Ever since that experience I've kept a supply of spruce moth imitations in my stash of handmade flies. Not only did I learn about matching a food source for cruisers, but I learned about what happens when too many fish exceed the carrying capacity of a body of water for them to thrive.

A more recent learning experience while fishing for cruisers occurred when I fished a shallow farm pond in western Iowa out of my float tube during a mid-September Sunday in 2013. I latched onto something I didn't expect. Two weeks earlier in the same pond I landed six largemouth bass, all twenty- to twenty-one inches, and kept two for baking later in a tangy Asian sauce. This day I kept a twenty-two-inch but less weighty male bass, and fifteen ten- to twenty-inch bluegills for future suppers. I was tired. I had smoked my perfunctory three cigars. The afternoon was drifting toward 5:00 p.m., time to return home to complete the farm chores before supper.

I paddled around the farm pond for the last time. When I was near the inlet that fed the five-acre pond, I noticed a swirl in approximately foot-deep water covering the sediment that had collected in the shallows. I wondered, *Can I catch another big bass and "call it a day" before heading home? But really big largemouth bass don't congregate together; they almost always are territorial and keep competition away.*

I maneuvered toward the inlet until my flippers touched bottom and I couldn't paddle any closer. As I readied myself to cast a size 6 black fly toward where I had observed the swirl, several disturbances appeared on the surface simultaneously some twenty-five yards away in very shallow water. I observed the tips of a half-dozen dorsal fins before they disappeared underwater just as my fly reached the extent of its backcast. I surged with anticipation, but nothing happened when it landed on the outskirts of their assembly and when I retrieved my fly.

When I cast the fly again, it landed some seventy feet away and virtually in the same spot. Several larger fish than any I had caught this day lunged toward my handtied fly and one managed to grab it. I set the hook. From what I could see, all the feeding fish had dark backs and lighter-colored bellies.

Yup, these were channel catfish! I had seen one jump out of the water when I played it on my fly line earlier during the summer. Who would think that catfish cruise and leap out of the water!

It took me ten minutes to wear down this particular catfish. When I measured it at home it was twenty-eight inches long.

I've learned repeatedly that fishing for cruisers during a feeding frenzy is a little like farming during an era of substantial profitability. We seldom know what to expect and when the triumphs might end. Both can be risky adventures and great fun for as long as the rampant success lasts.

7

REFINEMENTS TO THE LITTLE BLACK FLY

My previous book, *Excellent Joy: Fishing, Farming, Hunting, and Psychology*, contained a chapter entitled "The Little Black Fly," along with directions to construct this productive fishing fly. My children, Shelby and Jon, gave the creation its name when they began fishing around ages six and three, respectively, over forty years ago. I made significant improvements to versions of the fly. An update on the directions for tying this rewarding fly is warranted.

Too few fishers know about this useful fly, even though I wrote about it earlier and have given away hundreds of the flies to anglers. The little black fly is the one that I and several of my fly-fishing buddies use most frequently. A float tube works best to approach fish in ponds and small lakes, but a pontoon or a canoe that moves about quietly can provide effective modes of maneuvering close enough to cast flies to entice piscine prey.

Usually, a single rendition lasts me the entire day unless I lose it on a snag or a fish breaks the tippet. Sometimes the fly can become so tattered toward the end of a busy outing that I wonder why it continues to catch fish. These are ones I don't throw away. There is something about these well-worn flies that obviously appeals to fish.

During an early July outing about a dozen years ago, Jon and I used variations of the little black fly to capture about thirty long-sided crappies and bluegills on successive days fishing in murky water. Jon caught the better share during our three-hour derby on Saturday, and I caught the majority on Sunday. We both used size 6 little black flies with Mylar strips tied into the front hackle. The addition of Mylar or tinsel strips is a refinement that has sometimes yielded even more fish than the original version, which was completely black.

Earlier that year, I caught a couple of the largest bass and a bunch of the biggest crappies and bluegills I ever retrieved on a little black fly with Flashabou strips. I thought I hit the mother lode of Iowa farm pond fish when I landed a twenty-one-inch, six-pound, eleven-ounce largemouth bass; a six-pound, fourteen-ounce bass; a half dozen foot-long crappies; and another half dozen ten-inch bluegills, all in an hour on a single size 6 little black fly with Flashabou tied onto the front end.

Two weeks later, I caught a twenty-two-inch female bass that had spawned earlier in the spring. I could place my softball-sized fist into her mouth. Added to the largesse were another dozen hefty crappies and bluegills, all taken within ninety minutes.

In August 2013, I landed my biggest largemouth bass ever, a seven-and-a-half pounder, on a little black fly with tinsel embedded into the chenille body. These are some of the bigger bass, crappies, and bluegills that one can capture in Iowa, made all the more rewarding when caught on a fly rod with a handtied fly.

It perplexed me when a popular fishing magazine reported that the favorite fly-fishing destinations of those who answered their poll selected the Rocky Mountains as the most cherished spot to fish, followed by waters off South Florida during the winter, and the French provinces of Canada in the summer and fall. I relish fishing the midwestern farm ponds as much as possible when the surface isn't frozen because there are more keeper-sized fish per cast in these waters than anywhere I have fished. But you have to know how to catch them. I also like ice fishing these same ponds, but with wax worms, spikes, and minnows. When I wrote the first draft of this chapter, I had not tried ice fishing with the little black fly. Only recently I gave it a try under eight inches of ice on an Iowa lake.

The little black fly was designed to resemble a minnow of no particular species. It seems to work well from ice-out until the end of open water as winter sets in. Minnows of one or more species are always available, but more often during panfish nesting that begins in May and may occur several times before ending in September. Smaller sizes, such as sizes 10 to 14 often work when young fry leave their bluegill, sunfish, bass, and crappie nests, or any other species for that matter. Predatory fish hang around nest sites where one or both parents guard their offspring and weed beds where the growing minnows seek shelter after they are on their own.

The many adolescent fish that prey on the fry can be a nuisance when smaller-sized flies are used, so it's efficient to step up to a size just larger than the juvenile fish can get into their mouths. Often, you'll feel a lot of bumps when retrieving a size 6 or larger fly as the youngsters snatch at it. The little fish grabbing at the fly seem to attract big fish. It's especially fun when the surface splashes as your quarry erupts topside in an attempt to throw the fly. I've often observed crappies, bluegills, and even channel catfish hoist themselves out of the water.

Fishers have to be careful not to jerk too hard when setting the hook and pulling in crappies because their mouths are so soft that one can easily dislodge the hook. We can't yank big fish like bass or soft-mouthed species to the net like the professional fishers do on television shows with their casting rods and twenty-pound test lines. It's much more fun when you have a challenging tussle with a fly rod and light tippet that requires final capture with a net or lifting it carefully onto your float tube apron than when you can yank a fish into the boat without having to use a net.

There are many variations of the little black fly. I first began incorporating tinsel into the little black fly about twenty years ago. I took a single strand of Mylar and wrapped it around the body, starting from the rear and working toward the head. I noticed that the shiny material resulted in more hits, especially in muddy water. Usually, the fly would remain intact for only a few fish, after which the tinsel strip broke. But even when the Mylar strand broke and dangled loosely, it didn't seem to stop fish from hitting the fly. That gave me the idea to tie a number of strands of Mylar to the hackle. I was onto something!

The recently added refinements to the little black fly are basically two easily applied modifications. The first is to add several strands of Mylar or tinsel, about as long as the fly, to the front hackle after everything else has been tied to the fly. Perhaps these metallic strands reflect light like the shiny scales of fish do or perhaps they simply act as attractors. Flies with metallic strands seem to be more effective on cloudy days and in muddy or weed-infested water than flies without tinsel.

The other adaptation I recommend trying is the use of black chenille with tinsel added to the chenille, to make the bodies of the little black fly. Some manufacturers add Flashabou as the shiny material to bass lures. This body material seems to resemble the reflective properties of fish scales. It enhances even more interest in the fly than only adding strands of Mylar or some other shiny material to the front hackle.

As promised, here are the directions from start to finish for tying the little black fly, but now with one or both refinements.

What size of hook should you use? It's good to have a selection of sizes ranging from no. 14 to 2, depending on the size of fish you are trying to catch and their habits. Generally, no. 6 to 10 flies are the best all-around; they imitate the size and movements of young fry. Larger sizes avoid catching small fish because they can't get the hooks in their mouths. There are times though when a no. 12 or 14 has consistently caught more big fish than a no. 4, probably because the minnows that big fish were feeding on were still fairly small.

Place the hook in a vice and put eight to ten wraps of thin lead wire on the shank of the hook. The lead wire and the hook itself give the finished fly enough weight to offset the natural buoyancy of the mink hairs or other material used for the hackles. Then, starting from the eyelet end and working backward, tie down the lead and make several revolutions around the back of the shank where the hook starts to curve. Use black waxed thread or monochord. It's helpful to put a little dab of fly-tying cement on the rear wraps to keep them from sliding on the hook shank.

The next step is to select and tie fifteen to twenty black mink hairs about two-thirds as long as the fly body onto the rear of the shank to form a tail. You can use black deer hairs, either natural or dyed black, instead of mink if sufficiently long mink hairs can't be found. On a size 12 or 14 hook, the tail hairs should extend approximately 3/8 inch beyond the point where they are tied to the hook. On size 4 flies or thereabouts, the tail should be approximately 5/8 inch or longer. Tie the tail hairs so they don't fan out excessively; the resulting assemblage resembles the form and movement of the tail of a fry when the fly is pulled through the water. Then use several thin strands of dyed black wool or chenille with Flashabou, Mylar, or other type of tinsel embedded into it to form the body of the fly. Wrap the wool or chenille strands to form the shape of a tiny fish's body, tapering larger toward the front of the hook. I've also found that black poly yarn or Z-Lon can be used to give a slight sheen to the body of the fly.

Now the fly is ready for the development of the front hackle, which resembles pectoral fins and can move when retrieved in water. Again, mink hairs or deer hairs, always black, should be used, and they should be about the same length as the hairs that were used for the tail of the fly. Gather about twenty to twenty-five hairs and tie them to the top half of the fly where the front of the body ends. This shape allows the hairs on the top and sides of the body to flex and to appear like pectoral fins as the artificial minnow "swims" through the water. Apply a few wraps of thread to hold down the hackle and then add eight to ten strands of Mylar or other tinsel to the hackle, about the same length as the body of the fly. Make sure these slippery metal strands are tied firmly, so make enough wraps and dab them with a bit of clear fingernail polish or something similar as the cement. Finish the head of the fly with knots of thread and dab it sufficiently with cement to hold everything in place.

I make several whip finish knots to complete the fly. Three or more whip finish knots are less likely to deteriorate from repeated use than only one knot. I tie the whip finish knot by hand rather than with a tool, because that's how I learned from my father-in-law to finish a fly. Apply three to four coats of generously dabbed cement, fingernail polish, or shellac to the front end of the finished fly, but allow enough time for each coating to dry before applying the next coat.

It's especially rewarding when the flies you've tied yield the fish that you are seeking. Most fishers I know who use the little black fly, including these latest adaptations, find that it works successfully on the many members of the sunfish, perch, and trout families.

Some fishers have told me they don't keep large bass that they catch, claiming they don't taste as good as smaller bass, bluegills, or crappies. I solved that issue in our kitchen and now usually have a few large, filleted bass in the freezer. I seldom keep females, even if they have spawned, because these are the "good breeders" of the next generations. I've found that the big bass slabs are a super main course of a meal when they are accompanied with a white sauce made of milk, garlic, and other homegrown or commercially available herbs, such as rosemary, oregano, coriander, and thyme. Add enough corn starch to thicken the sauce. If you feel brave, try Moroccan, Vietnamese, and Mexican spices too; they're all good.

First, fry the fish at 350 degrees Fahrenheit, preferably in a cast-iron skillet. Spread a thin sheet of melted butter or olive oil on the bottom of the skillet, just enough for the heat to penetrate throughout the flesh to make the exterior turn light brown and to deter the fish sticking to the pan. Don't use a lid on the pan for this stage. This stage usually requires about three or four minutes at most on each side, depending on the thickness of the slab. Then pour white sauce over the fish on both sides and fry each side for two more minutes with the sauce. Let the fish remain in the frying pan, covered, but away from the heat for a couple more minutes while you wait for everyone to join you at the table. Serve cooked potatoes with fresh sliced onions alongside, cooked rice, or couscous, and some type of green vegetable or salad as well. A full-bodied white wine or a mild red wine adds a nice touch to the meal.

Try the black flies with one or both shiny attractants on pike as well. They've worked well for me. I haven't heard of anybody catching muskellunge on this fly, but it wouldn't surprise me if it entices muskies too.

Give the "old" version and this refined version of the little black fly a try when ice fishing. Attaching a wax worm or reddish maggot, often called a "spike," results in even more hits under the ice. I think the smell of the insects attracts hits. In February 2023, I met a new friend who added bead eyes to his black fly creations; it also produces success. He regularly sends pictures of successful catches, usually crappies from under the ice. It's nice to know someone else has discovered their own version of the little black fly, along with improvements. End of report—for now.

8

BECOMING A GRANDPARENT

Our daughter was having her first baby in late fall, 2011. I would soon become a grandfather for the first time. Shelby asked her mother and me to help her and her husband for several weeks after their baby was born, and again when paid time off ended, until they could find full-time childcare.

Marilyn chose to spend the first three weeks after parturition—like many caring mothers do to assist their daughters—while Shelby recuperated from emergency Cesarean surgery. Marilyn helped little Alexandra get off to a good start in life, because Alex's dad had little paternity leave from his University of Utah genetic research work and Shelby had eight weeks of maternity leave.

When Shelby had to return to her rheumatology practice at Ogden, Utah, I would assume as many weeks caring for Alex as necessary until her parents found acceptable childcare services. I had some misgivings about caring for an infant, because it had been many years since I had diapered my children. I wondered, *Would my parenting instincts come back? Would I fail to meet the expectations of Alex's parents?* Most importantly, *Could I care for an infant that her parents and grandparents loved unconditionally?* I turned first to my midwestern friends, John and Susan, for advice.

They were experienced grandparents, yet I had reason to consider John's advice suspect. A few years earlier John was the object of a massive takedown by the local SWAT team at his North Dakota State University town where he was a professor.

For many years John reloaded shotgun shells and rifle cartridges. He and Susan enjoyed shooting guns as a hobby, plinking the many prairie dogs and magpies on ranches in the Dakotas and Montana to which they were invited to control the pests. I also wasn't quite sure how John's pursuits of hunting deer, shooting pheasants, and reloading his spent ammunition cartridges blended with being a well-liked professor of religion and philosophy at a major university, or how these hobbies qualified him to give me advice about becoming a grandfather. Nonetheless, I figured he had to be well qualified because he had married Susan, the highly respected president of the AgriWellness board of directors, for whom I served as its director. John and I, and frequently Susan as well, engaged in deep discussions of religion and current events honestly and without rancor, even when we disagreed. I admired John for founding the Northern Plains Ethics Institute and its journal. When Susan volunteered her husband's advice about becoming a grandparent, I liked her suggestion. John's encounter with the Fargo SWAT team wasn't a big deal.

A few years prior, John was test-firing reloaded rifle cartridges one February evening in his garage and backyard. John and Susan lived in a comfortable neighborhood a few blocks from the university. He fired percussion caps only; a backstop for real bullets wasn't necessary. *Bang! Bang! Bang!* Not quite satisfied with their performance, John went back into his garage to add more gun powder to each percussion cap. A while later he emerged with two rifles. *BOOM! BOOM! BOOM!* The noise resounded around the neighborhood when he fired the otherwise empty cartridges.

Suddenly a loud megaphone blasted, "Lay your weapons down. Lie down on the ground with your hands behind your back." The sound blared from all sides of the city block. Helmeted police officers carrying shields and machine guns busted through the front door of the house, yelling, "Are you alright ma'am?"

Already clad in her nightgown, Susan scrambled from under the ledge of the kitchen counter where she had crawled when the loudspeakers blared a few seconds earlier. With her hands up, she demurely faced the uniformed SWAT team.

Floodlights from an overhead helicopter completely illuminated the city block as cops thrust their boots onto John's hands and backside while he was lying prone on his lawn. When he was handcuffed, a police officer who recognized him uttered, "John, what the hell are you doing? Your neighbor just called us a few minutes ago to say there was a terrorist in your backyard and Susan was in grave danger."

When this incident made it into the *USA Today* newspaper the next day as the major news event in North Dakota, it made me proud to be acquainted with John and Susan. I kept an open mind to John's advice about becoming a grandfather.

A few years later, Susan, John, and I were all enjoying a little touch of Norwegian aquavit before bedtime. Susan and I were planning to deliver a series of workshops about behavioral health care to professionals and paraprofessionals in North Dakota during the following two days.

Susan announced to her husband, "Do you know that Mike's going to become a grandfather next month?"

"Oh, good Lord, the poor man," John chimed back.

"What do you mean John? Becoming a grandfather is a wonderful thing," Susan retorted bravely.

"Babies aren't any fun until they're at least four years old," John snorted. "They're just alimentary canals with openings at each end. You shovel input into one end and clean up the output at the other end. What's fun about that?"

"Well," Susan indignantly replied, "somebody had to take care of you, John! You were a baby once!"

"Yeah, but I got over it quickly," John proclaimed. "I was able to take care of myself well before I was four years old and I've managed myself properly ever since."

Enough said, I thought to myself. *I'll consider advice about becoming a grandfather from other sources too.*

I thought of my friend, Ken, a psychologist in Colorado. Ken, my graduate school roommate before I got married, introduced me to Marilyn. Ken visited us at our newly constructed home a few miles west of Charlottesville, Virginia, in early spring 1978, about ten weeks after our son, Jon, was born and when Shelby was three years old. I was a professor in the Psychology Department at the University of Virginia.

"Would you like to hold Jon?" Marilyn offered to Ken a few hours after he had arrived at our abode in the eastern foothills of the Blue Ridge Mountains.

Ken thrust his arms forward, as if someone was about to give him a piece of lumber to hold. Marilyn placed Jon into his stiff arms.

Jon focused his eyes directly onto Ken's eyes with obvious uncertainty and Ken reciprocated with a similar gaze. "How does this machine work?" Ken asked.

"Oh Ken," Marilyn cooed, "you have to hold him so he feels secure." Marilyn adjusted Ken's arms and showed him how to draw Jon's swaddled body close to his chest.

Jon squirmed and issued a loud fart.

Shelby and I, who were observing this with considerable wonderment, both giggled and Marilyn laughed heartily.

"This engine smells," Ken exclaimed, as he uncomfortably pushed his bundle into my outstretched arms.

"It was just a little gas!" Shelby exclaimed. Even at her young age, Shelby, as well as her parents, had well-trained noses able to discern the difference between a healthy fart and the smell that accompanies more solid expulsions.

No, Ken isn't the person I need for grandparenting advice, I concluded to myself.

As it turned out, Ken became a wonderful father himself a few years after the Virginia episode, and eventually a similarly caring grandfather. John was already a proud father and grandfather several times over when we discussed my imminent grandfatherhood. I could tell early on that John and Ken were devoted to their roles as fathers and grandfathers. I turned to them for advice several times during later years.

However, at that time I wondered if I would have to start my search anew for someone with whom to air my uncertainties about becoming a grandfather. I wasn't sure if the instincts to undertake good parenting were still within me. And so, I thought, *Here I go into grandfatherhood without the mentors that I probably will need. Perhaps I can draw on the tender loving care my father gave Shelby and Jon before he passed away from a heart attack prior to their kindergarten age. I can also practice the generous and patient nurturing given by Marilyn's father, Walt, to our children, and me. That means showing our grandchildren the gifts of trying hard, being honest and accountable, enjoying the outdoors while camping, and maybe raising their own food as much as possible, as well as fishing and hunting when—and if—they are ready.*

Thus far, our grandchildren have similarly believing fathers and mothers who espouse the values and life skills for their progeny to which Marilyn and I exposed their parents, and which includes healthy doses of experience in the outdoors, truthfulness, respect for others in the same fashion they would like to be treated, willingness to work hard—even under adversity—and trust in God.

9

THAT WAS TOO CLOSE

Scott is a good fisherman, a good fly-fisher, and a good person. He is the kind of friend everyone wishes for: honest, generously helpful, and funny—with clever, left-field humor that extends a party. He is optimistic, and he owns a boat, which I don't. I don't know why it is that when Scott hangs around Jon and me, some kind of life-altering experience seems to happen to him or all of us. One of Scott's life-imperiling experiences occurred a few years ago in Arkansas and didn't involve his boat.

Scott accompanied Jon and me several times when we took our annual season-opening trip from Iowa to fish for trout in northern Arkansas. This also was Scott's last trip with us to Arkansas to fish the Norfolk River and the White River, which it joins a few miles below the Norfolk Dam. These are hallowed trout waters that can be best fished from some kind of floating craft. The river flows vary, depending on whether some, all, or none of the electricity generators are operating on the dams. When no generators are operating and the river flow is low, the trout and the occasional smallmouth bass are concentrated in the ample holes of the river bottom.

We timed our trips to coincide with the start of the major league baseball season. We listened to the radio broadcast of our favorite team, the Chicago Cubs, as they almost won their first game of the year, and then we recapped the day's events as we took turns driving. We motored through Springfield, Missouri, the home of the original Bass Pro Shops, which had been closed for several hours already. At Mountain Home, Arkansas, the service station we stopped at later wasn't staffed either, but its pump allowed us to insert a credit card to pay for fuel.

We reached our rented cabin with a key taped to the front door at 3:30 a.m. next to the shore of the Norfolk River below the dam where four electricity generators operated on a variable schedule.

Jon brought along Hayden, a ten-week-old, bouncing, yellow Lab he hoped would replace his aging and cherished hunting dog, Nugget. Hayden stayed in her kennel in the loft where Scott and Jon slept. Mostly this was to keep her from tearing apart our cabin while we were gone during the day, but she had the run of the place while we were around. Hayden peed only once inside our cabin, near my bedroom door close to the lawn outside, which is forgivable because she meant well. It was partly my fault because I didn't open the door quickly enough.

The first day fishing the Norfolk portended to be strenuous, for all four generators were operating full-tilt and a heavy water flow inundated the river. The water would be so high and swift that rivercraft would speedily drift down this renowned stream, making fly-fishing for trout challenging. It would be difficult to hold one's position near promising holes; we usually had to find sheltered coves or stationed ourselves on the downstream ends of islands. Jon and I owned pontoons, but not Scott. He volunteered to pick us up later in the day at what was called the handicap-accessible dock seven miles downstream, where we would find him waiting or fishing nearby with his fly rod in hand.

Jon and I set off in our pontoons, which we guided with fins on the feet of our waders. Although Jon and I occasionally stopped at islands to fish where the river confluences joined together just below the landforms, by early afternoon we almost simultaneously reached our destination even though we didn't fish together. Both of us had worked hard in the high water to catch barely enough thirteen- to fifteen-inch trout for supper. There are much bigger fish in the river. As we maneuvered our pontoons to the steps of the dock, we weren't fully satisfied even though we had enjoyed the outdoor experience.

Scott was glad for us, for he had caught a few trout—none big enough to keep—in the few pockets of water that could be waded into, off the main channel near the dock. Hayden, along with a little help from Jack Daniels, cheered us up back at the cabin. I offered to trade places with Scott the next day and to lend him my pontoon and paddles. We went to bed early.

When we awoke the next morning, the generators were turned off and the water level in the river was low—ideal for fishing. Trout would congregate in the deeper holes. Our spirits were high as I drove my Jeep to the put-in spot just below the dam. Although barely past 7:00 a.m., dozens of anglers and their hired guides were already loading gear into drift boats that would have to remain above the first rapids about a mile downstream, in water that was sufficiently deep to maneuver their vessels. Few outfitters had flat-bottomed craft that might be able to traverse the occasional dangerous, rock-strewn rapids and shallow stretches the entire route downriver to their take-out destinations. Jon and Scott were the only anglers with pontoons that could make the trip, along with the few flat-bottom voyagers.

Several suitably bedecked fishers were chatting amiably with a tall, slender, silver-haired man who was thumbing through fly cartons and periodically handing out something to smiling fishermen surrounding him on the stony shoreline. As I helped Scott and Jon inflate the pontoons and stow their gear, water bottles, and sandwiches, the friendly older gentleman made his way to us but steered toward Scott and Jon. I stepped closer to join in the discussion.

"Good morning fellows. Have you fished this river before?" he asked.

"Yes," Scott and Jon replied. "Several times, but usually when there was more water in the river."

"Have you ever used one of these?" the pleasant man asked, holding up an ivory-colored fly that imitated a sow bug.

"No," they answered, as they scrutinized the artificial sow bug the kindly man held in front of their faces. The fellow generously placed several imitation sow bugs into their outstretched palms, all the while clasping what appeared to be a fine bamboo fly rod under his left arm.

I noticed black ink writing on the varnished bamboo above a polished, stainless-steel reel that I judged to be costly. When a quiet moment in the conversation occurred, I asked him quietly, "Did you make your rod?"

"Why yes," the gentleman answered. "My name is on it," he said as he somewhat uncertainly handed it to me to inspect. He had a frown on his face.

Was he bothered by my inquiry? I wondered. *Was my demeanor offensive in some way?*

I immediately recognized his name on the fly rod as that of a well-known fly fisherman who lived in this part of Arkansas mainly to fish, for I had read articles about him in fly-fishing magazines. The rod was "oh so light" and springy, the most beautiful bamboo fly rod I have ever held; I told him so when I handed it back to him after carefully examining it for a few minutes.

The gentleman said "Thank-you" rather dismissively and quickly turned away. He wished Scott and Jon good luck with fishing, but he ignored me and didn't offer me advice or any of his handmade sow bugs, even though my waders and fishing vest were obvious signs that I intended to fish today, too. Again, I wondered what I had done wrong.

I helped Jon and Scott shove off the gradually descending gravel shore into water deep enough to float in their pontoons. I wished them well and asked them to call me on their cell phones if they needed something or couldn't locate me later in the day near the handicap-accessible dock. I made my way to my Jeep and trailer and drove the seven miles of narrow highway that followed the river downstream to the take-out point where I parked in the asphalt-covered lot. I had my essential fishing gear with me, including my own sow bugs, scuds, and hundreds of other homemade flies that either my deceased father-in-law, Walt, or I had crafted.

I fished first with my sow bugs in various sizes and shades of white, ivory, and pink in the pools close to the dock and parking lot. I didn't get any takes. As I hiked down the river I experimented with scuds, San Juan worms, micro jigs, zebra midges, a red-butted green nymph Walt had shown me how to tie, and several other nymphs of Walt's or my creation. These flies had worked well during previous trips to the Norfolk. Occasionally I had a hit and I landed a few small rainbows, but none worth keeping for supper. I tried the green woolly worm with a brass bead head and split pheasant-tail quills that had worked successfully during a previous excursion but only got a few tentative hits by smallish fish. Around noon my cell phone rang. Jon called to ask how fishing was going.

"Not too well," I replied. "The holes and the water look good but I'm not catching any decent-sized fish. I don't know what to try."

"Use the bla . . . fly," he said, as static interfered with his voice.

When I said I couldn't hear him and began moving away from a nearby cliff to get better telephone reception, Jon shouted: "USE THE LITTLE BLACK FLY WITH TINSEL ON IT." As I approached the middle of the river, Jon added, "I already got my limit on it and now I'm throwing everything I catch back. All the fish I kept are over sixteen inches."

"Wow," I exclaimed. "How is Scott doing?"

"I don't know; he's somewhere behind me. The last time I saw him was at the riffles well above the long 'catch-and-release' stretch that is always good for fishing. I'm at the upper end of the long stretch, but it's so low since the water was cut back at the dam that I'll have to get out of my pontoon to drag it downstream. The flat-bottom boat guides who got here ahead of me are making their passengers walk until the water is deep enough to float again."

"Okay," I responded. "Let me know how it goes."

I walked the shoreline back to the upper end of a promising hole I had just unsuccessfully fished, sat down on nearby rocks, ate my sandwich, and drank a bottle of water from my backpack. I lit a cigar and selected a flashy little black fly from one of the clear plastic electrical tape canisters I use to store flies in my fishing vest pockets. I made a test cast into the nearby hole.

The size 10 black fly with tinsel wrapped into the body swept toward the bottom end of the pool when I felt a heavy thump. As I pulled my rod upright, a rainbow trout about sixteen inches long slashed into the air just upstream from the tangled quagmire of uprooted trees and fallen branches that helped create the pool.

For the next several minutes the rainbow coursed back and forth from one side of the pool to the other, just above the jammed timber. I resisted the fish's continuous strains to prevent it from wrapping the leader and tippet around a tree branch. Gradually, the fish's tugs weakened and I was able to guide it into my outstretched net below the water surface. I was pleased as I thrust the gallant trout into my fish bag extending from my waders. I had not previously caught a trout on a version of the little black fly, nor had Jon until today.

I tried calling Jon on my cell phone to thank him for his recommendation but there was only static because the high banks along this part of the river blocked cell phone signals. I continued fishing other promising-looking spots downstream and succeeded in catching five thirteen- to sixteen-inch rainbow and brown trout over the next couple hours, all on versions of the little black fly. I made my way back to the dock and arrived there around 4:30 p.m.

After climbing out of the river canyon I called Jon to give him my fishing report. He was glad for our similar success with the little black flies. Jon was waiting for Scott, who was halfway to the dock when they had connected by phone an hour earlier. Scott still had to make his way through the wide but shallow mile-long stretch that is usually five to six feet deep when sufficient water is flowing. Scott, whose shorter legs were not accustomed to such strenuous physical activity, was having a difficult time dragging the pontoon wherever the river was shallow and rocky.

Jon was catching and releasing a good many trout while awaiting Scott. He was experimenting with various fly patterns, but any version of the little black fly was "the one" today. I told Jon how I was disconcerted by the gentleman who gave sow bug flies to Scott and him this morning, and explained that he was a respected fly fisher who was the subject of articles in fly-fishing magazines. Jon commented that perhaps the renowned fisherman thought I was old enough to not need his advice, and that the man was right.

To pass the time while waiting, I conversed with various fly fishers who were going back to their parked vehicles after spending the afternoon exploring many of the same holes I had sampled. A few had caught one or two trout of decent size, but most indicated little success. I struck up a conversation with a fly fisherwoman who accompanied a teenaged boy. The lady lamented about not catching any trout worthy for supper that evening. When I told her about the fish I caught, her ears perked up. She and her son, who avoided eye contact and verbalized nothing, often fished this area with mixed success, she said. They knew about the sow bug fly but it had yielded them only a couple small fish today. I mentioned how my little black fly had worked well. She asked to see it, so I gave both of them two little black flies apiece, one each with tinsel and one without any flashy stuff. I wondered if the boy had an autism-spectrum disability, but I didn't ask. The mother was very appreciative and her son shot me the briefest possible glance of acknowledgment as they trudged to their car.

Two hours passed without any word from Jon or Scott. Dusk was setting in. Around 7:00 I called Jon, who said Scott was still making his way through the long, shallow stretch. Scott had to drag his pontoon its entire way. He had lost a paddle going through the riffles above the long stretch and was tired and sore. I didn't mind the lost paddle, because I didn't use them, preferring flippers to maneuver in floatable water, but I was concerned that Scott had stumbled and was bruised from falling while walking in his flippers. Jon said he would wait for Scott to catch up and to make sure he was alright. They were still about a mile from the dock, he thought. To add to his unhappiness, Scott had not caught any fish.

I climbed into my Jeep to listen to the radio. The weather report indicated heavy thunderstorms with high winds and lightning were settling into our region. Distant flashes lit up the western sky, now dark enough to reveal their periodic bright pulses. The lightning displays drew nearer as I listened to the radio.

I became worried that Scott and Jon might have difficulty finding the dock or would be on the river when the thunderstorm hit. Knowing that being in water isn't safe if lightning is nearby, I telephoned Jon again to advise him of the possible storm. I was relieved when Jon said Scott had finally reached him and that he and Scott both had LED headlamps that would provide enough light for them to find their way even in complete darkness. Jon hoped they would reach the dock before the storm hit.

A few minutes later and to indicate where the dock was located, I parked my Jeep to face upriver so Scott and Jon could see its headlights. I called Jon again to ask if he could see the headlights. The last river bend was about a half mile upstream.

"No," Jon said as I flashed the headlights several times. He added that Scott was so worn out that he was swearing.

It would do no good to urge Scott and Jon to hurry, so I contented myself to listen to the radio and to meditate for a while. I worried about their safety. Every so often I turned off the Jeep's headlights to see if I could discern their LED headlamps, but to no avail. Except for the lightning flashes, it was completely dark.

The streaks of lightning were drawing close enough that I could hear rumbles of thunder to the west. Around 8:00 I called Jon for an update. When I blinked the Jeep's headlights, he said he could see them. Scott was so exhausted that Jon was worried he might injure himself; Jon said he would accompany Scott the rest of the way to the dock.

Minutes dragged on until the clock in my vehicle said 8:30, but still Jon and Scott had not arrived. I kept the Jeep engine running to charge the battery for its headlights. Periodically, I got out of my Grand Cherokee to peer upstream until I finally was able to detect beaming headlamps. The last vehicle other than mine had left the parking lot an hour ago. Even the die-hard evening fly fishers had abandoned the river long ago, despite knowing that fishing is usually superb before a storm.

Lightning bolts now spread across the entire western sky and thunder roared with each strike when I finally discerned Scott's mutterings around 9:00 as he slogged through shallow water toward the stairway under the dock that led to the parking lot. Jon had ahold of his left arm. I descended the steps with a flashlight to meet them.

Scott was cursing between labored gasps for breath. "I'll never go fishing again. Never, NEVER!"

He dropped his rod and plopped onto the bottom step, too exhausted to remove his flippers. I unhooked the bindings on Scott's flippers and accompanied him up the stairs while Jon carried Scott's and his own fishing gear and fish to the trailer during successive trips. After Scott was seated in the Jeep, I helped Jon carry the pontoons to the trailer and lash them securely. Thunder boomed so loudly it drowned out every other sound when lightning bombed the cliff just across the river.

Jon and I scrambled into the Jeep as the first huge drops of rain mixed with melting ice splashed onto the windshield. Soon, torrents of rain and ferocious gusts of wind blasted our vehicle and trailer so violently that I postponed driving anywhere. No one uttered a word. I silently thanked God for allowing Jon and Scott to reach safety and now prayed for protection for all of us. I worried that a nearby tree might crash onto our rig.

I felt relieved a few minutes later as the pounding rain and fierce winds diminished and when the lightning appeared to have moved east of us.

Scott was the first to speak, as I started up the Jeep's engine: "Never again. Don't ever ask me to go fishing with you guys. I thought I was going to die. I was praying my wife would be okay if I didn't live."

Jon softly voiced a reply, "I'm glad the storm wasn't as bad as it could have been. We could have still been out on the water!" After a pause he added, "Maybe fishing will be easier tomorrow so you can catch a big one, Scott."

"Bullshit! I'm never fishing with you guys again and maybe never with anybody else either," Scott fulminated. No one spoke the rest of the way to our cabin.

Supper was ominously silent as Scott had already crawled into his bed in the loft without eating supper. Jon and I ate fried trout and potatoes and devoured a salad of fresh garden greens I brought with us from home. Jon was also tired and contemplative. Hayden sensed the subdued mood and laid by Jon's feet while we ate. After supper I stacked the dishes in the sink; we all went to bed, Hayden too.

Well after the morning sun crept through the east-facing cabin windows, I heard Hayden barking in the loft to indicate she wanted to relieve herself outside. I decided it was time to make breakfast. I washed and dried the previous night's dishes and made breakfast for everyone of fried trout and eggs, toast, and fruit salad. Jon arose and joined me for breakfast, but it was a while before Scott appeared. He clung onto the banister as he stiffly negotiated his way downstairs around mid-morning. "I'm not leaving the cabin all day," he proclaimed. "Hayden and I are staying here while you guys go fishing."

Jon and I had checked the river and found all the generators had been turned on. The water level was high, so we decided to fish the pools below the dam that we could reach in our waders. We told our plans to Scott.

"I'm never going fishing again," Scott pronounced as he sipped his morning coffee. While I wouldn't blame him if he quit fishing with us after what happened yesterday, I knew Scott wasn't a quitter.

A period of silence lapsed. Then Scott announced, "That was too close. Next time I'm bringing my boat, and it won't be here."

Jon, Hayden, and I felt better, and yet I wondered, was another, more obscure—yet sublime—message intended from yesterday's happenings that I missed? Scott's boat, well, that's another story.

10

INDIGENOUS AMERICANS' ATTACHMENT TO THE LAND

As new archaeological discoveries of items such as bones from ancient habitat sites are analyzed, the findings usually push back the date when humans may have first entered the Western Hemisphere, probably by crossing the Bering Strait on land, sea, or ice. Historians agree that Asians initially settled into what is now Alaska sometime between 20,000 to 45,000 years ago. Adding to the debate about when and how the First People reached the Americas, archaeologists in Chile offer evidence that seafaring Pacific Islanders may have reached the west coast of South America while—or even before—Asians became residents of the New World in the Far North. The first Indigenous Americans were hunter-gatherers whenever and wherever they landed.

Growing food purposefully as farmers didn't occur until about 7,000 years ago in Central America and northern parts of South America, according to available archaeological evidence. Except for dogs that accompanied some human clans wherever they settled, taming and raising animals for food and other purposes occurred about 4,000 years ago, and probably first in South America.

Planting and harvesting maize, the forerunner of modern-day corn, began in Central America. These first American farmers selected maize plants during many hundreds of plant generations that exhibited the most favorable characteristics, such as an abundance of grain kernels that were originally on the flowering tassel, and later on lower branches of plants that had mutated and formed crude ears of corn.

Gradually, beans (the dry kind, not the popular string beans of to-day), squash, melons, tomatoes, peppers, potatoes, sunflowers, and many other plants were also grown for nourishment, medicinal use, and traded with neighboring tribes. Careful selection of plants within the various species they grew improved their yield, nutritional value, taste, and other favorable characteristics, such as tolerance for drought. As agriculture spread from the warmer climes of South and Central America northward to what is now Mexico, the contiguous United States, and southern Canada, farming practices also spread southward through most of South America. When necessary, slash-and-burn farmers in the Amazon basin moved periodically to new sites with fresh soil, and sometimes returned years later to former sites after de-cayed detritus restored the land's fertility. In the dryer areas of Cen-tral and North America, early farmers figured out how to irrigate their fields with canals, and to fertilize their crops with animal and human wastes, besides the detritus from previous crops.

Two key developments were to combine crops that supplemented each other and to rotate crops to minimize diseases that were more likely to occur when the same crop was planted annually on the same ground. Natives of the American Southwest combined corn, beans, and squash together into what are called "hills" today, but which were initially depressions in the soil designed to hold water. After the plants grew sufficiently, the farmers piled dirt around them to make small hills. They named these vegetables "the three sisters," because corn plants supplied stalks for the bean vines to climb, and beans furnished nitrogen, which the corn needed. Although planted inside the depres-sion, squash spread outside the boundaries and sent down supplemen-tal root systems as they grew, which diminished their need for water from their "hills." The large squash leaves also suppressed the develop-ment of weeds in untilled areas among the corn and beans by creating shade that discouraged the germination of undesirable seeds. An added benefit is that corn and squash furnished trace amounts of calcium, phosphorus, potassium, and organic matter that nourished the beans during future crop years. The saying that "something won't amount to a hill of beans" is wrong, because a hill of beans, corn, and squash truly represents successful farming.

Most Europeans and later-arriving Asian immigrants came to the Americas believing they would find opportunities to purchase land and other resources they needed to farm. Ownership had become the accepted practice in their homelands. With most of the land in their native countries owned by royal families, government rulers, religious institutions, and the wealthy, the New World offered possibilities for land ownership to former serfs. Immigrant slaves from Africa had no choice, however, but to work without pay for their owners. In many instances, slaves made their owners rich because the knowledge these immigrants and their successors possessed about growing such crops as cotton, tobacco, and sugarcane were vital to the success of plantation agriculture.

The original Indigenous people didn't understand the Europeans' concept of land ownership. The land, water, animals, and other resources of the earth were, and still are, considered divine gifts to be shared and conserved respectfully for future generations. My Indigenous American friends tell me that even the stars—actually, the entire universe—is a gift that can't be owned as property. They attest that Mother Earth is sacred. For them, Mother Earth embodies their concept of a supreme being. Even if they adopted Christian religions, their concepts of God, Creator, and Mother Earth have largely similar meanings.

Like many civilizations elsewhere on Earth believe, and as science has verified, life on our planet originated in bodies of water. Over vast time frames, the water, air, and land provided the gifts of plants, fish, animals, and people. Bison, birds, corn, vegetables, grass, and the forests represent essential elements to help sustain life. They weren't created to be owned, but to be shared as Mother Earth's sacred gifts. Sharing is essential for happiness and to become closer spiritually to a Creator.

When Europeans and other immigrants took control over tribal hunting and fishing territories, Indigenous Americans felt their deepest spiritual connections to Mother Earth were being desecrated. Forcible removal from their ancestral lands and confinement onto reservations violated their spiritual beliefs and the purposes of their lives. It's not surprising that such devastating violations of what was most important to the original inhabitants of what is now the United States and Canada led those people into profound disillusionment, despair, and what has been termed cultural and historical depression. Their experience of forced assimilation into a dominant society with different values contributes to having the highest suicide and addiction rates of any population in North America.

I learned much from the people I was invited to address in workshops about dealing with depression and suicidal tendencies that often accompany farming. I became friends with several members of Sioux tribal nations, Chippewa nations, and a psychologist who is Cherokee. I have had the opportunity to participate in several sacred rituals of these cultures and to implement them into my life. These marginalized people have taught—and continue to teach—me more than I have imparted to them.

Black farmers also continue to educate me. Several disenfranchised and successful Black agricultural producers asked for my help with their psychological trauma when they lost their farming opportunities in Louisiana and Mississippi a few years prior. They told me how they were pushed out of farming because favor was given by local financiers to white farmers. White farmers received operating loan approvals from local banks that also had guaranteed payments from federal banks sooner than the Black farmers. White farmers were able to purchase seed and fertilizer inputs earlier, and to fulfill production contracts with companies that purchased their sugarcane and soybeans earlier than their Black neighbors' products, thus earning better prices. Two of my Black farming friends were given awards as the top producers of sugarcane by their local farmer organization, but that was several years before they were squeezed out of farming by the subtle efforts of white lenders and merchants who undermined their success. I now understand the meaning of the term *systemic racial prejudice* better through my Black farmer friends, who are trying to hang on to the few remaining acres they own and to turn their operation into an educational center.

The historical trauma of racism in American agriculture is often not understood by persons who are not of color. My wife's father was a victim of such trauma. Walt was a second-generation Japanese American producer of seedless golden raisins, avocados, and citrus fruits in the Central Valley of California prior to the attack on Pearl Harbor by Japan in December 1941. He, and most persons of Japanese descent who lived in the western states, were confined to internment camps. When World War II ended, his opportunity to farm had been erased by white neighbors who had taken over his farm. Someone had burned down his barn, destroying all his farming equipment and his automobile. A positive event also occurred: he met his future wife, Michi, in camp, and they remained in Idaho after release, marrying, and starting a family. Michi was released first when a physician hired her to work as a nurse in the local hospital. Walt did what he could to stay connected with agriculture after discharge from the camp, first as a caretaker of lawns and gardens, and later as a worker in a potato processing plant in Idaho. His large and immaculately groomed garden produced beans, zucchini, tomatoes, and a variety of other vegetables, strawberries, and raspberries that immediately attracted my admiration after I became acquainted with Marilyn and visited her home.

The roles of Indigenous American and Black farmers continue to diminish, while the roles of Hispanic and Asian farmers in the United States are gradually increasing during the current century. According to the 2017 Census of Agriculture, which is the most recent data available as I write this, 95 percent of U.S. farm operators were non-Hispanic whites, who produced 95 percent of agricultural sales. Hispanic farmers accounted for 2.2 percent of agricultural sales, and Asians accounted for 1.3 percent of agricultural sales, both of which are increases since the previous census in 2012. Native Americans accounted for 0.5 percent of agricultural sales, but owned 5.6 percent of U.S. farmland, mostly sparse grassland and other land even less suited for agriculture. Farms operated by Black individuals accounted for 0.4 percent of agricultural sales and 1.4 percent of the agricultural producers. From 2012 to 2017, the number of Black producers increased 0.5 percent, but the number of Black-operated farms decreased 3 percent.

Most farm workers in the United States, about 2.5 million, are people of Hispanic heritage. They, and Asian immigrants during the past four decades, increasingly purchase small parcels of land whenever possible to raise enough fruits, vegetables, grains, and animals to meet the needs of their families. Whenever they have extra produce, they often sell it to buy more land and farm equipment. They help to fill a niche in consumer demand for locally raised and palate-pleasing food items. Some producers supply products that meet the standards required to be labeled organic, but they haven't completed the complex paperwork and inspections for certification as organic farmers. Overall, organic, regenerative, and other sustainable farms comprise the fastest growing type of agriculture in the United States, comprising about 1.6 percent of current farms, according to the USDA. Indigenous and Black Americans are gradually implementing this method of agriculture.

It wasn't by accident that the Lewis and Clark expedition team chose to spend their first winter in 1803–1804 among the Mandan people in North Dakota next to the Missouri River. The Mandans traded corn, beans, squash, sunflowers, and tobacco for gifts the explorers brought with them. The agrarian imperative was a strong force in the cultures of the Mandan Nation and for most other Indigenous Americans.

This is the same drive that motivates farmers everywhere, but sometimes it is expressed differently, including the various immigrants to the New World during the past five centuries. Indigenous Americans already had survival capacity in a less complicated world. Their methods of living, which included agriculture, enabled up to 40,000 inhabitants to flourish in cities of the Incas, Mayans, and at Cahokia in what is now Illinois, until unfamiliar diseases, probably brought to North

America by Nordic explorers, arrived around 800–1400 AD. More documentation is needed to clearly prove this hypothesis, but in the absence of more definitive historical evidence, it makes sense. My Mandan friends tell me that as recently as the 1830s, their tribe shrank from 3,000 to 300 persons due to smallpox, likely brought to their communities by French Canadian and American traders, but their numbers have greatly rebounded since then.

It is also not by accident that the most resilient tribes are those that maintain and teach their cultural practices. Their agrarian imperative instilled in them the initiative to do everything within their power to survive, and to take uncommon risks while enduring extreme hardship to adhere to their cultural practices—even during wars against overwhelming forces. The loss of their accumulated knowledge and human capital was tragic, not only for them but for everyone. That many Indigenous Americans are recovering their culture is a boon to all humanity.

11

LESSONS LEARNED ABOUT FARMERS' BEHAVIORAL HEALTH FROM THE 1980s TO NOW

Thirty or so farm couples gathered in St. Thomas Parish Hall for a potluck dinner and a meeting about the ongoing farm crisis, after mass on a chilly Sunday morning in February 1984, in a rural, western Iowa community of about 600 town residents and another nearby 400 farm people who called the community their hometown. About a dozen of the farm couples were parishioners at St. Thomas Church; the others were local families affiliated with the Methodist church in town or hailed from neighboring communities. Even though nearly all the meeting participants were acquainted with one another, their chatter was unusually polite and somber for folks who typically greeted one another with hearty handshakes, humorous comments, and loud discussions about the weather and the latest news.

After the ladies delivered their dinner dishes to the kitchen hands, they gathered in small, quiet groups while the men assembled in the back of the room. Most discussed what they might expect over the next few hours of the meeting. The farm couples had learned about the Farm Crisis Workshop from their church bulletins, the local newspaper, a local radio station, or by word of mouth.

At 10:50 a.m. I asked the participants to find seats at the tables, which were already set with dinnerware, glasses of water, and napkins, along with notepads and pencils. I outlined the schedule and promised that the meeting would end around 3:30 p.m., in time for everyone to get home for evening farm chores. A few minutes later I introduced Ken and Laura as farmers from a neighboring county, who were clients at Southwest Iowa Mental Health Center, where I was employed as a psychologist for three days per week. My therapy sessions with clients and workshops sometimes ran past scheduled hours, but I didn't mind, because I felt I was helping farm people who were in desperate straits.

Ken explained how until last November, he and Laura had operated a 640-acre farm, which included the 320-acre "home" place that they had purchased two decades ago from Ken's parents and was nearly paid for. They purchased an adjoining 320 acres in 1977, when the farm economy was sailing along, partly due to Secretary of Agriculture Earl Butz's policy of planting "fence row to fence row" to undercut competing agricultural countries during the Nixon and Ford presidential administrations of the 1970s. Relying partly on advancing technology and economy of scale, U.S. farmers could produce food cheaper than most agricultural countries. Russia became the major foreign purchaser of America's wheat. Successful farmers during that era generally purchased additional farmland, sought ever larger modern farm equipment, used borrowed money to finance purchases, and allowed inflation to increase their net worth. Farm profits rose, but so did the prices for farmland and equipment during this boom era. Nearly everyone wanted a share of the profits, which fueled rising prices on nearly everything and rising interest rates on borrowed money. This set of circumstances usually benefited farmers willing to take financial risks, until changes in the Federal Monetary Policy were instituted in 1980 to curb inflation, as described in a 1987 article written by J. T. Conlan in *Publix: The Journal of Federalism*. Many farmers had mortgaged their land to guarantee operating loans and to lengthen the time to pay off long-term debts. I remember paying an interest rate of 18 percent on short-term farm operating loans during the early 1980s.

That decade witnessed the worst farm economic chaos since the Great Depression of the 1930s. President Carter embargoed the sale of wheat to Russia in 1980 to punish the Soviet Union for invading Afghanistan, which drove down wheat prices and also negatively affected prices for other major commodities, including corn and soybeans. By 1987, farmland prices fell to 45 percent of their prices six years earlier. A federal Task Force on Agriculture and Community Viability estimated in 1987 that one-third of all people farming at the start of the decade were no longer able to farm. With fewer farmers and lower net worths of remaining farmers, a shrinking tax base created financial problems for rural counties and farm states, such as disruption of basic services, ranging from road maintenance to providing community mental health care. The recovery from the Farm Crisis of the 1980s took until the early 1990s. Ken and Laura were victims of these circumstances.

Ken had raised eighty cow/calf pairs of purebred Hereford cattle on pastures that he could rotate when the grazers bit off the grass in one paddock, along with enough hay for the cattle's sustenance over winters if heavy snow covered the remaining three hundred or so acres of cornstalks and soybean remnants left after Ken had harvested the crops. Laura worked as a bookkeeper for the local grain elevator to bring in additional income and to obtain family health insurance. That was before their banker required foreclosure on their operating loans, as well as the sale of half of their mortgaged land and all their treasured cows to pay down their new land loan. Ken had to take a job driving a semi-truck to supplement their now significantly limited farm income.

His voice cracking, Ken stopped talking several times as he described how their cattle herd thrived during twenty-five years of careful management, and how his cows and he took care of each other. He didn't have to drive the cattle into their pens and pastures—they followed him. Laura held his hand, with tears rolling down her cheeks, as did many people in the audience. Laura indicated how they found help after she read an article in their local newspaper that Southwest Iowa Mental Health Center offered counseling for $1.00 to $3.00 per hour, or free if necessary, and psychiatric medications at cost for farmers and their families who were overwhelmed by stress. The article mentioned that the suicide rate of farmers had doubled during the past three years, Laura said, and that anxiety and depression often accompanied financial restructuring or bankruptcy. Support groups, educational training in stress management, and programs like today's community meeting were available too, and without charge.

As Ken regained his composure, he slowly pronounced, "I wouldn't be here if we hadn't found Southwest Iowa Mental Health Center. Dr. Mike understands us. He's a farmer like us, but he also knows about mental health. We couldn't talk about that before. That's why we're here, to tell you it's okay to talk about your problems. It's a strength to seek counseling, and it only hurts you if you don't ask for help when you don't have all the answers."

When Ken asked if there were any questions, before taking a break for dinner, no one raised a hand, but during dinner, folks quickly clustered around Ken and Laura at their table, while others gathered nearby, waiting their turns to speak. Ken and Laura hung around for the rest of the meeting and conferred personally with at least half the audience during breaks and after the workshop ended.

At 1:00 p.m. I asked the participants to take their usual seats, while a physician explained what happens to our health when we undergo stress we can't control, followed by a banker who explained the steps involved in court proceedings pertaining to foreclosure on a farm loan. The Federal Deposit Insurance Corporation had declared his bank insolvent, largely because farming clients were unable to pay back loans. The farm couples empathized with him.

Following a very busy and noisy break, the meeting reconvened at 2:00 p.m. I explained how farmers were not in control of most of the factors that affected their finances, such as the weather, government policies, and market prices, but they controlled how they managed themselves. They could share their worries with others they trusted— or not. Their schedules, I said, are like a feed ration for raising cattle. The feed ration has to contain the right amount of carbohydrates for energy, protein for maximum growth, and various minerals to promote good animal health. The farm family's ration of scheduled activities should include time for talking openly with family members, recreating to escape from concerns for a while, praying together, and looking out for their neighbors and others in distress. They could take breaks from constant work and fretting on a daily basis by playing with their kids and taking short, inexpensive vacations to restore their individual perspectives and family well-being, such as camping and hiking together, or attending school sporting events that they might have withdrawn from watching. Mental health counseling from a professional who understands agriculture could be key to making it through this rural revolution. The more they learned about mental health and useful behaviors, the more likely they were to make sound decisions regarding their circumstances.

The symptom onset and remission through stages of adjustment to farm loss seemed to follow a pattern similar to Elizabeth Kubler-Ross's stages of grief and adjustment to the death of a loved one (i.e., denial, anger, going through the loss, slowly remitting depression while gradually returning to feeling okay, and acceptance). However, for farmers, their trauma was more severe in many cases and there were fewer rituals, such as funerals, to help farm people handle their losses. As Ursula Delworth and I explained in a 1990 article in the *Clinical Psychologist*, entitled "Clinical and Community Perspectives on the Farm Crisis," with the death of a loved one there is often a realization that its prevention is beyond our control, whereas most agricultural producers feel responsible for their loss of a farm, and especially when it's the family farm. Losing the family farm brings shame to them for not hanging on to what their forebearers struggled to acquire, and it usually eliminates the possibility of their successors becoming farmers. Research studies that were undertaken at several land-grant universities in the 1980s and onward to present day, collectively indicated that farmers rated the loss of a family farm as the most disastrous event they could experience, followed by the death of a spouse, the death of a close family member, a day when nothing goes right, machinery breakdowns, disease outbreaks, divorce, and on down the list. During subsequent research, which I undertook during the late 1990s, I learned that losing the family farm was harder on farm people than dealing with the death of a loved one, except when the loved one undertook suicide or was a child who died in a farm tragedy. It took me until the mid-1990s to realize that it may take eight to ten years to achieve recovery, with three to four years as the briefest we observed. However, farmers were never the same thereafter; losing the farm remained a lifelong regret.

In my 1990 article with Dr. Delworth, I explained that the first stage of losing the farm, the anticipatory stage, is characterized by increasing tension, worry, and denial that something foreboding might happen; it's also the second longest, with recovery taking the longest time, sometimes the remainder of their lives. The second stage entails the realization that loss of the farm is impending, which leads to internal bargaining, often including desperate strategies for hanging on to their land and other assets needed to continue farming. Much anger and worsening apprehension often accompany losing their hopes to remain viable as agricultural producers. The third stage includes the actual foreclosure period, which is the point at which symptoms of despair are most poignant. Suicide and the need for emotional support are more likely during this stage than during any other. During the fourth stage, realignment and acceptance of loss begin, but usually with significant depression initially, followed by gradually working through who and what are responsible for forced removal from their farm entirely, or massive restructuring like Ken and Laura faced to hang on to a portion of their agricultural heritage. The fifth stage entails finding new meaning, at which point it can be said that the individuals affected by total or partial loss of their farming operation have recovered; however, as I witnessed, survivors were never the same. They became low risk-takers, suspicious of good fortune, and likely to endure any future traumas. My maternal grandmother, who experienced the Great Depression, became so frugal that she kept quart jars filled with buttons she found or removed from clothing she had worn out, so that she could find the closest match to replace a button that was lost from any of her best dresses, rather than to purchase a new set of buttons.

As my presentation time during the workshop dwindled, I provided contact information about resources the meeting participants could access for various types of assistance they needed, such as the Iowa State University Extension Service for farm economic planning, and various church organizations for financial help, such as paying for utility bills. I asked everyone to take a slip of paper from the notepads on their tables and to write down something each person had that could not be taken from them, such as love from their families, personal faith, integrity, and so forth. While I played background music on my guitar, everyone came forward to pin their pieces of paper onto a bulletin board in the front of the hall. Many men and women sobbed, as they attached their written responses to the board. What were they feeling? Was it fear of unwanted circumstances ahead, or perhaps recognition that they weren't alone in their misery, or something else? The meeting ended with a prayer from the Methodist minister, but not everyone went home immediately. Many wanted to talk with Ken and Laura, and with me.

The Southwest Iowa Mental Health Center initiated the first mental health response in Iowa to the Farm Crisis of the 1980s, utilizing federal funds managed by the Iowa Department of Health and Human Services. I wrote the grant request for two years and later asked for, and received, a third year of funding. Other projects throughout Iowa soon followed, such as setting up the Iowa Concern Hotline in 1985, which employed telephone responders who understood the rigors of farming and could connect callers with available resources, such as legal advice. Other agricultural states, including Nebraska and Wisconsin, devised programs that included professional counseling that was free to agricultural people who couldn't afford to pay for it. Kansas offered mental health counseling that was provided by trained farm mediation specialists. In Minnesota, the state Department of Agriculture coordinated farm business consulting with mental health services. New York instituted a program that included business planning as well as professional counseling services that were delivered on the farms of their distressed owners. Joyce Barrett wrote the best summary of community responses to the farm crisis in *Mending a Broken Heartland*, which she penned after attending the June 1987 conference of the National Association for Rural Mental Health, during which we visited after my presentation. I remember my talk as a family event. My wife distributed written summaries of the Southwest Iowa Mental Health Center project and our two children ran the slide projector while I spoke. Overall, however, there was no template for what worked best. Health care providers and leaders in many disciplines, religious denominations, and businesses in rural areas across the country, and in Canada and other modern agricultural countries, tried approaches they thought would effectively reach the embattled farm population who often avoided mental health care because to many farm people it was a sign of weakness.

What did our farm crisis mitigation efforts at the Southwest Iowa Mental Health Center teach us? First, we thought that we had reached nearly every farm family in our three-county catchment area, 4,993 families, to be exact, about where and how they could obtain professional mental health assistance. Second, we found during the three-year project that there was an increase in farm crisis services at the center during the spring of the first year, which tapered off during the busy summer and fall seasons, but increased during the winter and early spring each year thereafter. Foreclosures on loans and bankruptcy proceedings were more likely to occur after harvest was completed, and after financial institutions could assess progress, if any, by farm borrowers in reducing their indebtedness. Third, project staff provided district-wide workshops on stress management, reviewed the signs of depression and suicide, and identified how to find available forms of assistance. Relying on grant funds, the center hired another full-time counselor with a farm background and a master's degree in behavior therapy. The two of us, and a psychiatrist with a national reputation for his psychopharmacology expertise, who also lived on a farm, provided the bulk of the regional counseling and educational presentations. We also gave invited presentations in Minnesota, Michigan, Kansas, Nebraska, and Missouri, for a total of 435 educational presentations during just the first eighteen months of the project, and gradually fewer over the last eighteen months. Fourth, even though the Southwest Iowa Mental Health Center had offices in all three counties it served, we found it necessary sometimes to provide counseling with clients at their homes, where they felt comfortable and where we could acquire a sense of the farming operation. The sessions frequently took considerably longer than the usual one hour. Project staff found that females were more likely than males to initiate the request for assistance. The average age of farm crisis clients was forty-two years. Fifth, as reported by Rosmann and Delworth (1990), when the project was completed, the diagnosis most commonly reported was "relationship problems," such as domestic and child abuse, quarreling within the family, spousal blaming, and anger, for about 40 percent of diagnoses. About half of the cases had more than one diagnosis for the primary client(s). Adjustment problems, which are temporary exacerbations of anxiety, depression, and other behavioral problems that remit when stress diminishes, accounted for 24 percent of the diagnoses. Anxiety disorders, including generalized anxiety disorder, panic, and post-traumatic stress disorder, comprised 11 percent of the diagnoses. Severe grieving was fairly common. Of 122 long-term cases, forms of depression, with major depression significantly more common than bipolar disorder, occurred in 33 percent of the cases, and usually after chronic anxiety wore down their capacities to cope with perceived threats. Substance misuse was the main diagnosis in 5 percent of the 122 extensively studied families, but excessive alcohol consumption accompanied 40 percent of the primary diagnoses. Alcohol, and more rarely hard drugs, were used to escape psychological pain more than physical pain. There was a marked absence of difficult-to-treat mental illnesses, such as psychotic disorders and personality pathology. Taken together, it appeared that the prognoses for recovery were good, if the farm families could work through their farm loss or farm loan restructuring. The agricultural population was reasonably healthy, in a behavioral health sense, and had to be, if they were to be successful farmers, ranchers, and agricultural laborers in the first place.

How did the United States as a whole respond to the Farm Crisis of the 1980s? To answer this question, let's begin with historical background about federal and private efforts to assist troubled farm people prior to the Franklin D. Roosevelt presidential era. The Smith-Lever Act was passed by Congress in 1914 and signed into law by President Woodrow Wilson. It established extension services at land-grant colleges and universities to assist farmers and anyone who needed information about how to raise crops and to process farm products for later consumption or sale. Times have changed. Only a tiny percentage of the extension services budget, funded as part of the most recent USDA Farm Bill, is earmarked for these educational purposes. Private forms of assistance to farm people in need of social, financial, and psychological support were limited to church organizations and local communities that sometimes rallied around unfortunate farm families, like Amish and Mennonite neighbors still do today.

During the Great Depression of the 1930s, many measures were passed into law at President Roosevelt's request, to assist agricultural producers affected by severe drought, low prices for farm commodities, and the inability of people farming marginal agricultural land to achieve a viable living. FDR's proposals included setting aside farmland for conservation purposes and receiving a small payment instead of raising crops for sale. Not farming agricultural land, especially if it was highly erodible, was deemed necessary in order to reduce production and thereby to enhance market prices, while improving soil and water conservation. During the 1930s, most farmers still undertook plowing soil and planting crops upside and downside hills, so soil erosion by rainstorms was common on the rolling land that comprised most of the farmland in the United States, as was wind erosion in drought-stricken areas, and both forms of soil erosion on marginal farmland that we now know should probably never have been tilled and instead maintained in its original prairie grasses and other plants. The farming practices of minimal or no tillage, installing terraces to hold water from flowing down hillsides, planting on the contour, and planting alternating strips of different crops, such as hay and oats that discouraged erosion between crops that required cultivation (e.g., corn and cotton) hadn't become widely accepted yet, but these methods became more popular from the 1940s onward.

Other measures that Roosevelt proposed, and were passed by Congress, included payments to farmers for storing grain, the establishment of the Farm Credit Administration to allow farmers a longer time to refinance farm purchase agreements, and at lower than usual interest rates, and to set up federal work programs to employ displaced farmers as well as other people who couldn't find jobs.

The Farm Crisis of the 1980s brought about significant reforms for dealing with bankruptcy. Revised federal statutes allowed farm owners to retain forty—instead of five—acres, along with a house, a car or truck, essential furniture, and everyday household items. Through much effort by mediators of farm disputes and lenders, relations between farmers seeking loans with lenders have become much more collegial rather than adversarial. A revised code of ethics for lending practices to agricultural producers was developed and implemented. I wrote its first draft sometime around 1990, at the request of an agricultural lending group. Most of my suggested reforms persisted, which included: (1) borrowers should be allowed to have someone join the borrower in their deliberations with lenders, as an extra set of eyes and ears for the borrower, and to provide constructive support to the borrower; (2) all the people in the negotiations should sit around a table and in the same type of chairs, so that superiority is not conveyed by the seating arrangement; (3) the people in the discussion should be visible to other bank staff for safety reasons, while also maintaining privacy of speech; and (4) the lenders and borrowers should both take responsibility in the development of a business plan that is acceptable to both parties and in follow-up reviews.

The Farm Crisis of the 1980s led to federal legislation during the 1990s while there was an era of slow recovery of agriculture from its earlier doldrums, and a decade when attention was devoted to making farming less risky by developing crop insurance options, subsidizing long-term agricultural loan payments as a last resort if a viable farm operating plan could be agreed upon, and expanding options for placing crops into long-term storage and borrowing against them as collateral. Moreover, a network of Centers for Agricultural Safety and Health, funded by the National Institute for Occupational Safety and Health, was established at a dozen major universities, including one at the National Center for Agricultural Medicine in Marshfield, Wisconsin. Much emphasis was placed on making farming safer through education in a newly established field, agricultural medicine, as well as local community education, such as farm safety day camps, a specialized AgriSafe Network of clinics to assess farmers' physical and mental health, the Certified Safe Farm Program of offering reductions on farm homeowners and liability insurance, if the farm met criteria to become certified as having met standards that insurers helped develop, and to work with farm machinery manufacturers to reduce injury and death hazards by designing safer farm equipment. The National AgrAbility Project was also launched during the 1990s to assist injured farmers to return to their chosen vocation after suffering serious injuries, such as amputation of one's legs.

Although the rates of injuries and fatalities of persons engaged in agriculture today remain the highest of any occupation, the annual number of injuries and fatalities of persons engaged in agriculture has declined in the decades following the 1990s, according to the U.S. Bureau of Labor Statistics. The National Agricultural Safety Database says the number of children who died in farming events has declined about 60 percent during the past thirty years. While the physical well-being of people involved in agriculture was improving during the 1990s and into the next millennium, their psychological well-being declined. In a 2002 article in the *Journal of Public Health*, Gopal Singh and Mohammad Siahpush reported that the rate of suicide by farmers steadily increased during the 1990s. This trend was also observed by Ramin Mojtabai in the *Journal of Public Health* in 2005, in which he mentioned that there was a decline of social-psychological supports for the decreased number of agricultural producers as a result of the 1980s Farm Crisis.

The USDA and the Internal Revenue Service have long considered farmers, ranchers, migrant farm laborers, and permanent workers in the production of food, fibers, and renewable energy, such as wind and biofuels, to be farmers, as well as fishers, foresters, lumber harvesters, hunters, and plant nursery operators. The USDA conducts its Census of Agriculture every five years, with data pertaining to 2022 as the most recent census currently.

In September 1998, there was a day when the price for market-ready hogs reached the incredibly low price of eight cents per pound, live weight. Congressional leaders and federal agencies, such as the Office of Rural Health Policy (ORHP), became alarmed about the possibility of recurring economic and overwhelming psychological strife on financially impacted farmers. The ORHP offered several million dollars to the Wisconsin Office of Rural Health and the Wisconsin Primary Care Association to bring together leaders from seven Midwestern states (Iowa, Kansas, Minnesota, Nebraska, North Dakota, South Dakota, and Wisconsin) to strategize about how to best assist the agricultural population with crisis mental health services. Many invited participants were leaders in their respective states who tried various approaches to helping their state's agricultural producers as they coped with the 1980s Farm Crisis. The invited participants came together to share their expertise about what they had learned. I was one of Iowa's representatives during the formation of a seven-state consortium called the Sharing the Seeds of Hope (SSOH) program, and I participated in follow-up in-person meetings and telephone conferences. Funds were disbursed to each state to provide services they deemed best, such as

low-cost or free counseling, recuperative and educational retreats for
economically distressed families, community meetings that brought
together local farmers and businesspeople to figure out long-term local solutions, such as constructing a local grain-processing facility to
produce ethanol within their communities, and other creative ventures. Having formed a new nonprofit organization that was incorporated in Iowa to assist distressed farm families, AgriWellness was
designated to manage Iowa's portion of the grant and shared funds
with the Iowa Concern Hotline and with professional providers who
agreed to offer counseling sessions to farmers and their families for a
reduced fee. My ongoing polling of farm families showed that the loss
of a child in a farming tragedy was as stressful as losing an entire farm,
but so was the death of another important family member involved in
the farm operation.

By 2000 it became clear that the Wisconsin Office of Rural Health
and the Wisconsin Primary Care Association could not continue to operate the SSOH program, because these two state entities were man-
dated to serve only the people of Wisconsin, so the leaders of these
two organizations convened the project leaders from the seven states
to meet in Minneapolis to figure out the next steps. Alternative entities were invited to submit proposals for administering the remaining
SSOH funds. Iowa leaders recommended AgriWellness for the job,
but with new bylaws and a new seven-state board of directors. Other
leadership options were proposed as well; however, the representatives from the seven states chose AgriWellness, and me as its director,
to carry on the SSOH work.

Over the next fifteen years, AgriWellness became the leading organization in the United States that was trying to figure out how best
to assist farmers everywhere with their mental health issues. All the
AgriWellness staff participated in writing many grant requests to various federal agencies, state offices of human services, nonprofit corpo-
rations and foundations, and to many for-profit companies. Relying
on a contractual basis with the Iowa Department of Human Services,

AgriWellness recruited and trained Iowa's first disaster crisis counselors to help the state's residents recover psychologically from disasters, such as floods and tornadoes, when the Federal Emergency Management Agency (FEMA) determined that federal assistance was needed to augment state and local recovery efforts. We also identified and helped some 450 new residents adjust to Iowa after relocating from Louisiana following Hurricane Katrina. We drafted a new Iowa Disaster Behavioral Health Plan that became the template for several subsequent renditions. It was critical to match the characteristics of the people affected by a disaster when employing crisis counselors after disasters in order for the counselors to relate culturally with the disaster victims. My colleagues and I wrote many journal articles about assisting residents in rural and agricultural regions, and for the Disaster Technical Assistance Center maintained by the federal Substance Abuse and Mental Health Services Administration. AgriWellness sponsored conferences every two years called The Clock Is Ticking for Rural America: A Behavioral Health and Safety Conference, which attracted 130 to 240 participants from around the country and occasional visitors from Canada and Australia, which had established their own programs to aid distressed farmers.

The AgriWellness Board of Directors determined to figure out the behavioral health services that most effectively aided distressed farmers, ranchers, farmworkers, and their families. Plans were drafted for each state to offer a range of services: (1) farmer-friendly hotlines or helplines; (2) the provision of counseling by licensed professionals; (3) training the professionals to work with agricultural people if they weren't already familiar with the unique cultural aspects of their agricultural clientele; (4) the provision of up to five free counseling sessions; (5) community education programs about mental health; (6) weekend retreats for families during which the parents learned about managing their stress and farm business, while their children learned how to accommodate household stress; (7) social marketing of available forms of assistance to farm people through the distribution of educational literature; (8) outreach through state and local media; (9) establishing useful coalitions within each state that could furnish required funding streams from state and local governments, private foundations, and other entities that could maintain the services after federal grants ended; (10) advocacy contacts with others; and (11) support groups for embattled farmers and their families.

Only four of the seven states (Iowa, Nebraska, North Dakota, and Wisconsin) had operated statewide farm crisis hotlines or helplines continuously from the Farm Crisis era in the 1980s. By early 2005, the other three states (Kansas, Minnesota, and South Dakota) set up statewide farm crisis telephone and email services, information clearinghouse websites, and follow-up services, including the provision of free or subsidized counseling from trained and licensed professionals in any mental or behavioral health care field.

Utilizing grant funds from the federal DHHS, the AgriWellness office collected monthly reports from our seven state partners for a twenty-six-month period from September 1, 2005, through October 31, 2007. During that time frame, there were 43,852 contacts with the hotlines and helplines, as reported by Shari Stucker and me in 2008 in *NARMH Notes*, a short-lived publication of the National Association for Rural Mental Health. Some people may have contacted our partners' hotlines and helplines more than once. I also presented our findings at the 2014 Conference of the International Society for Agricultural Safety and Health, held in Omaha, Nebraska. My presentation was included in the proceedings of the conference and the details are reported here.

The racial background/ethnicity of the callers who contacted the seven state farm crisis services included 86.0 percent white non-Hispanic people; 2.7 percent African Americans; 1.9 percent Native Americans; 1.1 percent Hispanic people; 0.6 percent Pacific Islanders; 0.6 percent Middle Easterners; and 7.5 percent with other racial backgrounds/ethnicities, or were not reported. The racial background/ethnicity of the callers approximated that of the residents in the seven states, except that 3.5 percent of the region's residents were Hispanic, according to the 2000 U.S. Census.

Of the callers, 51.1 percent were actively involved in farming, ranching, or working on farms; 40.2 percent were the spouses of people actively involved in agriculture; 1.1 percent were children in an agricultural household; 4.8 percent were displaced farm people; and the remainder had other roles in agriculture.

Callers reported the following reasons for contacting the hotlines/ helplines: 24.6 percent were concerned about marital and family relationship issues; 27.7 percent reported difficulty coping on a daily basis; 27.7 percent reported feeling depressed; 5.5 percent reported their own or other family members' problems with alcohol, drug, or gambling addictions; 14.3 percent reported stress about finances; and some reported other concerns or more than one concern.

The telephone and email responders at the seven statewide farm crisis centers asked the persons who initiated the contacts if they, or someone in the household, exhibited suicidal behavior. The trained responders reported 685 persons (1.6 percent of 42,852 callers) who indicated suicidal behaviors. Seventy-seven of these persons reported a suicide plan. Another 56 persons had attempted suicide. If there was reason to suspect the need for immediate assistance, the responders followed up by contacting an adult family member, a caregiver, or law enforcement as a last resort. I remember a situation in which the Iowa Concern Hotline contacted me with the name of a person whose family had sought my professional services. When the call was transferred to me, the individual exhibited slurred speech and indicated having swallowed a bottle of sleeping pills. While keeping the caller on one telephone line, I tried but failed to reach a family member, so I contacted the sheriff in the caller's county some 75 miles distant from my office. I explained the situation and said I would keep the caller on the line until the sheriff responded. A few minutes elapsed before I heard the caller drop the phone and collapse onto the floor while we were talking. I tried to get the caller to answer me but was unsuccessful. When the sheriff arrived at the home several minutes later, the sheriff picked up the phone and learned that I was waiting for confirmation of a hand off. The sheriff and a deputy transported the comatose person to the nearest hospital where treatment took a few days and was successful. I consulted with the family a few times thereafter. The farm couple expressed profound gratitude several times.

During the 26-month study, 7,238 counseling sessions were provided to people who requested a paper voucher that could be given to a recommended professional in exchange for a counseling meeting. Some sessions were undertaken at the homes of the people needing help. Home visits allowed the counselors to see their clients in their own territories. The counselors reported demographic information and the diagnoses of their agricultural clients, but no personal identifiers, to their state farm crisis coordinator, who passed the information along to the AgriWellness office. We learned that the service recipients were mostly (97.3 percent) white non-Hispanic persons. Our project did not effectively reach racial and ethnic minorities. We attribute this partly to the counselors being mostly white non-Hispanic professionals. The diagnoses made by the service providers included the following: 3.6 percent marital relationship/parent-child/other relationship problems; 44.5 percent adjustment problems; 32.5 percent depression; 10.7 percent anxiety disorders; 4.2 percent alcohol and other drug addictions; 0.6 percent pathological gambling; 0.1 percent psychotic disorders; and 1.5 percent personality disorders. The diagnoses of the persons receiving professional counseling roughly matched the diagnoses of the 122 intensively studied families in the Southwest Iowa Mental Health Center project about twenty years earlier, when combining marital relationship problems and adjustment problems. Both diagnoses share some commonalities. Moreover, there was considerable agreement between the reasons callers indicated when they contacted their state hotline/helpline and the diagnoses rendered by the professional counselors.

Besides the availability of farm crisis hotlines/helplines, and counseling that could be offered like an employee assistance plan (EAP) for farm people, what other best practices emerged from our 26-month study? We found that employing providers who understood farm culture, through undertaking training that the program provided, or because they were already familiar with culture of the people they served, was critically important, as was matching the racial and ethnic backgrounds of the professionals with the persons needing assistance. We found this to also be important to the success of FEMA-funded crisis counseling programs that helped victims of disasters in Iowa to recover.

We learned that community education programs were well received, according to anonymous evaluations we collected from 7,515 persons who participated in educational meetings and workshops at the local level. Another 760 persons participated in weekend retreats and workshops for farm families. The retreats were costly, partly because grant funds paid for a hired person to manage the farm in the absence of the farm family, such as milking cows twice daily, besides paying for weekend accommodations, but the farm families praised the retreats for helping them regain their perspectives and learn valuable skills. Conducting social marketing of available services was important, for we distributed 165,977 pieces of literature about stress and how to find help. Placing the information in places that farmers visited, such as their county USDA farm service agencies and on bulletin boards of local coffee shops and restaurants where farm people gathered, seemed to reach the intended people most effectively. Our state partners found that their brochures and magnetized refrigerator door contact cards often ran out at these settings and had to be replaced. Conducting outreach contacts through local media, such as newspapers, radio, and television programs that farmers were familiar with helped to break down the negative stigma about seeking help when needed. We also found that it was important to provide information about the signs of stress, depression, suicide, and how to find assistance. The building of coalitions and undertaking advocacy with farm organizations and government officials were difficult to assess; however, I became convinced that the media, such as respected farm magazines, newspapers, and television programs, deserve much of the credit for farmers now becoming accustomed to talking about personal issues and mental health with other persons with whom they are comfortable. Lastly, it's easy to recognize the value of providing ongoing support groups to farmers in need of understanding. Almost 100 percent of counseling clients and support group participants said they would recommend these forms of assistance to other farm people.

Our project services and findings were designated as best practices by the U.S. Department of Health and Human Services in *Rural Behavioral Health Programs and Promising Practices* in 2011. They became the foundation for the Farm and Ranch Stress Assistance Network that is now a part of the current Farm Bill. Key provisions are: (1) farm telephone helplines and websites; (2) community education; (3) support groups; (4) outreach services and activities; and (5) provision of services by persons who understand the cultures of the people they serve. Another recommendation was to provide home delivery of assistance in a situation in which a farm resident is homebound.

It has become clear that beneficial services for distressed agricultural producers must achieve five "A" grades: (1) available at times and places suited to agricultural producers, such as during evenings, weekends, and on rainy days; (2) affordable, so as to not worsen financial problems or insurance coverage, that is, like an employee assistance program for farm people; (3) attuned culturally to the needs of farmers, ranchers, and farmworkers when the providers understand agricultural behavioral health and if possible, match the race and ethnicity of the clients; (4) accessible within reasonable driving distance, or by home visits, and sometimes now via telehealth; and (5) acceptable because the professional counselor has credibility with the clients because the counselor knows what to do to make their lives better.

Over the years I have learned much about suicide from the people I serve. Farm people recognize suicide as a major problem. It has become clear that the factors that increase the risk of suicide by farmers include the simultaneous experience of three or more major stressors. A summary is warranted: (1) farmers are a hardy group, but most can't deal well with more than two serious problems at a time, such as the death or incapacitation of a person who is essential to the farm operation, combined with a disease outbreak in the livestock herd, living alone, substance misuse, or other significant stressors; (2) exposure to toxic pesticides (especially organophosphates) increases the risks for depression and suicide, as has been well documented by Lorann Stallones and Cheryl Beseler at Colorado State University; (3) I look for several danger signals by asking distressed farmers about the following: Does the farmer verbalize feelings of hopelessness? Has the farmer lost interest in practically everything except their own dreadful feelings? Is the farmer unable to laugh or take pleasure in anything recently? Does the person make dramatic threats, such as "I'll shoot my livestock before I let the court have them." Does the farmer experience the "lump in the throat phenomenon" in which the person wants to cry, but can't break down to cry? Is the person avoiding public events, such as church services or kids' school activities that he/she usually attends? Does the farmer demonstrate very flat affect? Does the personal appearance of the farmer and/or the farm seem unkempt? Is the farmer unable to sleep or sleeps very poorly for three or more nights in succession? And is it tax season, time for a loan payment, planting, or harvesting?

If a farmer, regardless of gender, reports two or more of these signs of serious depression and potential self-harm, it becomes important to negotiate with the farmer who can be contacted to be physically present so that the farmer is never alone. This might be a trusted family member, a nearby neighbor, or friend. I also require that the at-risk person call me daily with a progress report and when in distress. If I am not available, I provide several suicide hotline telephone numbers, such as 988, the closest farm crisis service, the nearest hospital emergency room, and sometimes the Farm Aid Program contact information (even though Farm Aid is not a hotline, it can offer support). We set up a plan of remediation during follow-up therapy sessions. It is demanding on me or any person, but saving a life is more important than becoming tired; however, I have had to learn to manage my own compassion fatigue.

The question should be asked: Is farmers' understanding of mental health improving? The American Farm Bureau Federation commissioned Morning Consult to conduct polls of 2,004 rural residents, including 81 farmers and farmworkers, in 2019, 2020, and more recently. Major findings in 2019 include:

- 30 percent of farmers said poor mental health is a major problem for them or their workers
- Two of three rural respondents and farmers said they know where to seek mental health assistance and they know the warning signs of a mental health condition
- 82 percent of farm respondents said their mental health is important to them and/or their family
- 91 percent of farmers/farmworkers said financial issues and fear of losing their farm impact their mental health
- Rural residents and farmers/farmworkers would like their primary care providers and mental health service providers to have specialized training about rural life and agricultural behavioral health

Each year the poll has yielded slightly more positive results. In comparison to a generation ago, farmers have become more knowledgeable about their behavioral health and less afraid of seeking assistance when needed. I know of one farmer coffee klatch that asks a different member of the group to bring an article about mental health each Monday morning when they meet. They look forward to their discussions.

12

SANDHILLS' GOOD, BAD, AND UGLY

My 2004 Jeep Grand Cherokee rumbled over the cattle guard worn shiny by many previous vehicles that had traversed the entryway from the asphalt county road. We followed a rutted half-mile-long dirt path toward the Lucky Lady Ranch. Jon, my thirty-year-old son, and I aimed to hunt prairie chickens and sharp-tailed grouse for the first time. We towed an eighteen-foot boat with a forty horsepower outboard motor that Jon had borrowed from our buddy Scott. When we weren't hunting upland gamebirds, we planned to use the boat for fishing on nearby Sandhill lakes and Merritt Reservoir twenty miles to the northwest.

We knew this area fairly well, having first fished Merritt in 1983 and many times since, as well as Big Alkali, Hackberry, and Watts lakes, which are part of, or adjacent to, the Valentine National Wildlife Refuge. Even though regulations prohibit keeping any bass from Watts Lake, I like Watts a lot. Its water is clean and translucent, although stained by pondweeds that engulf the entire lakebed and furnish cover for a thriving multitude of plump bluegills as well as bass.

Hunting and fishing are allowed on most parts of the refuge except in sanctuaries where these activities are carefully regulated. I had booked a cabin for five days of hunting and fishing nearby. Jon and I brimmed with high hopes.

As we bumped along the sandy path and slowed for potholes, sorrel, dun, paint, and other variously colored quarter horses slouching lazily on our right raised their heads to check us out, while several dozen

Angus cows with robust calves, half as big as their mommas, grazed on prairie grass on the left side of the roadway. The Sandhill ranchers raised some of the best cattle in the world. They shipped most of their feeder calves to be fattened elsewhere because little corn was grown in this area to finish the beeves for market. The soil here is too fragile to be tilled for crops. Usually by that time of the year, late September, the pastures had dried up and turned brown, but on this particular year the cattle were up to their bellies in green grass all summer long. This is the way real cowboys think beef production should be, and the way many Americans think it still is, but isn't, outside the Sandhill area and a few other regions of the West. As we eased into the gravel parking area in front of a picture-perfect, log ranch house, we noted a black-lettered metal sign by the houseyard gate that announced "Salesmen will be castrated."

We strode to the front door of the ranch house to ask the hostess about our accommodations in the half-dozen guest cabins next door. She had mentioned that most of her guests were hunters or fishers when we spoke on the phone in July. We found a note and key taped to the door that directed us to the far eastern cabin as our quarters. I parked the Jeep next to the wooden post fence in front of our cabin so we wouldn't have far to carry our food and equipment. Nugget, Jon's devoted and aging yellow Labrador retriever, was glad to be let out of her kennel to stretch her legs and take care of duties.

As Jon and I finished carrying our gear into our quarters, a long-legged, tanned, attractive, twentyish woman moved the sprinkler hose to a not-yet-watered section of the front lawn. This was our signal, we thought, to find someone at home.

When we rang the doorbell, a long-skirted, tanned, attractive, seventyish woman answered the door and asked, "Can I help you gentlemen?"

"We're not salesmen," I stammered, somewhat purposefully.

"I figured that," the smiling lady said. "I see you found your cabin. Won't you come in? Please be quiet, because my husband isn't well.

He's sleeping in the next room. He has Parkinson's and we don't expect him to be with us much longer. All the kids except Cody are home so we can spend what might be the last time the whole family is together with Daddy. Cody is in the rodeo in Sioux Falls. He's a bulldogger and team roper. He'll be home after his events are over."

A long-legged, tanned, attractive, fiftyish woman sauntered into the living room to join in welcoming us, as well as the younger woman we had noticed outside.

"Come sit down. Before we go any further," the eldest of the trio declared, "please tell me if you voted for Obama in the Iowa caucuses last January. You don't have to answer that if you don't want to, but I noticed your Iowa address when you reserved the cabin and I wondered who you might be voting for this fall."

Jon and I exchanged uncertain glances. We didn't want to offend our hosts with our political views. Nodding toward the youngest woman, I cautiously suggested, "She's wearing a T-shirt that says 'Make love, not war,' so I think it's okay if we answer."

Gingerly, Jon responded, "We both supported Obama."

"I was so hoping that," the gracious lady chortled. "My daughter, granddaughter, and I were the only people who went to the county Democrats' meeting last month. I didn't mean to put you on the spot. I just want to talk to someone with similar political views!"

"Fancy that," Jon proclaimed. "The only Democrats in Cherry County, and we find all three in one house."

Everyone laughed and relaxed. "I'm Virginia," the lady continued. "This is Beth and her daughter, Erin, who just returned from the Iraq War . . . for the second time. Erin is in the reserves, but when you are a Democrat, around here many folks think of you as being unpatriotic. My other daughter will join us shortly."

While I knew Virginia wanted to continue this political conversation, I figured someone in the room might offend another, so I changed the subject. "How is prairie chicken hunting? Do you have any sharp-tailed grouse?"

"We have lots of prairie chickens," Virginia said. "Please don't shoot any around the ranch here, because they're my pets. I buy bags of shelled corn to feed them during the winter in the pasture out front. There are lots of the birds in the hills that you can hunt."

Virginia continued, "Are you going for them by yourselves or do you have a dog? It's a lot better hunting if you have a dog."

"Yes, we've got Nugget." I added, "She's a yellow Lab."

"Yeah," Jon vouched. "She's getting up in years but she's still a great bird dog. She's in her seventies in human years. She's hunted and retrieved thousands of ducks and geese and nearly as many pheasants and quail. If there are prairie chickens and sharpies out there, she'll find them!"

Jon and I both tensed with excitement. But our obvious exhilaration didn't deter Virginia. "You will be doing a lot of walking. You'll probably see deer, maybe jackrabbits too. But . . . tell me, why are you supporting Obama for president?"

For the next half hour, Jon and I explained our rationales for supporting Barack Obama for U.S. president during the upcoming fall election. The other daughter, who had Beth's figure and the same tan, joined us. Virginia, her daughters, and granddaughter seemed so eager to talk to kindred spirits that they sometimes cut us off mid-sentence to add their insights and worries about the direction in which our country seemed to be heading. Beth brought beers for everyone to fuel the conversation.

As the ranch family's need for comfortable ideological discussion became satiated, during a quiet moment Virginia solemnly voiced, "Bob is seven years older than me. We always had such a clean life, I mean, everything seemed pure—the air, the water, our lifestyle. We're not big drinkers. I don't know why he got Parkinson's so young. He was still in his sixties. When Bob couldn't run the ranch anymore, we rented out the pasture and hay ground and that's when I started my cabin rental business."

"Farm and ranch people seem to have a high rate of Parkinson's," I commented. Virginia perked up again.

I told Virginia and her family members what I knew about suspected links to certain insecticides and herbicides, as well as to heavy metals and the effects of repeated blows to the head that people, such as boxers, other contact sport athletes, and people who work with livestock, sometimes experience. Jon told them he worked for an organization that promoted rural health care and how it was for him growing up on our farm. I explained my efforts to understand the behavioral health of people involved in farming and ranching. "Parkinson's disease is still largely an idiopathic illness without clear causes," I said.

While I ticked off a list of toxic substances, Virginia and her daughters asked each other if Bob had used any of the suspected substances, but they responded, "No." Were there toxic pesticides in the water on the ranch that everyone and their livestock drank? "No."

However, their deep, sandy soil was very porous and allowed the underground movement of fluids of all types, including the possibility of seepage from sources of toxicity that might not have originated on their ranch, or even nearby. Again, they concluded, "No, the soil in this area has never been tilled and exposed to agricultural chemicals. The closest industrial site is more than thirty miles away and no neighbors use pesticides, except for parasites on their cattle." When Bob was in the army he didn't serve in Vietnam, where many soldiers claim they were exposed to Agent Orange, a substance linked to Parkinson's symptoms in some studies. They wondered if Bob had received too many blows to his head while working with cattle, but they concluded "No" again. They expressed concern about Cody. As a professional steer wrestler, his head often got banged around. They recognized that Parkinson's seems to have some heritability. "Is it something we did or failed to do?" they wondered. Our discussion was terminated when Bob awakened. It was suppertime.

We said our good-byes, after getting directions for the best route to take through the ranch to the distant sand hills that ringed the entire spread some six to seven miles away.

The next morning Jon and I arose well before dawn. We gulped a hearty breakfast, Nugget as well, and soon were on our way in my Jeep. We followed a barely discernible path around a slough and a pond that Virginia had called "Fish Lake," covered with countless waterfowl, mostly ducks, but also white pelicans, loons, and grebes. Plovers, terns, and long-billed curlews skittered away from our vehicle. The path meandered through many hundreds of recently wrapped big round bales of native grass hay. A red-orange Massey Harris tractor, dating to the 1950s and attached to two nine-foot mowers hooked in tandem to cut an eighteen-foot hay swath, was still parked in the field.

We scattered dozens of fleet prairie chickens from the outskirts of the path. Nugget quivered with excitement, and I must say I did too. We respected Virginia's request to not shoot at her pets, but our anticipation was surging. After winding our way some six miles into the surrounding hills, we were stopped by a four-strand barbed wire fence, attached to crooked red-cedar posts interspersed with two steel posts for every cedar timber. We parked next to the fence halfway up the side of the first hill and loaded our twelve-gauge shotguns. We stuffed containers of water and sandwiches in our orange hunting vests, along with food and water for Nugget. Jon tied leather booties to Nugget's feet to protect them from prickly pear cactus thorns.

A brilliant sun emerged over the surrounding wind-produced escarpments as we hiked up the first hill, staying about 150 feet apart. Clumps of golden dried grasses, yucca with gray flower stalks, poison ivy, wild rose bushes still retaining their red hips, dusty green miner's lanterns, and mounded ant hills were scattered throughout the terrain. There were many sand blowouts as well, barren across their five- to fifteen-yard expanses. Wind had scooped out these bowls. As we were driving the day before, we had noticed how some Sandhill landowners tried to stop their spread by placing rubber tires in evenly spaced patterns in the empty sand; sprigs of grass were growing in some established tire plots.

More than a hundred centuries ago, easterly flowing winds swooping off the Rocky Mountains some three hundred miles to the west picked up the tiniest pieces of dirt in what is now western Nebraska and transported the dust eastward. The larger and heavier particles stayed behind to form the sandhills. The wind-borne dust mostly remained aloft until it encountered the first major longitudinally running obstacle, the extensive groves of trees along the Missouri River, which restrained the wind and allowed the minute particles to gradually accumulate over many successive centuries to form the Loess Hills of western Iowa. Some dust also was carried eastward by rivers that emerged in the Sandhill region and emptied eventually into the Missouri River, which flooded each spring and usually lowered thereafter. During dry periods, the flood plain dust was whipped into the air on windy days and added to the layers of loess soil, accumulating in deep deposits on the east side of the Missouri River. Landowners along "the Big Muddy" and eastward for about forty miles, where I farmed have the best remnants of the sandhills. These minuscule particles form a gigantic sponge that holds water even at the tops of our hills, but the surface dries quickly after rainfall. Our soil is rock-free, varying from a few inches to a hundred or more feet, and highly erodible. We have to protect our soil from wind and water erosion with minimum tillage practices that keep plant material on the surface, side-hill terraces, and grassy strips to hold the soil in place. Besides abundant corn and other crops, we can grow the same plants that flourish in the Sandhill region and the Western High Plains—tall and short prairie grasses, Ponderosa pines, Black Hills spruce, and aspen. Some would say we have the best and most uniquely formed soil in the world.

The morning progressed as I contemplated these matters. I had to stop every couple thousand feet to catch my breath on the steep sandhill inclines. Metoprolol medication kept my heart from exceeding 110 beats per minute. I had been taking this medication since my unusual tachycardia episode and placement of stents in two coronary arteries in 2005. The altitude here is some 2,500 feet higher than in western Iowa, so oxygen is sparser. I was not in as good shape as when I raised cattle on our farm, feeding daily 150 head and handling some 16,000 small bales of hay and straw yearly. I rented out the row-crop land and reluctantly sold my prized Simmental cattle in the early 2000s, so I could concentrate on improving the behavioral health of people involved in agriculture in my area and to pursue lecturing around the United States and abroad. I began to write more and lectured around the country, but mostly at the University of Iowa, where I held a staff position that eventually merged into adjunct professor. It always seemed the cows got out of their enclosures only when I was gone from home; Marilyn had to get them back into their pens or fields and fix the fence when the part-time hired hand was off. That arrangement wasn't going to work.

Jon and Nugget used my rest periods to check out nearby clumps of woody brush and other birdy-looking areas. A covey of juvenile prairie chickens about the size of bobwhite quail burst out of a waist-high, wild plum thicket, whirling in all directions. Jon fired twice and knocked down a bird, which Nugget promptly retrieved. I scrambled to a higher vantage point to observe where various birds landed so we might have another chance at them, but all sailed over ridges and hills and I couldn't visually follow them to where they alighted.

"Wow, I've never seen birds flush so wild," Jon gasped. "Did you see how fast they flew?"

"Yeah," I panted. "And did you notice they landed where we couldn't see them set down? They all made sure they were over a hill. These birds aren't as tame as the ones back at the ranch."

Every prairie chicken we flushed and failed to knock down flew over a hill and out of sight. I supposed this was a survival mechanism they developed to keep them from being followed by coyotes or other predators. When Jon and I pursued them to the hilltops where we last spotted them gliding, we often encountered them on the far sides of the ridges, near the top, and in some type of cover. They seemed to favor hunkering together in wild plums or the rosebush and poison ivy swatches that offered snacks as well as open views of their surroundings. I surprised birds several times as I transcended a ridge and peeked over the top. As soon as I stepped into their view they bolted on foot or burst skyward. Sometimes they flushed several hundred feet ahead, well beyond shooting range. Once, I got a couple shots at desperately maneuvering birds and scattered a few feathers, but I didn't kill any. Jon was more successful; he cleanly dispatched three colorful prairie chickens. Nugget, who roamed closer to Jon than me, retrieved all of Jon's trophies. She had flushed all of Jon's birds.

During the early afternoon we surprised a huge jackrabbit, the biggest I have ever seen, and the first Jon had ever encountered in the wild. It loped away without us firing a shot. We used to have what we thought were too many jackrabbits in my part of Iowa, but not anymore. They began disappearing in the early 1970s when coyotes moved into the area, displacing foxes into secondary status. Red and gray foxes were not fleet enough to capture the fast-moving hares, but perhaps coyotes, with their superior intelligence and endurance, figured out how to tag-team and run down the creatures. Or maybe other factors than coyotes were responsible for the jackrabbits' disappearance, such as the loss of habitat as farmers planted row crops fence row to fence row during the 1970s. I last saw a jackrabbit in my home county twenty-five years ago.

When we were adolescents, my older brother by two years and I hunted jackrabbits on our farm and neighboring spreads on Sunday afternoons during May after the corn was planted and before the alfalfa fields were tall enough for the animals to hide there. During the daylight hours the hares often hid in grass-covered ditches in the cornfields. These swales were not plowed, so as to prevent erosion from runoff during heavy rains. As we tromped through the ditches, we flushed big hares and sometimes managed to knock them down as they bolted away. I noticed that the nearby emerging corn plants occasionally were bitten off at ground level, which I attributed to the jackrabbits. Dad always inquired how many we shot—usually two or three in an afternoon—when we returned home from our afternoon hunts in time to help with evening chores.

Before the jackrabbits disappeared in the 1970s, community hunts were organized on winter Sunday mornings. Pastors would announce the hunts from the pulpit. Men and boys old enough to carry guns rushed home to eat dinner—not "lunch"—and regroup at 1:00 p.m. Up to forty participants, all carrying firearms of various types—but mostly shotguns—gathered at the local eating and drinking establishment to plot the day's escapades. Most retreated to the same gathering point after the hunt, with other recreational pursuits in mind, but not me, for I had evening farm chores at home like milking cows by hand and feeding 4-H calves.

The hunters spread out along the four sides of a section of farmland and walked toward the center, flushing the jackrabbits into a loosely formed but ever tightening ring of shooters, until those nearest the hares could dispatch them. If a fox also was discovered within the ever-tightening circle, the hunt became all the more exciting, for the person who shot the fox could earn a bounty from the county auditor's office and sell the pelt. The hunts were needed to thin out the jackrabbit population before coyotes populated the region. Besides, many hares were butchered and their meat was mixed with pork sausage to produce tasty burgers that were made even better with considerable libations to wash them down.

On this first day of hunting the Sandhill country I estimated I had walked about ten miles, but it felt like more. Jon probably had walked fifteen miles. Nugget and I were so dead tired when we returned to our vehicle at 4:00 p.m. that we could hardly get out of the Jeep to scout the marsh around Fish Lake. The clean air and pristine conditions of an undisturbed slough perked us up a bit. We flushed a great many ducks and fowl of all types from the cattails and slough grasses before making our way to our cabin. We didn't want to shoot any waterfowl—we just wanted to consider future hunts when the waterfowl season was open.

Jon still had some reserve energy when we got home, so he skinned and butchered the prairie chickens he shot and placed them in a bowl of water on the floor of the washroom located behind the ranch house. I began to make supper.

I had always heard how scrumptious prairie chickens were reputed to be. Before Iowa became farmland, as many as several thousand prairie chickens per square mile inhabited the open prairie until their habitat was destroyed by plows. Commercial hunters as well as settlers slaughtered the birds for their meat until they became nearly extinct in the state. Now the birds are being reintroduced into several substantial restored prairie tracts.

As Jon was cleaning his knife, he heard Nugget cough. Nugget always accompanied him everywhere. She had devoured three of the boneless breasts and several thighs; she was coughing from eating too fast. In Nugget's opinion the prairie chickens were scrumptious and she might have thought she had earned them!

Jon rescued portions of one bird that I roasted for supper. It tasted mighty fine, along with the hamburgers I also had to fry. While Nugget slept contentedly on her bed, all Jon and I could do was laugh and console ourselves with beers. We talked about the next day's plans.

The next day Jon and I arose before dawn and with Nugget, still stiff from the previous day's sojourn, we set off for the hills east and north of Merritt Reservoir. The day was cloudy and portended rain. We took the boat with us in case fishing was a better option than hunting on slippery ground. Over the years we had taken many walleye from Merritt and even more smallmouth and largemouth bass, crappies, and bluegills. We figured our bodies, and Nugget's, would not last as long as yesterday.

We stopped at Merritt Dam Bait Shop and Service station to fill the boat's fuel tank and purchased a map of the Samuel R. McKelvie National Forest that surrounds the reservoir. The bait shop operator said all the cattle had been removed from that area several days ago and herded to their winter pastures, so the hunting should be good. We unhooked our boat in the parking lot and set out for the hills in my Jeep.

The terrain was more rugged than the slopes around the Lucky Lady Ranch. Some stretches of what our map said was a four-wheel-drive trail were forty-five-degree inclines and declines. The trail was replete with yard-deep washouts and boulders big as hundred-gallon barrels. Cattle had stripped the land nearly bare, and only a few grass stems and unpalatable forbs remained for prairie chickens in which to find cover. We hoped for no rain, because we could be stuck there for a while if it stormed. Eventually, we reached a flat-topped knoll with some grassy flora, sagebrush, and sumac, where we decided to leave our vehicle.

We took note of our bearings. There was a windmill in a coulee a quarter mile to the south. Usually, windmills were spaced two or three miles apart and ran continuously, pumping fresh water for livestock and wildlife all summer long. When the drinking tanks were full, excess water drained onto the surrounding ground and eventually seeped back into the well. Most wells were shallow, less than twenty feet deep, because the water table was so close to the surface. Some wells were artesian and didn't require a pump. We knew if we got lost, we could find the latitudinal and longitudinal coordinates hammered with punch mark indentations into the northeast angle iron strut of any windmill. It was pretty cool that surveyors and landowners had marked windmills this way so folks could figure out their locations without a map, and to identify the windmills. All one had to remember was one's home range and township in order to determine where you were in relation to home. In our case we had a U.S. Forest Service map as well.

Jon and I marched along the top of a long ridge, one of us on each side of its crown, and Nugget between us. We figured any fleeing birds would likely pass in front of one of us. An hour later the ridge ran out and we crossed a valley to another parallel running ridge. By noon we still had not encountered any birds. We decided to rest a while and to eat lunch under a thick grove of small pine and spruce trees a few hundred feet ahead. As we drew nearer to the dense hillside cove, we spotted a black form rise amid the foliage, but still partially hidden in the dark underbrush. *Is it a bear?* we wondered. While uncommon, black bears inhabit some parts of Nebraska. The form didn't move.

We had our guns. There were two of us and one of *it*, so we weren't unduly alarmed. As we stepped toward the cove, a tall, wild-eyed, black bovine bull briskly trotted out of the cover toward us, snorting and with his neck arched. He was a big guy—at least a ton in weight. Maybe Salers or Chianina genetics mixed with his Angus blood made him so tall and high-strung. When we stopped, he stopped, forty feet apart. We surveyed each other. If the bull charged us, there were no trees nearby for us to climb or hide behind.

"The man at the bait shop said all the cattle had been moved to winter quarters," Jon commented.

"Yeah, I'll bet the cattle drovers couldn't find this guy. He was probably hiding. He won't come out of the hills until winter sets in, when he has to find food and shelter. Then he might show up in somebody else's cattle herd," I suggested.

"He looks mean," Jon volunteered.

"Did you see how quick and athletic his movements were? I don't want to mess with him. Let's stand closer together and act tough so he gets the idea he'll have trouble if he charges us. And keep Nugget behind you so she doesn't provoke him," I directed.

Jon sidled up beside me, with Nugget heeling behind him. I stomped my foot on the ground and held my gun up, with my cap atop, to look taller and more threatening.

Suddenly, the bull wheeled and trotted over the hilltop at a fast clip. "Whew," I sighed. "I thought we might have trouble for a moment. He's a dang good quality bull physically, but I don't like his attitude. I wouldn't keep him around."

When I raised Simmental breeding stock on our farm, I scored all the cows and bulls on a scale that rated their dispositions. Cows that became mean when they calved and bulls that were aggressive were eliminated from the breeding program because I didn't want to pass these moderately heritable traits along to cattle my customers purchased. I was especially chagrined when my neighbor, who was handling chores for me while I was gone on a speaking trip, was severely injured by an over-protective cow that thought he was separating her from her day-old calf. She came from even-tempered lineage but she had a dangerous temperament that didn't show up until her second calf was born. I soon sold this cow/calf pair.

"Maybe he's a good coyote chaser," Jon offered. "Out here nobody keeps an eye on the cattle daily and they have to fend for themselves."

"Yeah," I said, "but I don't like the way he's a loner. He's not with his cows. He might have some throwback characteristics to more primitive ancestors that make him dangerous to handle." We ambled toward the small grove, sat down under the trees, and quietly consumed our sandwiches and water.

Jon broke the silence, "I wonder where the birds are."

"Maybe we should try the other side of the reservoir," I offered. "Should we pack up and drive over there?"

"Anything has to be better than what we're finding here," Jon agreed.

It took us nearly an hour to hike back to our vehicle, and another half hour to traverse the rugged trail to its entryway. Sodden gray clouds were billowing overhead. We reached the asphalt highway as the first big drops of rain splashed on the windshield. A short-lived thunderstorm cut loose. We were glad we were on a hard-surfaced road, because we would have spun off the slippery and treacherous trail we had just negotiated.

Thirty minutes later we parked at the base of less intimidating slopes on the southwest side of Merritt Reservoir. The sky had cleared; bright sunshine was drying the soil. Jon and Nugget headed to the far side of a long ridge heading north, while I took my time to crisscross the closer side of the ridge. I was becoming weary. I kept an eye on Jon when I occasionally topped the ridge. I spied him and Nugget another half mile away on the next ridge. *There's no way I can keep up,* I surrendered in my head. I trod slowly, taking in the sweet smells and sights of abundant prairie grasses, goldenrod, sagebrush, rabbit brush, and an occasional blowout penstemon, which is thought to be endemic only to this part of the world. Although I was enjoying myself, I was so drained that I wondered if I could make it back to the Jeep a mile away.

Taking my time, I stumbled down to the base of the hills. I hoped I wouldn't fall as I struggled to lift my feet over decaying cacti and yucca plants. I slowly slogged to my Jeep, grabbed a soda from the cooler, and slumped into the front seat. When Jon and Nugget didn't arrive within an hour I began to worry a bit. *Were they alright? Had they encountered another bull?* I rejected this supposition because the hills had not been grazed by livestock. Nonetheless, I worried.

Just as I was about to set off to where I had last seen them, I spotted Jon making his way toward the Jeep along the base of the hills next to the reservoir. Every so often he stopped, turned, and waited for Nugget to catch up. She was a good 150 feet behind him most of the time. The sun that had come out after the storm was descending behind the hills when they finally arrived at the Jeep. "Did you get any birds?" I asked.

"Nope, didn't see any," Jon responded. "Nugget is completely done in," he added.

"I think we should go fishing tomorrow," I volunteered as I drove home. We picked up the boat where we had parked it. When we arrived back at our cabin, no one was outside the ranch house. A pickup truck was parked in the front yard. We speculated that Cody was home. Although we wondered how Bob was doing, we didn't want to intrude into their personal affairs.

The sun was coming up when we awoke the next day. Nugget was feeling better. We decided to hunt during the morning on wildlife refuge land next to Hackberry Lake and to go fishing during the afternoon. After preparing what we needed, including the boat, we set off on what we surmised would be a great Valentine National Wildlife Refuge adventure.

These hills were nearly as intimidating as those we had encountered yesterday, and the outcome was the same. Even with binoculars, we spotted no prairie chickens. I flushed two mule deer bucks that sprang in their characteristic way of lifting and setting down all four feet simultaneously in long pronks as they bounded away. We noticed eagles circling lazily over the prairies and marshes next to Hackberry Lake.

After lunch we found our way to a sloping concrete ramp leading into Hackberry Lake. The lake was clogged with water plants. There were distant open-appearing channels, just like we sometimes found on Watts Lake, but boaters could only use electric motors or human-powered craft on Watts. After shoving our boat off the trailer, I parked our outfit while Jon started the outboard motor. Just as I was ready to heave myself into the boat, the idling motor sputtered and stopped. The outboard propeller was completely wrapped with pond weeds. Jon spent fifteen minutes leaning over the stern, clearing coontail and milfoil from the propeller and its shank. I hoisted myself into the front of the boat. When Jon pulled the engine cord, the motor came back to life again. We backed about twenty-five feet away from the concrete when the engine choked once more. I had my waders on and the water was only about four feet deep, so I jumped overboard and untangled the debris.

Jon spoke, "This isn't going to work. We might as well give up trying to fish here."

Jon tipped the motor forward so it wouldn't entangle in more weeds while I dragged the boat to the concrete ramp and backed the trailer into the water under the front of the boat. After loading everything, we decided to stop by Watts Lake on our way back to our cabin.

Watts was choked with plants, too. We were determined to try our float tubes anyhow. We managed to tear routes through the weedy mess to what appeared to be less congested water a couple hundred feet from the shoreline. When we reached the clearer area, only the surface was free of plants. Milfoil was everywhere and my usually predictable little black fly quickly got caught on shallow submerged plants during every retrieve and before a fish could snatch it. "It's no use trying to fish," I somberly pronounced. "We'll have to wait until spring, before the water plants start to grow in order to fish here again," I consoled myself and Jon.

That evening, over supper of foil dinners cooked on smoldering hot wood coals in the outdoor fire pit, we decided to hunt the hills around the Lucky Lady Ranch the following day. Unlike anywhere else, we had flushed prairie chickens here earlier, so we were somewhat optimistic about our prospects tomorrow. Virginia visited our cabin. She told us Cody was home and Bob's condition had not changed. Virginia said hunters had shot lots of prairie chickens last week in the area we planned to hunt the next day. Our spirits lifted.

The following morning we arrived at the base of the same surrounding promontories where we had hunted two days previously, again before sunup. We parked a couple miles north of where we had initiated our hunt several days prior. We wanted to explore territory we had not yet hunted, as well as to check the spots where we had discovered birds previously.

Only the thickets, grass, and shrub clumps where we found birds previously held prairie chickens again, but the birds were warier. They flushed as we approached within three hundred feet of their havens. We got off a few shots apiece. Jon knocked feathers out of a bird; it crumpled earthbound a couple hundred yards away, just over a hillock. When Nugget got to the location where the bird went down, and when Jon and I joined her, the bird was nowhere to be found. Eventually we gave up the search. We noticed a coyote loping off in the distance. Maybe the coyote had been watching us all along and captured the wounded bird before we could find it. I summed up the situation, "I think I know who is wilier: the prairie chickens, the coyote, or us— and it's not us!"

We hunted all day. Twice Jon had to pull prickly pear thorns out of Nugget's feet. The thorns had penetrated her leather booties. We found lots of haunts where bird droppings indicated that chickens or grouse had roosted or rested recently. We got sweaty in the warm autumn sun, with our chaps on to protect us from thorny shrubs and rattlesnakes. We stripped down to our T-shirts and stuffed our jackets and outer shirts into our hunting vests. We used up all our water on Nugget and ourselves and were glad when we returned to the Jeep, dead-tired around 4:30 in the afternoon to fill our water canteens and enjoy sodas.

After a late breakfast the next day, we readied our fishing equipment and headed to Merritt, with the boat and Nugget as well. Jon and I were thinking along the same line when we commented simultaneously, "Today we have a boat dog." Nugget barely raised an eyebrow. It was 10:30 a.m. when we purchased minnows and worms at the bait shop.

As we were unloading our boat at the ramp sloping into an inlet on the west side of the reservoir, we noticed the water level was about ten feet lower than when we had fished Merritt in previous years. We supposed the reservoir had served its purpose—to provide irrigation water for downstream crops, even though there had been fair precipitation in this region for most of the growing season. A large cabin cruiser, about thirty feet in length, was high-centered on some kind of underwater structure about a quarter mile from the ramp. Two smaller boats were connected by tow ropes to the larger craft. Every few minutes their motors revved up and the water roiled furiously, but they couldn't budge the heavier cruiser.

A friendly, white-haired couple was also putting their pontoon boat into the water. The lady said they fished here often. The man warned us, "Be careful to go around the area where that boat is stuck. There are lots of sand bars out there, everywhere. You can't see them when you are on the water because some are just under the surface. Don't go too fast, because if you hit one it will stop you real quick, like it did that boat out there. You can ruin your engine, or worse, wreck your boat."

Jon lifted Nugget aboard; she found a place near the bow and sprawled on the aluminum floor. I shoved off, jumped in the boat as best my sore joints would enable me, and collected myself on the middle seat. Jon took control of the motor at the helm and backed the boat away from the ramp. As soon as he turned the boat around, Jon gunned the motor. We sped around the marooned craft and its unsuccessful rescuers and headed to the upper reaches of Merritt. We hurried past a cove on the left where we frequently had caught many smallmouth and largemouth bass, bluegills, and crappies during previous outings. There was a campground next to the inlet. It was now a shallow, weed-choked, unfishable marsh. We motored up the main arm of the 2,900-acre lake, when it is full, to a narrow channel of the main inlet—the Snake River. We had fished this area before and had often found crappies and bluegills next to a cliff where many boulders strewed the channel along its base.

Jon halted the boat and dropped anchor. We tossed night crawlers into a conglomeration of submerged rocks. Five-inch bluegills tried to gulp our worms but most couldn't get their small mouths around the hooks. We tossed back into the reservoir those that managed to swallow the worms. We played around a while and decided there were bigger fish elsewhere.

Jon gunned the motor as fast as it would go. We raced toward Merritt Dam, where we hoped to catch walleye that fed along the rocky inclines of the dam structure. We had caught walleye there in past years. When we passed our intake ramp well off in the distance, the big cabin cruiser was gone. Somehow, it had been freed from the sandbar. Jon kept our craft in the middle of the body of water, where the reservoir probably was deepest.

Whump! We were nearly thrown off our seats by the forceful thump. Jon cut the accelerator. Almost as quickly, we were free again, and the boat motor idled while we gathered our composure. Perhaps our momentum helped us traverse a sandbar. We were shaken by the unseen hazard.

"Don't drive so fast," I admonished. "You heard what the man said at the boat ramp. I don't want to be stranded out here."

Jon defended himself, "I followed the middle of the channel. I didn't think there were any dunes out here, but I was wrong."

Nugget went back to resting and Jon resumed heading toward the dam, at half-throttle.

A few minutes later, we reached the hundred-foot-deep water near the dam. "How about if we try minnows and troll along the dam," Jon suggested.

"Sounds good," I replied. Our hopes for catchable fish returned. I handed the minnow bucket to Jon after grasping a lively two-inch baitfish for myself. We slowly coursed back and forth along the dam. We consumed sandwiches and sodas. We put on fresh minnows and experimented with worms and leeches. We tried letting our baits rest on the bottom of the reservoir and we trolled the shallows next to the slope of the dam. No hits. As evening approached, we still had not experienced any tugs on our fishing lines.

"Do you think we ought to head back to shore?" I suggested.

"No, walleye start to feed when nightfall comes," Jon answered. "I want to catch at least one decent fish. Remember how we used to catch them around this time when we fished from the dam?"

"Yeah," I replied while remembering our catch of a half dozen walleye several years earlier and from the dam. "But I want to be able to see where we are going when we head back to the boat ramp," I added.

"We have lights on the boat, so don't worry," Jon advised. I relaxed.

An hour later it was past evening; my watch signaled 8:00 p.m. and we still had no hits. I started to reel in my bait.

"We might as well give up," Jon proclaimed. He reeled in his bait also and then headed our craft toward the boat ramp a couple miles somewhere northwest. Jon found the switch for the lights, but when he flicked it on, nothing happened. "Uh-oh, the lights aren't working," he pronounced somberly.

"Yikes, we could be in trouble," I cautioned. "Take your time so we don't get hung up on a sandbar and stay toward the east shoreline until we get past where we hit the sandbar earlier," I said with some uncertainty.

We could see three dim lights in the distance where I thought the boat ramp was located. One of the lights moved around, as if someone was carrying a flashlight. That gave Jon an idea. "Hand me my duffel bag with my fishing gear," he requested. "I've got a headlamp in my bag."

Jon rifled through his duffel bag and found a headlamp. When he strapped it to his head and switched it on, it cast a weak beam about fifty feet. This would have to work.

The lights to the west disappeared. There was no moon. It was pitch-black except for the stars and the dim beam from Jon's headlamp.

Slowly we motored toward where we thought the boat ramp was located. I could make out the Big Dipper and Polaris in the northern sky, so I knew we were generally headed in the right direction.

When we reached what we thought was the inlet leading to the boat ramp, we could discern no lights, and all we could make out with Jon's headlamp was a weedy marsh. "Are we lost?" Jon ventured.

"No, let's keep following the shoreline on our left until we come to the ramp inlet. If we keep doing this, we have to come to the inlet that has our boat ramp. Just take it slow so we don't get hung up if we run into sand."

I silently prayed. I reckoned we had to encounter our inlet or familiar-looking water. Maybe we would eventually spot the lighted campground onshore. I also knew if we found the inlet with an island in the middle that we used to fish successfully for bluegills, largemouth and smallmouth bass, and more on past trips, then we were too far north and could turn around and come back south. I figured we had not gone that far north yet. I kept my anxiety to myself.

We kept moving northward slowly, staying about two hundred feet from the shoreline. About twenty minutes passed. The tree-lined shore on our left opened into an inlet. As we rounded the bend we could see two creosoted utility poles with lights. My Jeep and the boat trailer were parked next to one of the poles. "We made it," I shouted. "Stay to the right as you enter the bay so we don't get hung up on the shoal where the cabin cruiser got marooned."

"I knew where we were all the time," Jon bravely proclaimed. "I knew the ramp had to be on our left. If we followed the shoreline we would have to come to it eventually."

"You and I were thinking the same thing," I agreed. I silently offered a prayer of thanks.

It was 9:30 p.m. when we left the parking lot by the ramp. On our way back to our cabin we nearly hit a porcupine waddling across the blacktop road whose quills could have pierced our tires if we drove over it. I wondered, *Is this another nudge from a higher power?*

We ate a light supper and decided to head back to Iowa in the morning, after one last hunt on a promising stretch of the refuge we had driven past a couple times during our trip.

We arose well before morning light and packed up. I visited the ranch house to pay our bill after the lights went on and when I figured someone was up. Virginia, in a long duster, greeted me at the front door.

"Did you shoot any prairie chickens?" Virginia asked.

"No," I replied. "But Jon got four in the hills where you told us to hunt, but none elsewhere." I told her about the many places we hunted.

"I saw your boat. Did you get any fish?" Virginia asked further.

"Yeah, but we didn't get any keepers. They were all too small," I answered. "We tried Hackberry Lake but it was so weedy our boat propeller got tangled up and we couldn't use it. Watts was so congested we couldn't maneuver with our float tubes," I answered.

"I have an airboat you can use, if you come back," Virginia announced.

I paid the bill and thanked Virginia for her and her family's hospitality. There was a pause.

"You helped us, both of you," Virginia said. "We didn't know why Bob should have to die—he's so close to going. We thought there was something we did, or didn't do, that contributed to his illness. You and your son helped us figure out we didn't cause this. We just don't know what caused his Parkinson's. We can accept that better now. Thank-you." She squeezed my hand.

I told Jon about my conversation with Virginia as we drove to a section of the refuge we hoped would yield us some last shots at prairie chickens prior to our departure. We both said little as we contemplated the past several days.

After a three-hour workout in the hills without seeing a bird, we both talked little as we loaded Nugget, our guns, and our gear into the Jeep and headed toward home. As we reached the blacktop road leading away from the refuge, I observed, "Some trips are like movies . . . you never know how they are going to turn out until the end."

"Yeah," Jon chimed in. "This was like Clint Eastwood's movie *The Good, the Bad, and the Ugly*. The 'good' was the first day when I shot four prairie chickens; the 'bad' was when Nugget ate most of them and when the bull wanted our lunch; and the 'ugly' was when we didn't catch any fish, shoot any more birds, and last night on Merritt."

Silence pervaded for a couple minutes until I broke the spell. "You want to do this again next year?"

"Yup," Jon replied.

13

NONPLUSSED

For about three years in the early 1970s, Ken was my roommate while we pursued our doctoral degrees in clinical psychology at the University of Utah. Living with Ken was a fete and a feat, for he posed many challenges, some of which resulted in my betterment and some of which I'm unsure. Ken could be esoteric, provocative, insightful, and a lot of fun. We remain close today.

Ken introduced Marilyn to me. One evening in January 1971 when nothing seemed to be going right for me, he took me to Marilyn's apartment. They were acquainted because Ken was a friend of Kathy, Marilyn's roommate. Kathy apparently had gone downstairs in their apartment building to purchase a soda when Ken and I arrived. The door was unlocked when we knocked. Ken announced, "Let's go in, because Kathy said she would be right back." We didn't know Marilyn was ill, so we talked a while in the darkened living area until Marilyn emerged from her bedroom in a long heavy robe, without makeup, hoarse, and looking the worse for wear. She was in her second year of the master's degree program in psychiatric nursing at the University of Utah.

Marilyn had such severe laryngitis that she could hardly speak, along with a sore throat. It took only a few minutes for me to figure out that she needed a remedy for her conditions. I asked her if there was any honey and lemon in her kitchen, which she confirmed. Soon I made a warm palliative for her ills. As Marilyn admitted years later, I was the first suitor who had offered to take care of her, while she, a nurse, was accustomed to taking care of nearly everybody else, including suitors she had dismissed.

Marilyn and I married one and a half years after we met, and we remain bonded partners for life after the unusual introduction.

Ken had all kinds of good motives about people, protecting the environment, and fly-fishing. I thought his positive motives stemmed from his mother, who was a schoolteacher and grew up on a farm in southwestern Minnesota, and from his equally benevolent father, whom Ken looks like today, with silver hair and a trim physique. Ken developed a unique approach to life. He attracted other people to help take care of him, although he has always been competent in his own right. It was especially tough for Ken when he lost his devoted wife, Carla, to cancer after forty-five years together.

Two generations removed from working the land, Ken was inquisitive about agriculture; he would inherit part of his mother's farmland eventually. He was an accurate observer of things around him. He wasn't aghast that I had helped lead a sit-in at the University of Utah Administration Building in 1969, to express opposition to the Vietnam War, and the course that most Utah politicians and some appointed administrators were taking about economic, racial, and gender equality. His views were somewhat similar to mine. He liked it when I introduced him to Jane, who, like me, was a graduate of the University of Colorado in psychology and played the guitar. We sang together in a number of amateur performances in Boulder. Jane lived and worked in Denver.

I offered to help Ken move to Denver to pursue employment he had already lined up and partly to reside in the same city as Jane, after he finished his PhD requirements in December 1972. Ken needed to be at work on January 3, two days after the move. Meanwhile, heavy snow was falling across the intermountain region.

We loaded Ken's rented moving van with all but his Volkswagen Squareback on New Year's Day. There wasn't an easy way we could load his vehicle into the truck, although there was ample space, because all the loading docks were closed for the holiday. Ken searched for ways to drive his VW into the rental truck as the last item to be loaded. Eventually, he found a spot at a local railyard that allowed us to back his vehicle next to the dock and possibly to drive it into the moving van. We busted through foot-deep snow into the railyard. Ken backed the rented moving van next to the four-foot-high dock. Then he drove his VW up the ramp onto the dock and angled it toward the truck. The dock was too narrow—only eight feet wide—to allow him to fully turn his aging but functional car into the truck. To make matters worse, we couldn't find any planks over which he could drive his vehicle into the truck across a two-foot-wide gap between the truck and the dock.

I couldn't offer good advice, so Ken drove his vehicle toward the open back end of the rental truck, thinking the car's front wheels might somehow transcend the space between the dock and the truck, but instead the front wheels lodged between the dock and the truck, unable to move. Upon my suggestion, Ken eased the moving van ahead a couple inches, to allow his vehicle to freely move up and down. I suggested a plan.

Ken crawled into his Volkswagen while I maneuvered myself under his vehicle, grabbed the front axle, and lifted it up about a foot on my shoulders. I was very glad the motor in his VW was in the rear of his vehicle, making my end easier to lift. I hoisted the car's front end sufficiently to allow Ken to inch forward carefully until the front wheels rested entirely in the truck. That done, he backed the moving van closer to the dock and drove the rest of his vehicle easily into the van. We shut the truck's rear door. By then it was almost midnight; we needed to be on the road the next day as early as possible.

Driving conditions were terrible the next day as we crept on I-80 across Wyoming on icy surfaces and with a blizzard hampering our vision. We arrived in Denver around 4:00 a.m. the following day. After a couple hours of sleep in the moving van, Ken and I unloaded his Volkswagen at a grocery store unloading ramp and moved his other belongings into an apartment that he had rented. I became ill and recuperated the next day at his apartment before taking a commercial airline flight back to Salt Lake City, while Ken undertook his first day of work at his new job.

The end of the saga is that Ken got to Denver where Jane lived, but they didn't strike a romance. She seemed nonplussed about a relationship with Ken, although I never figured out why and, to Ken's consternation, neither did he. Nevertheless, the three of us had fun together for a while. The summer after Ken moved to Denver, Jane and Ken came separately to Utah for a fishing excursion with me to the Duchesne River in the Uinta Mountains, one of only three major east-west-running mountain ranges in the United States.

Marilyn and I were married by then. She had to work as a nurse at the University of Utah Hospital where she was employed, so Ken, Jane, and I headed to the Uinta Mountains by ourselves on the Friday morning before the July 4 holiday.

Federal and state plans were underway for the declaration of parts of the Uinta Mountains as a "wilderness area." Simultaneously, there were efforts to divert most of the south-flowing Duchesne River from the Uinta Mountains into the west-flowing Provo River to provide additional water to the burgeoning metropolises of Provo, Salt Lake City, and various suburbs. Until the partial diversion occurred later, the Duchesne emptied entirely into the Green River, and ultimately into the Colorado River. We wanted to fish the Duchesne before any dams were completed.

Three eager fishers/campers packed our sleeping bags, cooking necessities, and tents to head to the central Uinta wilderness area. It was late June; the streams were still receding from spring runoff in the mountains.

By 11:00 a.m. we parked his mostly still functional Volkswagen Squareback at the designated parking lot and hiked with our backpacking equipment up the Duchesne River Valley several miles, arriving at a sagebrush-filled flat with a few pines along the river, just below a much steeper canyon. After making camp, Ken and I headed upstream with our fly rods and the handtied flies that I gave him, while

Jane headed downstream with her casting rod, a carton of nightcrawlers, and a book.

Ken and I leapfrogged each other for three hours, moving ever farther upstream along a wild, late spring runoff that likely would be significantly less volatile a couple weeks later. I fished from treacherous landscapes on top of truck-sized boulders into tumbling waterfalls and only slightly more placid pools just below them. Ken hiked to various other stretches about which I never learned, except that he didn't catch any fish. I caught a fourteen-inch brown trout, which was a decent accomplishment in this raging water.

Ken and I headed to the slower-moving river pool, some fifty feet wide and one hundred feet long, next to our campsite. We spent an hour casting into the deep green water that appeared at least fifteen feet deep. Both of us caught a twelve-inch rainbow trout apiece. It was time to see how Jane was doing and to prepare supper.

As we strode down the riverside trail, eventually we spied Jane's white shirt. She was reading her book and holding her casting rod in her other hand.

"How was fishing?" Ken asked.

"Not bad," Jane replied. "I caught a few."

Jane arose from her comfortable seated position to yank a metal stringer of fish. There were five 13- to 15-inch rainbow trout attached to her stringer.

"Wow, you caught more fish than Ken and me combined," I exclaimed. "What did you catch them on?"

"A little piece of worm that I put on the hook while I was reading my novel," Jane explained. "I'm nearly done with my book."

Ken seemed dumbfounded and had some other thoughts on the tip of his tongue that he didn't express, but which I knew from living with him for several years were best left unsaid. Nonplussed, I reassessed my impressions about the superiority of fly-fishing and using my own personally tied flies.

Jane reeled in her bait and retrieved her fish chain. It was silent the entire way back to our camp.

We enjoyed fresh trout fried in butter for supper, along with cooked potatoes, carrots, and onions, and a bottle of wine that Jane had toted to our campsite. The next day all of us fished closer to our campsite; again, Jane caught the most trout.

I'm not sure what happened on the drive back to Salt Lake City the next morning. I suspect that the relationship between Ken and Jane changed significantly after the Duchesne fishing event. Whatever it was, they parted, and Ken went on to marry Carla and to have two wonderful daughters. If Jane ever married, I don't know. She moved to Alaska to teach special education students and we eventually lost touch. What I know is that this episode taught me a lot about what fish want for food when the spring runoff is still high—and a lot about humility.

14

WORKING WITH CATTLE

B ovines were the next livestock after sheep and goats to be domesticated by our farming ancestors around 9000 BC, first in Asia, and later in Europe. Domestication of pigs followed and horses were soon tamed as well. A couple thousand years later and many centuries before Christopher Columbus reached the Western Hemisphere, Native South Americans tamed llamas to carry burdens. They also raised llamas and the smaller alpacas for their delicious meat and the soft fur that underlays their tougher outer hair. Alpaca fur, especially, could be made into warm and unweighty clothing. America's first farmers also kept guinea pigs, turkeys, and other large birds as pets and for food when necessary, but no bovines or bison were available to the South and Central Americans until Spanish explorers brought tamed cattle with them in the 1500s.

The first bovines to be tamed were *Bos indicus* cattle in southern Asia, which are ancestors to zebu and Brahman cattle today. *Bos taurus* cattle were domesticated in the colder climates of Europe and northern Asia. Both types of cattle descended from aurochs and brought genetically acquired attributes with them, such as the capacity of *Bos indicus* animals to wiggle their skin to scare away flies that landed on them. *Bos indicus* animals had mild temperaments that allowed humans to tame them to milk them and to pull agricultural tools such as plows. *Bos taurus* descendants were selected first for their meat, and later they became draft animals and sources of milk as their dispositions moderated through selection of those with the most desirable traits. When *Bos indicus* and *Bos taurus* animals were interbred and selected for specific purposes, they became the forerunners of most of the modern breeds of dairy animals, such as Holstein and Jersey cows, as well as modern-day beef animals, such as Hereford and Angus cattle. Indeed, selective breeding was practiced to refine offspring in the Aberdeen Angus breed for their black color, absence of horns, and the palatability of their meat. Some breeds, such as the Simmental, were selected for the purposes of furnishing milk and meat, and for their docile demeanor so that they could be handled by children as well as adults in Switzerland where the breed originated; worldwide, the Simmental is the second most popular breed, following Angus. Charolais cattle, which today are highly appreciated for their desirable cuts of meat, were selected in past centuries for the dual purposes of serving as draft animals and for food in France and neighboring countries.

As for pigs, I don't dislike them. My family raised swine while I was growing up. I cleaned their farrowing pens, raised pigs as 4-H projects, and helped Dad vaccinate and castrate weanlings. I savor good pork on the grill and in other cooked fashions. I also know that pigs would be happy to devour my carcass if I became unable to defend myself while in their pen, whereas cattle wouldn't eat me.

I raised only one pig while farming myself. I found a stray animal while I was checking my fields one June afternoon. I placed a lost and found advertisement in the local newspaper and questioned my neighbors, but nobody claimed the animal, so I kept it until it was at the age to turn into pork chops and sundry other edible cuts.

As for horses, they are the subject of another chapter.

Actually, I am a fairly good judge of pigs and other farm animals, such as sheep, chickens, saddle horses, dairy cows, and especially beef cattle. I was a member of the winning Shelby County 4-H livestock judging team at the 1964 Iowa State Fair.

While I think I know something about cattle, I can't tell anyone riding in a car or truck with me on the highway the make, model, and year of most motorized vehicles we pass on the road, but if I spot a bovine critter a quarter mile away in a field while cruising along, I can offer a reasonably accurate estimate of its breed, sex, weight, body condition score, and—most important to me—its quality as a meat producer. Please don't tell my wife or anyone else who might ride with me on a roadway, because I have been successfully faking that I know something about cars and trucks for much of my adult life.

I learned a lot about mutual regard and trust from a first-calf heifer that was giving birth and needed an episiotomy because her labia restrained her calf from being born. She had never been previously roped, restrained, or haltered; surprisingly, she walked calmly into the twenty-by-twenty-foot calving pen. I tossed a lasso over her head, but I didn't have to restrain her in any way and removed the lasso as the two-year-old animal allowed me to perform the operation without sedation and while standing quietly. I was very grateful because the surgery required an unusually long incision for the calf's head to emerge. After a couple hard contractions, and a few tugs by me on the calf's protruding front legs, a newborn calf flopped onto the straw-covered floor. The new mother turned around carefully and greeted her baby by vigorously licking it. It raised its head and they bonded while exchanging olfactory cues during several deep breaths. I sewed the new mother's labia together without any medication or restraint. She acted like the episiotomy didn't hurt and went about her business while I was present and touching her. I couldn't comprehend how this previously unrestrained heifer allowed these procedures and said so to my teenage son, Jon, who had assisted with the procedures by being available in case I needed help and handing me medical equipment. He aptly summarized what had just taken place: "She trusted you."

I've experienced such trustful circumstances in different ways and at other times with my cattle. One such episode occurred when I salvaged a newborn calf that had fallen into standing water during its efforts to gather its legs under itself to arise. When I arrived on the scene with my ATV while checking the birthing pasture that warm, rainy April night, my searchlight trained onto a cow that was mooing softly to encourage her faltering offspring to stand just upside of water ponding in one of several terraces I had installed in the fields to reduce erosion from heavy rainfalls like this episode. Just as I arrived on my four-wheeler, the baby calf flopped over in the accumulating runoff and was struggling to raise its head above waterline. I jumped off my ATV and ran to the calf.

This mother cow was usually somewhat protective when she had a newborn calf, but now she allowed me to wade into the eight-inch-deep water to rescue and carry her baby away from danger. She kept her nose just a few inches from her calf and me; she did not bump me even when her calf struggled a bit in my arms. She lowed softly in a reassuring way to her baby, and perhaps to me as well. I set her calf down on safe pasture ground a couple hundred feet away from the terrace. As the mama cow licked her newborn, it struggled to its feet to search for its mother's udder and its first important nourishment, colostrum. The Simmental cow stood still while her calf latched onto a teat. As I returned to the ATV, the rain stopped. When I drove past the cow and calf at a respectful distant, the mother visually studied me intensely, as if to say reassuringly, "All is okay now."

Other lessons also have been formative and beneficial. I learned to be a fairly good roper and could lasso a cow from a horse or from my ATV.

A number of years ago during an early April day, I needed to treat a 250-pound bull calf that had a navel infection. Frost covered the ground; sloppy soil sucked my boots wherever I walked. I strode in foot-deep mud and manure with my lariat in hand into a feedlot pen and cornered the calf that needed a dose of antibiotics. The calf grew skittish as I moved closer.

It bolted when I got within fifteen feet of it. As the animal sprung along the fence in front of me, I quickly threw a loop ahead of the fleeing calf and lassoed it. Planting my feet firmly, I prepared for the rope to become taut, and it did as it settled on the neck of the calf racing past me. The animal had enough momentum to thrust me head over heels into the muck. I hung on to the rope, although I ate a lot of mud and was covered from head to toe with slop. I prided myself on being able to capture the calf on a headlong run.

I gave the calf the antibiotic shot it needed. I thought I was a decent roper.

A few years later, one of my registered Simmental calves developed pink eye from the hordes of summer flies that usually hang around cows and calves. I rode my four-wheeler with my veterinary kit and a lariat to the pasture where the animal was part of a herd of cows, calves, heifers, and a bull.

The animals were standing on a hilltop to catch any flowing breeze on this hot day. After parking the ATV, I cautiously walked toward the herd and waited until the calf I wanted to treat was within roping distance, some twenty feet away.

As I flung the loop, it encircled a 1,200-pound yearling heifer standing next to the calf I was seeking. I lassoed her perfectly! She ran and I couldn't hold her as she dragged the rope and me behind her.

Eventually, I caught and treated the suffering calf by cornering it next to a fence, but for the next several days I tried without success to grab the rope trailing behind the now-cautious heifer as she came to drink water or to eat grain from a bunk from which I tempted her and her herdmates to get close to me. Jon had no success either when he checked the cattle while I was at work.

A week passed before I was able to grab the rope the heifer was dragging as she drank from the only available cattle waterer. I was hiding behind a plank fence with sturdy posts next to the contraption. I wrapped the lariat around the closest post. Gradually, I cinched the animal ever closer until I could unhook the metal clasp of the hondo to free her. I was glad she didn't have to drag the rope anymore, but I reappraised my roping ability.

That's how cattle are; they can teach us lessons we need.

15

HORSE SENSE

Most people who like horses have stories to tell. Having lived and worked with horses much of my life, they taught me lessons I can best describe as "horse sense."

My first lesson occurred at age four. I proudly "drove" Dad's team of Belgian draft mares during July oats harvest while my father and a teenaged lad used pitchforks to load bundles of shocked oats onto a flatbed wagon to be hauled to a McCormick-Deering threshing machine that separated the grain from the straw and was shared with two neighbors. I yelled "giddyup" or pulled back on the reins to slow their pace so Dad and his helper had enough time to stack the oats bundles on the wagon. Helping with farmwork at this young age might be termed child abuse today, but back then it was normal. I felt appreciated and enjoyed the important work.

When an inch-long, blood-sucking, female horsefly landed suddenly on the rump of one of the horses I was handling, I yelled to Dad. It bit the horse painfully. She vigorously swished her tail and bucked, unable to shake the fly. Dad shooed the horsefly away, but it kept coming back and landing on the same spot after he had chased it away.

The Belgian mare tried to run wildly as the horsefly continued tormenting her. Her behavior alarmed her yoked mate, who joined in the escape. I pulled with all my four-year-old strength on the reins and shouted "whoa," while Dad ran to catch the runaway outfit. Our rig disappeared over the hill leading to the horse barn a quarter mile away.

I should insert here that a runaway team of horses was, and still is, a dreaded circumstance that has resulted in many carriage or farm equipment tip overs and injuries to people and horses.

Just as the horses approached a closed wooden gate leading to their corral, they skidded to a stop, nearly thrusting me off the front of the half-loaded wagon. Dad eventually caught up with us as I wiped away tears, while the horses' chests heaved, as well as Dad's, to gather their breath. The event was the talk among the threshing crew for the rest of the day, but it was the horses that deserved the credit, and I knew it, even though several of the threshing hands said I was a brave boy.

Dad soon purchased fly drapes from one of the few remaining harnessmakers still around during the early 1950s. The drapes were made of four-foot-long, shoelace-like strings that hung down from a heavy cord that ran lengthwise from the horse's neck to its rump when flung over the harnessed draft horses. The strings jostled in the wind and whenever the animal moved, thus dispelling flies and mosquitoes from landing on the horses; yet the fly drapes allowed the horses to cool off while they worked.

Years later I learned running is one of the ways horses rid themselves of biting insects. These horses knew what they were doing and meant no harm to me or Dad, or any deviation from their work expectations. I also learned that only female horseflies load up on blood so they can store enough energy to lay their eggs.

While growing up, my two-year-older brother, Joe, and I frequently rode the draft horses, or our quarter horse, named Trix, for fun, to herd cattle, and to set gopher traps after the last hay crop was harvested. We usually saddled and rode Trix together after we arrived home from school on fall afternoons. While Joe sat astride Trix in the saddle, I rode behind him on the saddle blanket, holding onto Joe's waist to avoid falling off. We checked pocket gopher traps we had set the previous afternoon in alfalfa fields on our farm. The pesky rodents are called pocket gophers because they have a fold of fur-lined skin on each cheek into which they stuff food for carrying into underground storage rooms of their burrows that were dug well below frostline for winter. Old and freshly dug gopher mounds made cutting alfalfa hay difficult because any mounds of mud gummed up the hay mower's sickle, so we wanted to trap as many gophers as possible before the next spring. When successful, we euthanized the gophers we captured and cut off the front claws.

We were paid a bounty of ten cents for every pair of gopher claws we turned into the Shelby County auditor's office at the courthouse. The lady at the auditor's office counted the claws, which had been preserved with salt, with her bare hands. Our esteem for her rose greatly. When we earned $14.40 one fall, our feat was published in the local newspaper and earned us much admiration from other farm boys at school, and from Dad. The next year our uncle asked us to set traps on his land as well.

Joe made Trix gallop during a cloudy mid-November afternoon when we arrived home from school late. Our parents had to drive us to school and pick us up afterward; Dad had been unexpectedly delayed that afternoon. We hurriedly searched for new gopher mounds located in a series connected by underground runways into which alfalfa roots grew and were harvested by the pocket gophers. We would likely arrive home after dark and still had to milk several cows. As we galloped around the hayfield, Trix stepped into a badger hole. Badgers have gophers on their menus; holes dug by badgers in search of gophers have broken the legs of many horses. Trix stumbled and somersaulted. When we landed on the ground, Joe was uninjured beneath the saddle horn and cantle. I had been thrown aside. Trix rose to her feet. None of us were hurt, but when we climbed onto Trix again, she took more time to look out for badger holes while we searched for gopher mounds. Dad wondered why we arrived home after dark. As we milked our dairy cows and talked, he understood. Trix, Joe, and I were more careful after that lesson; we never fell again.

Having grown up with horses, when my family moved from Virginia to our Iowa farm in 1979, I wanted my children to experience the same enjoyment that I had with these animals. I purchased a filly and a seasoned eighteen-year-old mare, both registered by the American Quarter Horse Association. I joined the association to register the colts we raised.

I used our horses to check cows during calving season until I figured out it was easier to get a new mama to follow her calf as it rode in a cart trailing a four-wheel ATV where she could see and smell her calf than when it was slung over a saddle. During harsh weather, newborn calves needed protection in a barn. It also was easier not having to saddle a horse than driving the ATV with its headlights and a movable searchlight around the calving field at night.

Our horses were relegated to pleasure-riding. The filly that I broke to ride gave me a few bruises until she realized I was the boss. She accepted being ridden decently, but she needed to be taken out regularly to retain her skills. This was difficult for Shelby and Jon, because they were involved in music, sports, 4-H, and more. Sometimes I had to give the filly a reminder lesson before one of the kids would ride her. The older mare figured out how to dump the kids by purposefully scraping their legs when she went around fence posts too closely and by running under low-hanging tree branches. The wily animal never tried these tricks when I rode her. I began to wonder if we needed the horses, especially after getting bucked off a few times by a colt produced by the older mare, as I broke the youngster to ride.

During the following summer, a neighbor called me one day to say one of my bulls was running with his cows; he asked me to get the animal out of his pasture, which adjoined mine. I took the ATV to separate the bull from his new harem and drive him through a gateway to my farm.

Each time we drew near the gateway, he bolted and charged the four-wheeler. I had to hightail it away to avoid getting butted. The bull trumpeted to his new kingdom as I returned home to retrieve the experienced quarter horse mare.

Now on horseback when I encircled the bull, he predictably charged us to confirm his newfound status, but the experienced mare dodged him adroitly every time and chased after him, sometimes biting him on his tailhead when she drew close enough. After twenty minutes of this game, the bull wore down and stood facing us, gasping for breath.

I flung my lariat at him like a whip. He turned and steadily ambled toward the gate he knew he should use to exit.

Enough said. The horses remained with us for a few more years until the kids' interest in riding was replaced by teenagers' activities that were deemed more important. All of us learned lessons from horses, but I'm pretty sure I learned the most.

16

YIKES

The first time I fished Henry's Fork, a tributary of the Snake River in Idaho, was in September 1973. Marilyn and I had married the previous year. Our friend, Klea, who taught surgical nursing at Weber State University in Ogden, Utah, invited us to her summer cabin for the Labor Day weekend. Marilyn had finished her second year of teaching in the same program as Klea, in psychiatric nursing; I was finishing my doctoral work in clinical psychology at the University of Utah. Klea, a dozen years older than Marilyn and me, was—and still is—an intelligent, funny, and delightfully irreverent person. She enjoyed the outdoors. As a liberal politically, Klea was atypical of the majority of Utah's Mormon residents. The three of us hit it off from the start.

Together we drove to her cabin among the loosely strung-out conglomeration of summer homes that the local post office designated as Moose, Idaho. Klea's cabin was a couple miles from where Henry's Fork gushes as an artesian spring large enough to meet the water needs of 300,000 people. It joins an even larger fork some eight miles downstream after emerging from Henry's Lake near West Yellowstone, Montana, just west of the national park with a similar name.

Klea said the fishing was great. Although she didn't fish herself, her neighbors attested to big brown trout and whitefish in the permissible-fishing section of the stream below the spring. Klea liked eating trout and the landlocked coho salmon that annually migrated up Moose Creek past her cabin to their nesting haunts. Marilyn and I accompanied Klea to acquire salmon from the U.S. Fish and Wildlife Service after collecting their eggs and milt. With Klea, we canned the salmon later in our excursion, but for now, all I could focus on was fishing Henry's Fork. I purchased my Idaho fishing license at Mack's Inn, where the Moose Post Office was located. Before sun-up the next morning, I hiked in my waders through a half-mile of tall grass meadow to a fast-flowing and mist-enveloped river. Sandhill cranes issued their eerie cries, adding to the mystical atmosphere. I was the only person in this wild earthy place.

Streamside, I attached a handtied dry fly onto my fishing line and cast it forty feet upstream into the rushing water of a long, dark, scooped-out hole. A large brown trout jumped a foot out of the water after my fly as it landed but it didn't seize the fly. I figured I would have to lower my profile against the awakening sky, so I slipped into the river near the lower end of the hole where the water didn't appear deep enough to overflow my chest-high waders. I congratulated myself for fishing the fabled Henry's Fork of the Snake River for the first time in my life. I anticipated a good day of fishing. As I cast upstream, trout and whitefish practically snatched my royal coachman fly. Within two hours I hooked a couple dozen fish and kept three of my five-trout limit, all sixteen to twenty inches long, and two eighteen-inch whitefish. I gradually made my way into a deeper part of the hole; water was just a couple inches from coming over the top of my waders. I heard a loud splash behind me.

Turning to see what caused the commotion, I was surprised by a nearly black bull moose with five-foot-wide antlers gazing at me some forty feet to my rear and in water up to his belly. He didn't seem perturbed as he slowly encircled me on my left, keeping his distance. He entered the deeper headwaters of the dark pool some eighty feet upstream and began feeding, thrusting his head underwater repeatedly. Each time he raised his muzzle, strands of vegetation hung from his chomping jaws.

I continued to fish as the moose gradually drew closer. He pushed into the deepest part of the pool until he was ten yards in front of me and water covered all but his neck and head. I cautiously backed away but remained in water above my beltline.

While his head was underwater, I cast my fly a few feet in front of the grazing moose. When he raised his head as I was retrieving my fly, abruptly he snorted and stomped toward me as rapidly as the six-foot deep water allowed his heavy frame to move. I scrambled quickly to the shore a few feet to my right and hurled my body onto the grassy bank. I scurried to a nearby large, dead, but still-standing pine and hid behind its gray trunk. My fishing rod lay next to my feet but my line dragged downstream.

For the next several minutes I didn't care if my fishing line was becoming entangled in the river vegetation. Periodically, I peeked around the tree to observe the moose, still grazing in shallower parts of the pool I had abandoned. It dawned on me that this was the early part of rutting season.

A smaller bull moose entered Henry's Fork a hundred feet upstream. The big guy spied the other possible threat to his domain and slowly made his way upstream, head and antlers alternately tilting and waving ominously from side to side. I used the occasion to reel in my line and decided it was time for lunch.

Both bulls gradually stalked upstream, keeping several yards distance from each other, and disappeared around a bend in the stream as I finished my sandwich and a soda. *Yikes,* I thought to myself as tension drained from my body, *I hadn't expected a moose to charge.* After a short rest I went back to fishing various holes in the river, but I periodically surveyed the surrounding terrain to make sure I was close to a tree until I caught my limit of trout and returned to Klea's cabin. When I arrived back at the cabin during the early afternoon and told Marilyn and Klea of my adventure with the aggressive bull moose, Klea commented sardonically, "We would have come looking for you if you hadn't come back by nightfall."

During a separate but similarly dangerous fishing excursion, Jon and Scott drove from Des Moines to meet me at Brookings, South Dakota, on a Friday evening in early November a dozen years ago. I was already at our motel when we met, after teaching a seminar for health care providers in Sioux Falls earlier in the day. Scott brought his eighteen-foot boat with its forty horsepower outboard motor so we could go after walleye the next morning on Lake Thompson, some fifty miles west of Brookings.

We arose on a cloudy and blustery Saturday. After breakfast we drove our vehicles to Lake Thompson, hoping to catch a bunch of fish before an impending cold front arrived. We knew fishing often peaked just before a storm.

Lake Thompson, one of the largest natural lakes in South Dakota, is renowned for its walleye, pike, and perch fishing. It was currently at its maximum depth of about twenty-six feet, but has been known to become shallower and even dry during prolonged droughts.

As we unloaded Scott's boat at the marina on the east side of Lake Thompson, thick clouds were building to the northwest. The weather forecast predicted changeable temperatures and showers. We had our rain slicks with us. The water was choppy when we left the dock, but soon we had trolled several hundred yards into the nineteen-square-mile lake.

I was the first to hook a fish, a two-foot-long northern pike. We expected to catch walleye and perch, which are even better eating than pike. While releasing the pike into the lake, brisk wind gusts suddenly struck our slow-moving boat and turned us sideways. Whitecaps quickly formed and sloshed water over the gunwales of our boat.

We could see hills on the far western side of the lake about four miles away and decided to head toward their direction, where we hoped there was protection from the mounting wind. As we drew a couple hundred yards near the western shore, large drops of rain turned into ice and snow pellets, soon leading to a blizzard. We could see only about ten yards. Scott, who was piloting his boat, announced, "Boys, I think we better turn back." We had already donned our life jackets and checked to make sure they were securely buckled.

While Scott was turning the craft around, a huge wave struck us broadside, thrusting Jon and me off our seats and almost upsetting the boat. Scott regained enough control to allow the violent wind to push us from behind as he maneuvered to minimize the waves washing into the boat's hull. Swooping waves loomed several feet higher than us during their undulations as we rose and descended some eight feet with the rising and subsiding surface tension. Scott steered in the general direction the northwesterly wind was taking us. We felt somewhat safe until the wind mounted even more and began hurling water over the stern. Jon and I scooped out water with bait pails, as Scott's boat pitched up and down in the turbulent swells.

Gradually, our boat accumulated several inches of water in the bottom, despite Jon's and my best efforts to bail it out. We had no idea where we were headed. We were in deep—and worsening—trouble.

After what seemed an interminable length of time, but was probably less than a half hour, our boat scraped bottom and then crashed against big boulders. We could barely make out a shoreline a few yards away through the heavy snow, but where were we? Scott switched off the outboard motor.

Massive waves slammed our boat sideways into glacially deposited rocks as big as cars, scattered next to the shoreline, and splashed torrents of water into the vessel. Scott's boat could be smashed into smithereens by the incessant waves. Using our oars, we tried to push the craft off the rocks and headways into the wind, but the force of the unrelenting waves repetitively thrust us back into the rocks. We couldn't maneuver. The boat was three-quarters full of water—another twelve inches and it would sink it.

Scott shouted above the unremitting wind and racket of the boat banging against the boulders, "Abandon the boat. Let it sink, I don't care. I don't want to die here. We might not be able to get to the marina."

Jon yelled back, "We don't know where we are. We might be close to the dock, but we can't see well enough to know."

Loudly, I volunteered to go ashore to ascertain any landmarks or where the dock was located while the guys scooped water out of the boat. I had donned chest-high waders for warmth before we left the dock earlier and was the only person who was partially dry.

Cautiously, I slipped off the back of the boat into the water between the boulders, while hanging onto the stern in case the water was too deep for my waders. The water level was just below my rib cage. Scott became less frightened when he saw I could touch bottom.

I waded ashore and scrambled along the lakeside bluff until I found a house under construction. No one was home, so I scurried alongshore until I spotted another house a couple hundred yards ahead. A light was on in this fancy and obviously new abode. When I knocked, a man came to the door. I apprised him of our situation and asked him where the eastside marina was located. He said it was about a mile northward and pointed toward the direction. He wished me luck and turned back to the football game on his television.

Minutes later when I arrived back at Scott's boat, he and Jon had emptied enough water inside the craft so the remainder was only a foot deep. I told them where the dock was located. We still could see only a few yards in the blizzard but the wind had subsided slightly. I asked Jon and Scott what they thought we should do.

Scott answered, "I'd rather let the boat drown than us."

Jon reckoned, "I think we can make it to the dock if we follow the shoreline far enough away so we don't bang into the rocks and if we take it slow."

I sided with Jon. Scott allowed Jon to drive his boat as Scott scrambled into the front of the vessel. Jon took over the outboard motor and gunned it. The boat wouldn't budge from the rocks.

Still in the lake and in my waders, I suggested I could push the boat while Jon and Scott shoved hard on the boulders with oars. Jon pushed with one hand on his oar and the other on the engine throttle. Scott shoved with an oar in one hand and accelerated the electric trolling motor on the front with his other hand. I shoved the stern with all my strength. With our coordinated efforts, the craft slid off the rocks. I followed it a few feet until it was headed sufficiently northwestward into the wind and lake. I clambered over the stern, staying clear of the churning propeller as Jon and Scott gunned their motors to continue our push into deepening waters.

When we were able to escape the stacks of boulders by a couple hundred feet, but could still visually make out the shoreline on our right, Jon steered the boat northward. We motored slowly. Jon periodically turned the bow into oncoming surging waves so we could brace ourselves and not upset when they crashed into us. Scott and I scooped out water. It took us a half hour to carefully maneuver along the barely visible starboard shore. Finally, we spotted our marina.

I have never been so happy to reach dockside. Hurriedly, we loaded the boat onto its trailer.

Scott and Jon drove off with Scott's boat toward our motel in Brookings and I followed in my Jeep. As I steered my Jeep, I became incredibly lethargic. I was hypothermic and the Jeep's heater was warming me up. I had never felt so tired in my life, even when I had my cardiac event several years earlier. When we convened at our motel in Brookings, Jon and Scott said they felt the same way. We thought our adrenaline and energy were completely depleted. We found our room and fell asleep for the rest of the afternoon. After we ate supper, we adjourned to the motel hot tub until we finally warmed up. We thanked each other. I silently contemplated a thanksgiving prayer in my mind for all of us being alive. Scott summed up the day: "Yikes. That was closer than I want to come to meeting my maker."

I got permission in early March 2014 to icefish a favorite farm pond on a bright Sunday morning, so I telephoned Jon, who was as eager as me to fish. Although he lived ninety miles away, he said he would pick me up at home around noon. For the first time in three months, the outdoor temperature was fifteen degrees above freezing. Jon and I cherished this healthy farm pond fishery that was twenty miles northwest of my home. We always shared our catch, dressed and ready to cook, with the owners, whom we also liked very much. They liked us, and they liked eating hand-sized fillets of bluegills and bass, too.

The final half-mile dirt road to the farm field where the pond was located had an inch of soft mud on its surface as we approached our destination. Another quarter-mile drive through a barbed wire fenced-in farm field over melting snow and muddy cornstalks was even more treacherous. Jon's Lincoln Mark LT truck slid almost sideways as we motored cautiously through an open gateway to the pond area. There were creosoted posts as big as tree stumps on each side of the entrance, which tilted precariously toward a deep ravine below the pond's dam. I hummed the Simon and Garfunkel song "Slip Slidin' Away" as we slowly wheeled a couple hundred more yards along slippery cornstalk rows on the steep hillside that sloped toward the frozen pond. Jon's sturdy four-wheel-drive truck didn't feel any too safe until we parked on a flat spot a few yards from the still-iced-over pond.

Melting ice water covered the surface, but the farm pond was still firmly frozen. Jon drilled fishing holes with his motorized auger through a foot of ice to reach water. All afternoon we kept moving from spot to spot around the small lake. Our electronic Vexilars detected fish below many of the holes into which we dropped wax worms and minnows, but only a six-inch bass latched onto a worm during four hours of experimenting at various locations. During warmer months we always caught fish from float tubes in this five-acre pond.

Around 5:00 p.m. we decided to call it a day. We had had fun just getting out of the house, talking, and enjoying the sunshine. Besides, I got to smoke two cigars. We loaded our gear and hopped into the truck.

Jon asked, and I agreed, if we should try to head up the steeply inclining field by cutting across the rows of cornstalks until we were well above the open gateway and then allow the gradient to assist us toward the gate through which we had entered to reach the pond. A few hours ago, only the surface of the ground was muddy. Now there was scarce snow to be seen and four inches of thawed mud everywhere, thanks to the warm afternoon sun.

Taking his time, Jon's truck climbed twenty yards up the hill before spinning out. After pausing, he gunned the engine and gradually got his truck to turn toward the gate a couple dozen yards downslope. The truck mostly slid downhill as we inched toward the gateway. It came, finally, to a halt on some tangled cornstalks a few feet from the slanted gateway we had uncertainly negotiated earlier in the afternoon when the ground was less slippery.

I got out of the truck to scout if we could make it through the gateway without sliding into the creosoted posts, or worse, into the ravine that lay some thirty yards downhill from the gateway. There was nothing to stop the truck from skating on the muddy ground into the ravine, even if Jon managed to get through the gateway without clipping the post on the downhill side. I waved for him to wait while I checked our options.

The ground was more level along the barbed wire fence to the left of the gateway, on the upside of a terrace and in a hayfield. The grassy surface of the terrace was firmer than the cornfield, making it a better route to the road.

If only the truck would stay above the sloping gateway and not slide into the ravine! Jon got out of his vehicle to survey the route I suggested; he agreed it was worth a try.

I watched from the hillside as Jon crawled back into his vehicle and slowly maneuvered it forward. Suddenly, his truck skidded downhill until he was a couple feet from slipping down the sloped gateway, when his truck lurched forward just enough, with all four tires spinning and the engine nearly at full throttle, to reach the level upside of the grassed terrace. He waited there a moment. I jumped into the front passenger seat. We followed the terrace several hundred yards until it ended near enough to our road that we could leave the sodden farm field. The hard-packed dirt road was drying from the bright sun; we finally felt safe. I thought, *Yikes, we could have had a disaster.* I composed a thank-you in my mind.

17

FARMING AND FISHING WITH MY PARTNER

Many of my significant life experiences have involved women. Farming and fishing have often been entwined in these life-changing experiences. Marilyn can verify that these experiences have been good for my character development, having lived with me for more than a half century.

Two-fifths of the world's farmers are female, mostly in highly traditional, impoverished third-world countries. While about 17 percent of the primary farm operators in the United States today are women, in most third-world countries, primarily the women feed their populations.

Like other farm boys who were involved in 4-H, I lost my share of first place finishes in the cattle show ring to girls, deservedly, although I didn't always think so at the time. A cute girl almost always seemed to win the beef showmanship contests; showmanship skill was evaluated by the same livestock judge, who was—and still is—almost always a man. Was the ability of girls and boys who showed cattle always appraised objectively and fairly? After losing a few times, I abandoned that kind of unproductive thinking and toyed with the idea of marrying an attractive young woman with whom to farm. That is, until I decided at age eighteen to become a Catholic priest.

For three years I ceased participating in the dating world. Even then, half of my best friends were women in my age range. We could talk about matters that were meaningful, often more deeply than my male friends and I could. Jane, whom I mentioned elsewhere in this book, was one of these persons, for she opened up my thinking about life's purposes other than serving as a Catholic pastor. Three years later and while attending the University of Utah in pursuit of a PhD degree in clinical psychology, Marilyn and I met. That Marilyn is a full-blood sansei Japanese American, and I am a full-blood fourth-generation German American, was unimportant to her, me, our parents, or anyone in our families. Marilyn and I have always loved each other faithfully as lifetime mates.

After Marilyn and I married in 1972, we moved to Charlottesville, Virginia, two years later, where my first postgraduate professional job was as assistant professor of psychology at the University of Virginia. We became parents to a daughter, Shelby, and a son, Jon. We built a house on 3.5 acres with a great fishing pond that we purchased seven miles west of Charlottesville, and which a couple centuries earlier was owned by Meriwether Lewis. Marilyn helped apply oil-based stain to the pinewood ceilings that she could reach with a stepladder, while I coated the rafters and tongue-in-groove ceiling timbers some twenty feet above our living area. She made curtains and many of her and my clothes, including my favorite shirt back then, a bright floral cowboy shirt that always won positive comments. I raised a huge garden that enabled us to can and freeze a lot of vegetables, and we relied on the venison I butchered and the fish I caught for a substantial portion of our basic food.

Working long hours, often into the evenings, I made strides at teaching undergraduates and graduate students at UVA, and I successfully obtained research grants that provided employment for several graduate and undergraduate research assistants, and to two PhD clinicians who assisted for a few hours weekly with supervision of graduate students' therapy with research clients. Marilyn taught behavioral health nursing when she had time around the births of our children until they were about a year old; I could sometimes be home to care for the kids when Marilyn was gone from home, and we had a competent day care provider in our neighborhood when we needed assistance.

Yet, not everything seemed right. Marilyn commented frequently when I went outside our house to observe the sky at night; "You care about the weather, don't you? You're a farmer through and through, aren't you? I always wanted to marry a farmer with a PhD, and I got one." That settled it. We both preferred to live in the countryside and raise our children on a farm.

We revealed our intention to move to a farm the following year when my parents arrived for an invited visit the day before Jon was born on January 19, 1978. We had asked my parents to care for Shelby, then three years old, while Marilyn was in the hospital and I was at work. When we made the announcement, Mom was surprised and asked, "Why? You have it good at the university and your salary will be going up every year."

I replied, "We've been thinking about it for three years. We want to raise our children on a farm and there's no better place to do this than in Iowa, where I grew up."

Marilyn added, "We also want to be around family."

Following a lengthy silence, Dad spoke up: "It's your decision. Much as I want you to move to Iowa, I don't want to influence you one way or the other."

Mom ventured another comment: "You're young and just starting your family and your lives together. You both have a lot of spirit and can build another home."

As the evening went by, during supper and while going over household matters when Marilyn and I would both be away, we talked about what "home" meant. Home, I felt, was the community where my parents and remaining grandparent lived, and where a brother took over the farm where my brothers and I grew up. Home, for Marilyn and me, signified ties to the land we owned and to the outdoors. Marilyn was capable of making a house look and feel like home wherever we lived. Upon arriving in mid-May 1979 at our four-square white house built in 1893, Marilyn set about making the house into a farm family home. While she decorated, sewed, and handled the household, I planted our first Iowa garden and finished planting corn and soybean fields with an old four-row planter. Dad rode with me for my first two rounds on the tractor and then pronounced, "You're on your own." Dad had a heart attack that ended his life a year later. I still needed his advice.

My father gave us a medium-sized tractor, and I purchased two small used tractors and a new "big" machine with a cab and considerably more horsepower than my other tractors. We purchased a two-seat pickup truck large enough to carry a fourteen-foot camper, and I bought Dad a smaller pickup truck to enable him to drive his own vehicle when Mom needed to use their car. Most of my farming equipment purchases consisted of used items, such as a hay baler and a disk. I built three hay racks and mounted them on running gears. Over the next fifteen years, I constructed four cattle sheds, two storage sheds for farm equipment and a shop, two grain storage facilities, and our new house in 1987–1988. I started our purebred Simmental cattle business in 1982, which became my favorite agricultural enterprise over the years. I learned much about living closely with the land and farming organically; it felt good.

Marilyn had a lot to do with building a new house in the late 1980s, not only with its design and decoration, but with the prospect of a new home altogether. Our ninety-year-old farmhouse was drafty and had no insulation in the walls. I covered the windows with clear plastic inside and outside before winter each year, to insufficient avail. One cold December night Marilyn set a bucket of water next to the window of our bedroom on the north side of the house. When we arose the next morning, a skim of ice covered the water. That did it! No more new barns until we had a new house. Marilyn's insistence on a new house reminded me of a Hamlin Garland short story about a farm wife in the late 1800s who converted a new barn built by her husband into their home while he was away from home purchasing more cows. When I mentioned Garland's story to Marilyn, she demanded that we look at house plans. She had cut out pictures of houses she liked. I drew up the blueprints of a home we agreed had everything we needed, but its construction cost was beyond our means. That was in 1986, while we and many farmers were recovering from the worst farm crisis since the Great Depression. Marilyn sought the advice of a certified architect; his plans were a reworking of what I had drawn earlier, and his construction plan was more expensive and his design fee was completely out of line, in comparison to my free services.

A few months later, Marilyn brought out photographs she had taken of our current house. As we looked at them, she suggested, "What if we add on to our house?" I extended the roofline of our existing home over what would be the addition, and I added a high clerestory area with a chimney and proposed an attached garage. Marilyn said, "I like the way it looks." I also suggested the placement of a new kitchen, a new front entrance, a fireplace, a music room, a den, and an upstairs master bedroom suite. As I explained my thoughts, Marilyn encouraged me to continue my design work. "It doesn't look like it was added on to an existing structure," she commented.

After Marilyn and the kids went to bed, I drafted a full set of architectural blueprints, including changes to our existing house. By 6:00 the next morning, the rough blueprints were ready for her review. She loved them. Over the next few weeks, we made some modifications; I drafted floor plans for each level of our new and old house, as well as views from each side, and specified the construction materials, electrical and plumbing details, and outdoor landscaping. We could use salvaged lumber, trim work, flooring, and several doors from an old farmhouse that a high school lad whom I employed, and I, tore down three years earlier. I spent the following two winters, whenever I had time after chores and on weekends, pulling nails and cleaning the salvaged materials for reuse. I also purchased thirty-two-foot-long used bridge stringers at five dollars apiece at various sales by the Shelby County Road and Bridge Department, which would serve as rafters in the new section of our home after cutting off the ends that had deteriorated. Now we could afford to build a new house. Although I managed the majority of the construction projects and helped build the new house as much as time allowed, I hired skilled craftspeople to carry out specialized tasks, such as the plumbing and electrical work, some of the heavy construction that required large machinery, and all of the brick and tile work. The young man who was my former employee had completed a program in home construction and carpentry at a nearby community college. He built all our cabinets and completed the trim work as his first post-graduation job. His attention to detail landed him many jobs thereafter. Marilyn set about once again designing an attractive setting that made guests comfortable and that suited our purposes. We installed a cast-iron cookstove that we used many times when our electricity was shut down by storms. The fireplace, with a unique system of distribution of air that I designed, along with R-64 insulation in the roof and R-30 insulation in the walls, didn't allow the house to drop below 46 degrees Fahrenheit despite a great many double-pane glass windows during a week without electric power between Christmas and New Year's Day. During and after the completion of our new home, and every year since, people would drive by very slowly on the road facing our farmstead and some would come up the driveway to inspect our new home more closely.

I also learned from my experiences with Marilyn when I asked her to help me with farm chores that there were limits to what I could expect. Sometimes I needed help to open and shut gates to sort certain cattle into a pen and to hold others back. When no one else was available as I began raising cattle, I asked Marilyn to operate the gate while I chased cows, one at a time, down the alley of the corral. I would yell "Let this one (e.g., a pregnant cow) out," or "Hold this one (e.g., a cow that had already calved)." Usually, Marilyn did okay.

On this particular Saturday morning in early April, the frozen ground was thawing, helped along by recent rains. The cattle yards were a muddy mess. My part-time hired hand was off for the weekend, and the kids were too young to assist, so I asked Marilyn to help get a first-calf heifer into the calving shed. The bovine was inexperienced with birthing and needed a dry, warm place for parturition, where I could help her if necessary.

Marilyn's task was to shut the gate after I herded the animal into the yard next to the calving barn. I could take it from there.

Marilyn pulled on her boots and put on a warm coat, gloves and a hat before she slogged into the cattle feed yard where the very pregnant heifer with a water bag beginning to emerge from her rear end was eating her breakfast of ground hay and ear corn with the other cows. I opened the gate to the yard by the calving barn and asked Marilyn to hold the gate open until I could drive the soon-to-be-mother into the yard and then to shut the gate.

I singled out the animal and herded her into the yard. I yelled for Marilyn to swing the gate shut, because the animal had turned around and was already heading back toward the opening. Marilyn tried but couldn't lift her feet from the suctioning mud and manure.

"Hurry," I yelled. Marilyn pulled her right foot out of her boot and stepped with her stocking into the soupy mess, then fell on her butt in the slurry.

By now, the heifer had escaped from the holding pen. Laughing, I commented, "All you had to do was swing the gate shut, not walk with it."

"Do it yourself," Marilyn replied. "Help me up," she added as she headed to our farmhouse.

That was the last time Marilyn helped me sort cattle for many years. I figured out how to drive cows as a bunch into a pen and to let all the animals out of the gate myself except the one I wanted to hold back. We bought a sheltie that summer, who became the first of several cattle dogs and a part of our family.

I also had to rely on Marilyn to drive the tractor on the baler when no one else was available to help with the haying tasks during our first few years of farming. I showed her how to operate the gears and the switch to turn the tractor's power take-off that propelled or stopped the baler while I stacked the bales on the hay wagon behind the baler. Our young children stayed in or near the pickup truck where we could see them while we baled hay. They were in charge of serving lunch, which they enjoyed as much as we did.

For three years of Saturdays and Sundays (about four times each summer) when we needed to load the hay onto wagons, Marilyn ran the baler. She didn't figure out how to swing widely enough around corners to pick up the windrows of hay. I had to jump off the hayrack to sweep up the hay she left on the corners by hand and throw it into the baler intake.

I was glad when Jon was strong enough by age five to operate the clutch on the tractor. He had to use all his strength to press the clutch down, but he already knew about operating gears, power take-off, hydraulic levers, and all the other switches on our International 806 diesel tractor. Jon quickly learned how to drive the baler around the corners without missing any of the windrows. He became our baler operator for the next ten years until he was strong enough to take his turn stacking bales on the hayracks.

There weren't any rules about when a farm child could operate machinery when Jon became our baler operator, or when Shelby and Jon hoed soybeans with me, beginning around age ten. Sometimes even Marilyn joined us when the weeding was difficult; we enjoyed the camaraderie and breaks as we swigged water and ate cookies together during one of the worst farm jobs, "walking beans." Some farm kids were more capable than others at the same age, such as myself. I first drove a tractor at age five and was required to milk cows by hand at that age, but only during the evening chores until I was eight years old. Thereafter, Dad expected me to help with morning chores as well as other farmwork, including the dreaded "walking corn" task of pulling weeds in all the cornfields during early August with Dad, our hired hand, and my older brother. I didn't consider any of the farmwork to be overly harsh, although I disliked walking corn while carrying a machete to cut weeds. It was a sweaty job during the hottest time of the year. We wore long-sleeved shirts and wide-brimmed straw hats to minimize corn leaves from swishing and sometimes cutting our bare hands and faces. Corn pollen collected on our wet clothes and in our eyes. Plus, we had to keep an eye out for feared black and yellow spiders that could cause painful bites, as I knew from experience.

Working hard was fun and I felt I contributed to the success of our family farming operation. Shelby and Jon, now in their forties and making their own successful livelihoods, often say that farmwork shaped their character and capacity to deal with tough circumstances.

So, when Marilyn asked me why I never said anything to her when she left swatches of windrowed hay on the corners that I had to pick up, I replied, "Because I thought you would quit." At that time Marilyn wasn't experienced in farming, but she became increasingly more competent driving trucks and keeping an eye on the weather, as well as relaying directions to our farmhand. Now she reports to me about how the crops look after driving along farm fields. Marilyn can spot a disease outbreak in a soybean field as quickly as I can.

There are some things in farm life that Marilyn developed a knack for, and a few more that capitalized on other forms of expertise, like fishing. Although she enjoyed paddling our canoe, she said she didn't really enjoy fishing. However, she got into the action quickly when we fished together in Canada.

In celebration of our fortieth wedding anniversary, Jon and our daughter-in-law, Amanda, invited Marilyn and me to Canada, along with her parents, for a fly-in fishing trip. The guys convinced our mates that this was an opportunity to explore the Canadian wilderness while staying with accomplished fishermen, cooks, and all-around outdoorsmen. None of the women had flown previously in a small seaplane, and they were eager for the new experience.

We flew out of Kenora, Canada, to a remote lake in northwest Ontario on a Sunday morning in early August. We arrived at a clean, three-bedroom cabin built on the shoreline of an island in the middle of a several-thousand-acre pristine lake. We were the only human inhabitants within a ten-mile radius.

While our mechanically inclined son got the boat motors revved up, the rest of us unpacked our food and gear inside the comfortable cabin. Within an hour we were "on the water" searching for walleye and pike.

With complete honesty I can say that we ate walleye fried, baked, or cooked in chowder for at least two daily meals during each of the next six days. On the first day, Marilyn caught a twenty-five-inch walleye, the first fish during her lifetime. This energized the men to show the ladies who the "better" fishers were.

Didn't happen! At the end of the trip, Amanda, who claimed to have fished only once previously, landed the most walleye, while Marilyn claimed the biggest walleye.

The men consoled ourselves with the fact that we can be sensitive, decent, and good cooks while on a fishing trip. We cleaned and cooked all the fish and prepared most of the meals at the cabin. We enjoyed lazy evening boat rides with our partners to locate the prettiest sunset views before the darkness set in around 11:00 p.m.

The husbands kept the motorboats in tip-top running condition. Jon and Amanda emptied the garbage on a separate island some distance away, so bears wouldn't be attracted to our cabin. The guys scrubbed the cabin counters and floors for the next group of fishers. We didn't eat any beans.

However, and this is important, our partners did their part. They kept the cabin organized; they cleaned what the guys had missed; and they basically looked after all of us and made us feel reassured. They were our reason for asking them to join us. As a popular song says, "Love is in the air."

And yes, unlike earlier visitors to our cabin who wrote in the guest book, none of us drank too much alcohol. The preceding party of seven guys claimed they had consumed twenty-one cases of beer and nine gallons of hard liquor during six days and nights. After all the hard liquor was gone, one guy bet everyone else that he could drink a gallon of milk in one sitting. Thirty minutes after he had reached his goal, he was sick. He wrote in the cabin guest book, "I didn't feel better until I shit a cheese brick the next morning." He didn't mention if it was mild or sharp cheddar, but apparently it freed up enough space in his innards so he could consume his share of the remaining beer.

I wrote in the cabin guest book, "I hope our wives will accompany us on another fishing trip here."

18

NUGGET AND HAYDEN'S EXCELLENT ADVENTURE

We always had a dog on our farm to help with cattle chores and watch over our farm. We had Casey first, then Cary, and Sachi, who were much loved members of our family. They lived inside our house as pups and on the porch or in barns as adults, depending on the weather. We developed deep bonds with our dogs, as well as our kitties. Our dogs and cats were friends too, so it was natural that our children, and now our grandchildren, like dogs and cats.

When Jon was twenty-four years old, Nugget became his first canine companion and hunting dog. He learned about Nugget, a yellow Lab who was four years old, from Jim, a licensed outfitter and guide for Cabela's. Nugget had already established a well-deserved reputation for masterfully pointing and retrieving hundreds of upland gamebirds and almost as many ducks and geese. Some of her accomplishments appeared on televised outdoor channel broadcasts.

Jon had hunted pheasants with Nugget and Jim once, prior to learning from Jim that he wanted to sell her because he had assumed a new employment position that didn't involve guiding hunters. For six weeks Nugget lived in a four-by-eight-foot chain-link pen in a garage owned by one of Jim's hunting clients. She could roam around the house's yard only when her caretaker was at home in the Des Moines area, where Jon and Scott also lived.

When Jon visited Nugget to look her over, it was late summer. She greeted him with a few tail wags and sad eyes. The next day he brought her to his home.

Nugget often visited our farm with Jon; the three of us mostly hunted pheasants together. Jim accompanied us on a couple of hunting excursions. Nugget and I became close, and Marilyn also established a bond with Nugget, who responded to her commands as well as mine. Hunting trips with Nugget always resulted in many pheasants, ducks, and geese for our freezer or to eat fresh. Our son-in-law, Shale, also liked when we hunted together, whether with or without Jon. Nugget joined us on fishing trips, holidays, and sometimes stayed with us when her regular family was away.

As Nugget approached eleven years (seventy-seven human years) of age, Jon's wife, Amanda, gave him Hayden as a birthday gift. Hayden was also a yellow Lab, but with a redder coat; she came from a long line of fine hunting dogs. Hayden was a ten-week-old pup when she accompanied Jon, Scott, and me on a late March fishing trip to the Norfolk River in northern Arkansas. She slept in her kennel in the same upstairs bedroom as Scott and Jon, and she ran incessantly around our cabin when she was out of her kennel.

Hayden was fun to watch and play with. Without Nugget around, Hayden had an opportunity to associate with us by herself, and oh, boy, did she! She hurled herself at us whenever we called her, sat next to us patiently waiting for scraps as we ate meals, and she chewed on dishtowels, shoes, and anything else she could find until we removed them from her.

When Jon left Nugget and Hayden with us overnight, both dogs slept on their doggy beds in our bedroom. Nugget would place her muzzle on my arm to awaken me when Hayden needed to be let outside to take care of duties.

Unlike Nugget, Hayden would reluctantly come when called and practically knocked us down when she obliged, as if to say with an indignant teenage voice, "What do you want?"

The summer after Hayden arrived, Amanda and Jon prepared for a two-week trip to Alaska. They asked Marilyn and me to look after Nugget and Hayden while they were traveling. Not wanting Nugget and Hayden to run loose or get hit by the many trucks on our graveled "county road" while we were at our day jobs, Jon and I constructed a sixteen-by-thirty-foot pen with cattle panels under a huge elm tree next to our house. We placed two portable kennels, lots of toys, and ample water in the pen. Nugget and Hayden seemed okay the first day Jon and Amanda were gone.

On the second day, I had to sternly order the dogs into their pen. On the following day after I was already at my office, Marilyn phoned me to come home to fetch the dogs because they refused to enter their enclosure until I grabbed them by their collars and scolded them. We wondered why they were so recalcitrant.

Fortunately, the next day was Saturday, and we were home all day. The July weather was terribly hot and humid; the dogs were glad to stay in the house except when I had outside chores.

That evening Nugget or Hayden asked every ten minutes or so to go outside, but soon barked to be let back inside shortly thereafter. Tiring of their demands, I made them stay outside after supper. I fell asleep in front of the television, while Marilyn watched her TV shows in our upstairs bedroom.

Shortly before nightfall a loud clap of thunder awakened me. I flipped on the Weather Channel and learned that a violent storm with high winds and hail was moving toward our home.

Alarmed, I asked Marilyn if the dogs were with her. She answered, "I thought they were with you."

I scrambled onto our front entryway and yelled for the dogs to come to our house, but there was no response. Reentering our home, I told Marilyn what was happening and that I would look for Nugget and Hayden with my Jeep.

As I pulled out of our driveway and headed westward on our gravel road, I spotted Nugget and Hayden trotting toward me with their tongues hanging out, but looking happy. Hayden and Nugget periodically bumped into each other, like two staggering drunks. I stopped my Jeep and opened the tailgate to let them into the back.

Neither budged. Then I opened the driver-side rear door. Nugget looked at me reproachfully as if to say, "Okay, but quit telling us what to do; I can take care of things fine." Both hopped onto the back seat. Hayden leaned admiringly into Nugget as I turned around and hurried home just as wind, heavy rain, and small hailstones began pelting our vehicle.

I didn't know how to explain what had happened until I called Jim. He said, "Nugget is the smartest and most respectful dog I ever had. She was trained to not poop or pee in her kennel, so when she was confined to a pen by her temporary keeper, she was humiliated when she couldn't hold it. Putting her in a pen reminded her of that humiliation."

Chastened, I thanked Jim and I never penned Nugget again. She could take care of things fine, and she did whenever Jon, Amanda, and the two dogs visited us.

During the pheasant hunting season that fall, it was apparent that Nugget had slowed down considerably. She watched Hayden, as did Jon and I, bound energetically through thick weeds and prairie grass, but Nugget efficiently pointed and retrieved most of the birds that we shot. Hayden learned caution from Nugget when racing through brushy cover and began to retrieve downed birds more satisfactorily.

The following summer I got a phone call from Jon one July day: "Nugget isn't doing well and probably won't live long, according to her veterinarian. Would it be okay if I bury her on our farm if she dies?"

"Of course," I said, brushing away tears. It was obvious that Jon was crying too.

The next day Jon called again to report, "Nugget had a stroke and can't see or hear, but she can smell. She can't stand up well. Amanda and I will bring her home tomorrow."

Mid-morning the following day, Jon and Amanda arrived with Nugget. They left Hayden in her kennel in the back of their pickup truck where she couldn't see what was happening. Nugget couldn't walk, so Jon carried her onto our front lawn where she could smell the sweet bluegrass. He brought two syringes, one filled with a sedative, and the other with a medication to stop her heart from beating. I had used my tractor with a loader to dig a three-foot-deep hole next to our farmstead and facing fields Nugget had hunted for most of her life. Jon liked the burial plot. I asked him If he wanted me to inject the medications, but he declined my offer.

Amanda held Jon's arm as he injected the sedative into one of Nugget's front legs. All four of us cried as Jon injected the heart-stopping medication next. Within seconds, Nugget appeared to be totally at peace. She no longer felt any pain. She was in a place where there were no dog pens. When it was clear that Nugget no longer had a pulse, I asked Jon if I should take Nugget with my tractor and loader to her burial site, but Jon refused; he carried her in his arms some three hundred feet to her grave. He threw the first handful of dirt onto her lifeless body; I used my loader to finish the job and packed down the dirt.

I tried my best to focus on Nugget and Hayden's excellent adventure.

19

HOT TUBS, KIDS, AND FARMERS' BODIES

"Is Grandpa going into the hot tub without any clothes on?" my four-year-old grandson, Mikey, asked his father with obvious astonishment. I was very gingerly stepping barefoot on a wood-chip path with a towel wrapped around the lower half of my body toward the hot tub in the backyard of the Santa Fe house his parents, Marilyn, and I had rented for the Easter weekend several years ago.

I was the first person in the family to "hit the spa" that day. The towel covered my swimming trunks underneath, but I could understand Mikey's worry.

Mikey's six-year-old sister, Alex, did little to alleviate her brother's concern when she hopped into the hot tub after me, asking, "Why is the water running over the sides of the tub?"

I had already lowered my body into the heated pool. Before I could answer Alex, my namesake grandson interjected as he climbed into the hot tub, "How come your belly button is so big?"

"I have a hernia," I explained, but my answer only prompted more questions.

"How did you get that?" both grandchildren asked.

"It's what can happen if you lift something that's too heavy," I answered. "I had surgery to remove a part of my body that had cancer, called the 'prostate.' The surgeon accidentally made the cut into my tummy too long, so it weakened the tissue around my belly button."

"You know what cancer is, don't you?" I added, and they nodded. "Afterward, when I picked up a heavy bale of hay, my tummy popped out, and I've had the hernia ever since."

"Does it hurt?" Mikey wondered.

"No," I answered. "It's one of the things that can happen when farmers don't pay enough attention when working, like losing my toes."

We had this conversation about my missing toes before, but both grandkids persisted in querying me further and commenting on my 1990 mishap. Mikey asked me to display my injured foot.

When I raised my right leg, the overflowing water subsided, but not the interrogation.

"You were brave," Mikey observed, albeit incorrectly.

"No, I made a mistake," I responded. "Your mother, Shelby, and your uncle, Jon, got into the combine our farmhand and I were operating and found my missing toes. They and our farmhand were very brave."

"Wow," Mikey said.

His sister spoke up: "I know what a combine is and how you lost your toes. I'm going to be a doctor like Mommy. She said finding your toes made her decide to become a doctor."

The in-pool conversation wasn't finished. Pointing to my chest, Mikey said, "You look like Grandma."

Oh boy, how could I explain this without compromising Marilyn's or my dignity? Let me just say that I postponed answering Mikey immediately and brought up the subject at the supper table. Big mistake! After everyone stopped laughing uproariously and wiped away their uncontrollable tears, including me, someone said, "That's what happens when you get fat."

That explanation didn't help a bit, as laughter surged again. Just so you know, I'm a bit overweight.

In retrospect, I have to commend Alex and Mikey for their innocent and complete honesty. They also looked out for me during the entire trip, particularly Alex.

I could barely walk, due to a pinched nerve or something else. Alex took my hand whenever we ventured to museums and such inspiring sights as the Loretto Chapel in Santa Fe and its multistory spiral staircase that was said to be constructed miraculously by a rancher/carpenter over a century ago, using only glue and wooden pegs.

I need a miracle, I thought.

Alex made sure I had my walking cane and waited with me on sidewalks and trails until my pain subsided enough to resume walking. Alex also spoke more loudly than usual because I could hear only half of what people said, partly due to otitis media that ruptured my ear drums a month earlier, and mostly due to aging of my cochlea, the internal spiral organ that detects sound.

Yup, my body isn't working properly, like many older—and some younger—farmers' bodies. My mind is okay, I think. I might need hearing aids and some kind of medical procedure to deal with whatever is causing me to walk painfully and with limited balance, but I will continue what I'm doing until nothing functions on me anymore. This is what many farmers decide as they age and answer their own—and their family's—questions about why they continue to farm.

Farmers don't readily quit what they feel they are called to undertake. When their physical capacities deteriorate, they still want to be useful. Sometimes this means farmers who are declining physically take on only advisory roles to those who follow in their footsteps. In other instances, they continue to work until their abilities to function decline to the point that they can't make meaningful contributions to the farming operation.

Reaffirming to me, more farm people currently request my assistance than ever before. Mikey and Alex also validated me when each said, in spite of any of my limitations, "I love you, Grandpa."

20

CROSSING THE BORDER

Virgil was waiting for Jon and me outside a Des Moines motel at 4:00 a.m., the day our Canada fishing adventure began. We crammed Virgil's considerable fishing gear and his tiny suitcase among our bags in the truck box of Jon's shiny, white, four-door Lincoln Mark IV truck. It was equipped with lots of chrome, a top-of-the-line package of extras, eight-inch lifts, and oversized tires; I practically needed a step stool to get into the super vehicle. After I drove this magnificent man-truck the first time, I awoke the next morning with macho black hair covering my chest, my voice an octave lower, and testosterone surging from all my pores. Okay, so I exaggerated a tiny bit!

We made good time driving north on I-35 and arrived in the Twin Cities in time for rush-hour traffic. We lost additional time when we pulled off the interstate highway to refuel Jon's vehicle. We needed to make a left turn but we could only turn to the right and then had to backtrack to the service station, making only more right turns. We had to make all right turns back onto I-35 too. It dawned on us that we were in the electoral district represented by conservative Congresswoman Michele Bachmann, at that time. "No turns allowed to the left," we laughed.

Jon and I had fished in Canada for walleye and other good-eating species several times previously. During one of my periodic conversations with Virgil, he said he had never fished in Canada. He added, "Catching all the walleye I can eat during an entire day at least once in my life is on my bucket list."

"Let's go to Canada this summer," I said. "Jon and I can show you where we can catch walleye, pike, and smallmouth bass until our arms wear out."

Virgil couldn't resist the offer, even though he'd had a heart attack and another stent implanted into a coronary artery two weeks before we left for Canada. Virgil and I met several years earlier when I asked him to help manage crisis counseling programs for people devastated by disasters like floods and tornadoes. He had a reputation as a highly skilled counselor. AgriWellness, Inc., the nonprofit program I directed, ran the crisis counseling program in Iowa at that time, through a contractual arrangement with the state. Virgil and I became good friends who were honest with one another, even when we joshed—which was considerable. I learned a lot from Virgil.

The two-hour ride in a 1946 Beaver float plane to our lake in northwest Ontario scared Virgil, but we had plenty of liquid sedatives to calm him after we landed. We had 4,000 acres of prime fishing water to ourselves. During previous visits Jon and I had named hot spots for good reason: the Fish Tank, Mike's Honey Hole, and the Hog Trough.

We caught and ate walleye every meal for a week, as well as a grand pike that Virgil roasted over a campfire with onions, peppers, cilantro, and potatoes. We kept ten walleye to take back to the United States after our week-long stay, two fewer than the limit of four apiece.

We took a more westerly route back to Iowa. When we arrived at the Pembina, North Dakota, border crossing with the walleye that I had filleted into twenty halves, we were surprised when two armed U.S. customs agents asked us to park our truck in their locked garage. The agents, both women around thirty years of age, demanded to know where we had been, how many fish we were transporting, and what we had been doing. We answered them fully. They placed us in a locked holding cell, took our phones, and said they would get back to us. We could ask on the intercom if we needed assistance. No one came when we asked via the intercom to use a restroom after waiting three hours.

The agents went through every item in our truck. They entered our cell and told us they used drug-sniffing dogs and long-handled mirrors (to scout the undercarriage of the truck) searching for drugs, but without finding any; they wanted to know where we hid the drugs. They accused us of hiding additional evidence when they found half a barbecued walleye we saved to eat as a snack. They asked how Virgil, Jon, and I knew each other.

A couple hours later, the two agents returned and told us we were in violation of federal fish transport statutes. They had called a federal game warden. Thankfully, we were allowed to empty our bladders, under surveillance.

The federal game warden told us he could charge us with either of two statutes: we had too many fish, because each filleted fish half was assumed to be an entire fish, which would lead to a $2,000 fine, or because we had not left enough skin on each fillet, a $300 fine per person. I had left skin samples, about a one-by-one-inch piece of intact skin (it's in the regulations if you read every page closely) on the fillets for inspectors to examine, but one or two fillets had slightly less than a square inch of skin. We could take our choice of the violations.

The federal game warden, named Wally, said he knew we didn't purposefully bring back too many fish from Canada and he knew from the pieces of skin on the fillets that they were walleye. He said he had to charge us nonetheless. A warning about how to prepare for future inspections at the border wouldn't suffice. We chose the cheaper option; we wrote out our checks payable to the U.S. District Court.

We aren't sure, but we think the border officials were racially profiling us, because of the nature of their questions and because Virgil is African American. They were probably disappointed when they figured out that we weren't drug mules transferring illicit substances across federal borders. The cynical part of me says that perhaps the border guards, and maybe Wally, enjoyed our seized walleye for supper because they had "earned their keep" that day. Another part of me was sort of thankful for them checking us astutely.

When we were allowed to leave the Pembina border station, I called Marilyn to explain we would be home about six hours later than expected. I asked her if she would welcome me, a federal offender, into our house.

"Of course," Marilyn said.

Oh well, I have done worse things in my life. I couldn't wait to get home, though sadly without the walleye I had carefully filleted and stored.

A little over a year later Virgil had another heart attack and passed away. I am so glad he had his once-in-lifetime experience catching and eating all the walleye he wanted. Maybe he is catching all the fish he wants in his hereafter. I miss Virgil, but perhaps he also is helping me to catch fish and to stay out of trouble. I hope so; I won't turn down any help I can get.

21

KIDS, FISHING, AND LAND STEWARDSHIP

"I got one," my seven-year-old granddaughter announced during a June 2021 fishing excursion with her dad, her two first cousins, and me. Her yard-long kid's fishing rod bent double and the line held as she slowly maneuvered a channel catfish almost as long as her fishing rod toward the dock where everyone congregated to watch the tussle. Her nine-year-old cousin carefully swept the fish into an outstretched net and lifted it onto the dock.

We were visiting a farm pond owned by a longtime farming friend and his wife in a neighboring county about twenty-five miles from my home. "Fish whenever you want," Tom and his wife, Hannah, always said when I called to ask permission to fish there. Asking permission became protection for myself as I aged, so someone knew where to look for me if I didn't show up at home before nightfall; it also was an opportunity to visit with my good friends. I knew this farm pond well, for I had caught fourteen- to twenty-inch largemouth bass, nine- to ten-inch bluegills, and my largest channel "cat" ever on a fly rod. I released female fish with bellies swelled by enlarging eggs back into the pond to help ensure the next generation. The owners carefully manage their pond and any upstream runoff with filter strips of several varieties of prairie grass, legumes, and other forbs. We flushed pheasants, quail, and butterflies, which the kids pointed out as we drove down the path to the pond beside a healthy green cornfield.

Lest I violate a fisherman's pledge, and out of respect for the rights of the pond owners, I won't reveal where this well-kept farm pond exists.

I know they will appreciate this gesture and what I have to say about their farming stewardship.

Jon's oldest daughter caught a nice bass and a huge bluegill later, but lost a monster largemouth bass that broke her reel first, and later the fishing line, while bringing it toward the shore. The other two kids managed to hook several bluegills, but landed only one fish during the retrieval. My grandson captured a bluegill as big as his cousin's bream. The well-acquainted cousins bantered excitedly: "Nice cast. I got a good one. Mine is bigger than yours. Quit bragging."

I wondered, *Were they already getting into telling fish stories? It must be a natural thing, because they didn't learn that from me.*

Jon and I baited hooks and untangled fishing lines until the young-sters got comfortable doing these things themselves or simply gave up when a huge tangle of line formed a bird's nest after an improper cast. That's how youngsters learn to fish. I also learned quickly to start over with the repairs to such messes by cutting off the tangled line, attaching a new hook, and rebaiting. A few times I had to ask for backup even though Jon was already busy with coaching the kids on how to cast their rods. He also was the official photographer. He didn't become impatient or frustrated. Jon even got in a few casts of his own before we left the pond as the kids fished together for three hours.

As we departed the pond in Jon's truck, he asked the kids if they wanted to fish again. A chorus of "next weekend, next weekend," erupted.

Visiting a Dairy Queen on the way home added to the fishers' happy moods. The kids were discovering how enjoyable everything is about fishing, even if you don't catch as many fish as others in the party, or none at all.

Jon asked the kids, "Do you know what you get when a big fish breaks your rod or reel?"

Silence. He explained, "You get a new and better fishing rod, like I did when a monster bass broke my first rod."

"Oh," the three youngsters responded, while contemplating the promise of good things to come.

Our conversation continued when we resumed traveling homeward. I mentioned that my grandchildren should thank the landowners who created this habitat for fish, wild game, and native plants when we stop by their home next time. My oldest granddaughter asked, "How did they get their good fishing pond?"

I explained how the pond was constructed with federal financial assistance for farmland conservation and flood control projects. I also explained how the owners planted grass and prairie flowers in an eighty-foot-wide swath of waterway farthest upstream that widened to about three hundred feet just above the pond. These management practices keep pollutants from flowing into the pond. Jon added that we only eat healthy fish from ponds and lakes we know are clean.

The discussion offered an opportunity to ask them why we eat the fish we catch and the pheasants, deer, and waterfowl that mostly only Jon captures these days when hunting. "Because it's good for you," my seven-year-old granddaughter answered, "and it's better than what you can buy in stores."

"Yup," I responded, and then launched into an explanation. "Do you know fishing and hunting are considered types of agriculture? Fishing and hunting furnish food, just like farmers. Before people became farmers long ago, everyone hunted, fished, and scrounged for food. In fact," I continued, "hunting and fishing gave the first farmers thousands of years ago many of the skills they needed to farm."

Silence. It dawned on me that my preaching to the grandchildren was above their heads. Like Marilyn periodically reminds me and says to others who are suffering through one of my lengthy explanations, "Ask Mike a question. Rather than give you a quick dictionary response, he gives you an encyclopedic dissertation."

My bad. The kids saved the day. I knew they were listening intently even if they didn't fully grasp everything I said, because they initiated into a game of who could be the first to spot a blooming wildflower along the highway.

The grandkids requested holding a fish fry featuring their trophies when we met next. Jon and I agreed. I cleaned the fish after they left for their homes. Becoming a fishing mentor to my grandchildren is no longer on my "bucket list."

Jon was only three years old when he and I went fishing together the first time. A popular family story is that he was born with a fishing pole in his hands. When he was five, he demonstrated his fishing prowess to our twenty-one-year-old farming apprentice from Switzerland. Joel lived with us for eight months. He and Jon cast worms into a seldom-fished farm pond that was loaded with bluegills and bass, while I cast my handtied flies with a fly rod when I wasn't needed to assist anyone. A cousin who farmed the land invited us to fish there anytime. We showed our appreciation by sharing cleaned and vacuum-sealed packages of fish with my cousin's family, like we did with everyone who allowed us to fish or hunt on their property.

Jon and I soon caught a couple dozen "keeper" fish, but Joel landed only five "keepers." While standing next to Jon on the water's edge, Joel repeatedly cast the same worms that Jon used for bait, and he tried grasshoppers as well. Finally, Joel exchanged fishing equipment and fishing sites with Jon. Poor Joel—he only seldom landed a decent-sized fish, while Jon could cast a bare hook into the pond and land a catch, but Joel became quite proficient and successful by the time he returned to Switzerland.

As I had done with my young son's catches, I cleaned and packaged the fish my grandchildren caught after they left. I couldn't have asked for a better introduction to fishing with my grandchildren, and to the importance of land and pond stewardship. Fishing and hunting are much more than capturing wild fish and game. The bonding that occurs while engaging in these activities together cements relationships and respect for all of nature.

22

WHAT MIGHT AGRICULTURE BE LIKE IN THE FORESEEABLE FUTURE?

Marilyn and I met Sara and Stefano outside our Rome hotel in early May 2017, in what became one of the most interesting days we have ever spent. Pursuing shortcuts on Italy's busy roadways, we scooted in our hosts' automobile about fifty kilometers to the ancient country town of Artena, located in the Apennine Mountains that stretch along most of the Italian peninsula.

There is an old Artena and a new Artena, however, they share the same town administration. Old Artena is demonstrating, and refining, what has contributed to its survival from the Medieval Era onward, despite several military invasions that destroyed many of the town's ancient structures and inhabitants. The World War II bombardment to drive out the Nazis was the most recent strife that severely damaged many ancient structures. Now partially restored, old Artena is perched high on a mountainside, while new Artena stretches out on the valley floor several hundred feet below. That old Artena is usually above the clouds, which periodically hover over new Artena until morning sunshine evaporates them, seems like an appropriate metaphor.

Sara Bissen, the managing editor of the *Journal of Biourbanism* (JBU), and I had been working for several months on an article about how rural and agrarian experiences influence people who reside in urban environments. Dr. Stefano Serafini, her husband, is the general secretary and research director of the International Society of

Biourbanism. At that time they were a two-person family, but as of 2024 they have a daughter that the entire community treasures.

Two mules with burlap saddles and their handler, Emilio, were waiting for Marilyn and me when Stefano parked the car in a small asphalt lot a couple hundred feet above the base of the mountainside village where the road ended. The animals stepped cautiously as they carried us several hundred feet in elevation up steep cobblestone walkways, for there are no streets that cars and bikes can negotiate, only many steps and winding five-foot-wide paved paths in old Artena where the Serafini family resides. It's no wonder the residents there are in good shape and live long—they walk everywhere. In so doing, they develop close affiliations with everyone, animals included, and come to know their fellow thousand or so residents in ways few people in modern urban and suburban habitats experience.

Sara feeds the mules carrots whenever they thump the front door with their muzzles, whether they are accompanied by their owner or not. The mules probably don't consider themselves as owned by Emilio, but rather as fellow neighborhood residents.

There is a new Artena less than two centuries old with nearly 13,000 residents on the more level plain at the base of this volcanic mountain range some one hundred miles northwest of Mount Vesuvius. Our destination was old Artena, known as Montefortino before 1873, which traces to the thirteenth century AD, and a few even older farms on the 2,500-foot mountain slopes above the town located anywhere the terrain isn't so steep that farm equipment would topple over.

The town was partially destroyed twice by papal armies in the early 1500s and totally razed in 1557 by troops loyal to Pope Paul IV, mostly because of political rivalries. When political differences finally simmered down, the town was entirely rebuilt.

The fourth and most recent destruction occurred during World War II, when Allied bombing missions obliterated old Artena's main church (one of four) where Nazi soldiers who controlled Italy after Mussolini resigned were thought to be hiding, along with several homes. Almost all of old Artena's structures that were damaged have been reconstructed, including the church that was demolished.

Somehow, old Artena has a capacity for survival. Maybe its survival can be attributed to strong feelings of community because everyone has to get to know and depend on one another in the village and surrounding countryside. A compelling urge infiltrates everyone to share in mutual survival functions, such as production and preparation of food, fuel, crafts that yield clothing, structures, education, medical care, and financial management, to name but a few essential ingredients for a self-sufficient community. Artena demonstrates an enduring agrarian imperative that its residents—and nearby farmers who are part of the community—all manifest. Most everyone has ties to the nearby farms, forests, and the Mediterranean Sea for food in local markets, wood for fuel, and foraging (mushrooms, wild boar, deer, and fowl abound, along with fresh and saltwater fish). Artena's sturdy buildings were designed to withstand earthquakes, wind, and water erosion over time, and are more able now to resist climate change than most modern buildings. Thick walls moderate temperature shifts to keep the inside cooler in the summer and warmer in the winter, thus requiring less supplemental mechanical apparatuses to create comfort.

There is no local police force in old Artena. It's unnecessary. Everyone knows each other's business; a suspicious person or event wouldn't go unnoticed or undiscussed. An amused town denizen commented that the residents looking out their windows are the police.

Sara and Stefano showed Marilyn and me local gathering spots, like the revered Catholic church at the top of the mountain that was spared during World War II, a coffee shop where the locals gather to exchange news and views, and a diverse farm on the more level mountaintop where the head of the family farming operation showed us fine Simmental and Romagnola cattle, geese, chickens, vegetable gardens, olive groves, vineyards, dairy ewes that supply the milk the multigenerational family makes into fine Pecorino cheese, and his prized Percheron stallion. Indeed, this stud would rival the Percheron sires that I've viewed at the Iowa State Fair draft horse shows, where the Percheron Horse Association of America periodically holds its national competition of the finest individuals, teams, and multihorse hitches in the breed. When we said "arrivederci," our agrarian host gave us a wheel of Pecorino cheese; he adamantly refused any payment and said in his broken English that our friendship was his reward.

Sara and Stefano then took us to the best restaurant we visited in Italy; it was in old Artena. While we dined there for three hours on a dozen courses and sampled local wines, the four of us discussed biourbanism and the content for the JBU article to which I subsequently contributed.

Biourbanism, I think, has a lot to contribute to how agriculture should be conducted in the foreseeable future, and possibly beyond. Biourbanism is a pretty esoteric subject matter to understand, but relevant to the future of mankind. In essence, biourbanism is a new field that connects the life sciences, such as biology and psychology, with integrated systems sciences, such as bioinformatics and ecology, into the design of ways that life might best exist in the future. According to the proponents of biourbanism, most life will be urban, hence the term *biourbanism*; however, it must integrate sustainable ways to produce the essentials needed to live, like food, homes, businesses, and environments that promote societal and political harmony, leading to survival in unpredictable future conditions. Biourbanism isn't only urban planning; it's world planning. It builds on concepts that all forms of life influence each other and proposes broad thinking and scientific investigation of how the entire life system works and can be managed optimally for the well-being of every person and all essential organisms.

The kind of thinking that biourbanism generates is macroscopic, incorporative, and dynamic, and it relates to understanding behavior and managing behavior optimally for the good of all—not just people, but all of life. When I proposed agricultural behavioral health as a new field that brought together agriculture with behavior science, I wasn't thinking that broadly, but now I can see its extensive implications.

Artena demonstrates biourbanism at its best. It retains its reliance on the surrounding agrarian community and centuries-old structures, but has added electricity, water, sewage disposal, and communication facilities (e.g., Wi-Fi). Artena integrates what I call the agrarian imperative into their biourban environment.

There is much more to learn from biourbanism that is important for future survival. By 2050, it's estimated that 70 percent of the world's 9.5 billion humans will live in cities. Much of agriculture will take place in urban settings and community living arrangements that incorporate towns and the surrounding countryside, such as Artena. Industrial-model agriculture will survive, but with closer scrutiny from consumers and governing entities, and only if it contributes to the survival of humans.

23

NEXT

The tragic deaths of five members of a large farm family on September 2, 1963, which officials concluded were brought about by the husband and father in the family, overwhelmed my little Germanic Catholic community and affected everyone, including my senior class of thirteen in which a classmate remained the oldest of five surviving children in the family. Now sixty years later, people in the community still talk about the event with uncertainty, sadness, and sympathy for the family. The forty-three-year-old farmer reportedly ended the lives of his wife and their infant daughter in the early morning hours before terminating his own life. Apparently, he scattered cyanide powder that was usually used to kill gophers onto his wife and their baby before shooting himself with a gun. According to one of many Iowa newspaper accounts, the oldest child in the family, a twenty-year-old daughter, was not immediately overwhelmed by cyanide gas from the toxic powder, for she drove the family car to summon the parish priest at the rectory approximately a half mile away, but she succumbed to cyanide poisoning a few days later. The next daughter, who was eighteen years old and had graduated from our school the previous May, was said to have called the county sheriff's office before she died from the cyanide gas while trying to resuscitate her mother. She and I were friends; we had talked together for well over an hour about three weeks earlier at the Shelby County Fair, where I was exhibiting market beef animals and other 4-H projects.

According to newspaper articles, an official investigation indicated the farmer had serious financial problems that threatened the loss of his family's farm. There was much speculation among local residents and in the news about the possible motives behind the family catastrophe, but no one knows for certain why the farmer undertook such devastating actions. The farmer is the only person who knows for sure, and even he may have been confused about his intentions. As I learned from my professional work with suicidal farmers, no one can fully and accurately judge a person who ends their life or the lives of others.

For many years I didn't know that this event would become a formative reason for me to become a psychologist. After completing high school, I attended Conception College, a seminary in Missouri, for three years, aspiring to become a priest. My parish and extended family had an extraordinarily high number of religious vocations. I viewed a pastor's role to entail much counseling, so I took every psychology course that this small Benedictine institution offered. Wanting to learn more about psychology, I attended the University of Colorado for summer school in 1967, where three of the courses I completed were about psychology and one was about the formation of public opinions. I felt like UC psychology professors reached out to me.

During that summer I also met Jane, a fellow guitar player whom I wrote about in a previous chapter. Jane had graduated earlier in June and was taking a couple graduate courses before launching a tour of Europe, during which she planned to stay overnight at youth hostels. I thought her plans were risky for an unaccompanied person, even though I had no experience on which to base my opinion. Jane turned the tables on me over a few beers at a pub that every past and present University of Colorado student knows well. She proclaimed, "You shouldn't be telling me this. You need to be a father in a different sense—a husband and parent; you should become a psychologist."

Although I dismissed Jane's recommendation at the time, I couldn't stop my internal debate during the next three days and nights as I completed my final course exams. I can still see it my mind: I walked to Chautauqua Park in southern Boulder around 4:00 a.m. during the third night and found a playground swing on which to rock back and forth while thinking and praying. *Oh, God, what am I supposed to do?*

I don't know what you want. Unless you give me a signal, I'm not going back to the seminary! Immediately, I felt at peace. This was my answer. I had been forcing myself to do something I wasn't meant to do. I had been pleasing my parents and what I thought were community expectations. I became a clinical psychologist. The rest of the story has already been written about in this book, except the part about how the demise of the local farm family influenced my life choice to assist troubled farmers and their kin. That connection came to me in 2009 during an interview with the director of the Iowa Psychological Association for an article she was writing. With insight that probably came from growing up on a Kansas farm and her relationship with her husband, a veterinarian who treated mostly farm animals, she asked me about the important events during my youth that influenced me to assist troubled farmers and farm families, as was the direction of much of my life's work. After a pause, I described for the first time what had happened to my classmate, her next older sister, and the family. Like many people in my community, and most farmers, I had buried a painful but significant event without fully realizing its importance in choosing my profession.

Much of my life's work as a psychologist has been to try to figure out why people farm, why they end their own lives in inordinate numbers—more than any other occupational group—as well as how to improve their behavioral well-being, their relationships with the land, their families, and their communities. Farmers know they can't control the weather, the markets for their agricultural products, or governmental farm policies, but they have considerable control over their behavior. My journey has been to understand the most important asset in agriculture, the people who farm. How do they view their own purposes in life? These efforts to shed light on how and why farmers behave as they do aren't meant to be intrusive into anyone's personal matters, including the family that bore the travail described prior, nor the residents of my community, nor anyone for that matter. We benefit from our own experiences and from science. Useful information needs to be available to everyone, so that we all learn more about managing our behavior.

The advances in understanding the behaviors of people who farm have at least two larger contexts: behavioral sciences and environmental sciences. These areas of scientific inquiry are expanding rapidly. The behavioral sciences encompass a relatively new approach to conceptualizing the future of people living on this planet and all life as we know it. The first behavioral science, psychology, and subsequent others, such as sociology and political science, are efforts to understand important dimensions of human actions. All these sciences are about as advanced as physics and chemistry were a hundred years ago. The new fields of behavioral genetics and bioinformatics are offspring mostly of new scientific arenas: genetics and information technology, combined with behavioral science. Nonetheless, since psychology emerged in the late 1800s, curious investigators and behavioral health care providers have figured out a lot about how to measure and manipulate behavior. To illustrate, behaviors can be measured quantitatively by their duration and time of occurrence, frequency, intensity, what precipitates their occurrence, and what follows thereafter, among many other variables that are just beginning to be understood. Behaviors also can be evaluated qualitatively, for instance, by such methods as naturalistic observations, structured interviews, or self-reported ratings made by the subject or by trained external observers who indicate their best judgments. Stated simply, quantitative measurements are about cause-and-effect parameters, whereas qualitative measurements are about the context and reasons for behaving. Both approaches are necessary to advance knowledge about behavior.

Along with behavioral scientists, professional providers of behavioral health care, and other insightful observers of events have learned something about how to manipulate human behaviors for therapeutic purposes, formation of opinions, marketing, and sometimes with selfish and unethical intent. An illustration of a therapeutic purpose is the Centers for Disease Control and Prevention's recommendation to undertake management of the behaviors associated with attention deficit hyperactivity disorder as the first treatment approach, and to include anti-hyperactivity medications only when teachable lifelong skills are insufficient to achieve the desired outcome. It's becoming common for people in advanced countries to consult psychologists and other behavioral health professionals to improve their business accomplishments and personal well-being.

The fields of ethics, history, marketing, behavioral genetics, and bioinformatics, among others, are advancing the knowledge base about the benefits and disadvantages of efforts to manipulate behavior. Understanding how to manipulate the behaviors of other organisms lags behind the manipulation of humans' behaviors. A key principle that is gradually becoming elucidated is that manipulations of behavior have always occurred throughout the continuum of life by actions that all organisms undertake, and which humans are barely learning how to control. Clearly, we don't understand enough about how human actions affect our planetary ecosystem, illustrated, for example, by the problems of global warming to which humans have contributed. That's where the environmental sciences come into play. Every behavioral event that occurs affects our environment and the course of history.

Just as all events of a physical nature, such as exposure to a warming planet, reverberate throughout the entire ecosystem of life, so do behavioral events. How any organism behaves affects the entire continuum of life. It's kind of like the proverb about how an unsecured nail on the shoe of a horse ultimately determined the outcome of a war in the Middle Ages, but in a behavioral sense. A farrier failed to secure a nail in a horse's shoe, after which the horse stumbled, which caused the knight riding the horse to fall, enabling an opposing warrior to slay the fallen soldier, which influenced the eventual outcome of the battle, and ultimately, the history of the countries involved in the conflict. All these events have quantitative and qualitative behavioral components, and they are not only physical events that happened to occur. These events involved the choice and behavior of the farrier, but it must be remembered that the knight chose his horse and to enter his country's army; the warrior chose to slay the fallen soldier, which assisted the successful warrior and his fellow soldiers in defeating their opponents in battle. Ultimately, the decision of the losing army to surrender and what happened thereafter were also choices by the losers and the victors. Generally, the higher the organism on the totem pole of life, the greater its influence over the behaviors of other organisms, but that isn't always the case, as we witnessed with infections such as the COVID-19 virus and its mutated forms. We must never overlook the influence of the behaviors of the tiniest organism on the full spectrum of life.

Given what we know about agricultural behavioral health, how does optimal management of behavior become key to the survival of farmers as they determine strategies for success within a complex, competitive environment? How farmers choose to manage themselves as producers—as well as how they assist their employees, livestock, and crops with behavior management—are critical to the outcome of the farming operation. Swedish researchers C. Lunner Kolstrup and J. Hultgren reported in the *Journal of Agricultural Safety and Health* in 2011 that the behavioral well-being of farm managers and their workers affects the profitability of the farming operation: livestock handlers who rated themselves as unhappy and troubled required more visits by veterinarians to their dairies than farmers who rated themselves as well-adjusted, thereby keeping expenses up and profits down. Dairies where managers and workers rated their well-being negatively had higher somatic cell counts in the milk their cows produced, thereby lowering the value of the milk. When the behavioral well-being of poorly adjusted farm operators and employees improved through the implementation of management-worker discussions or counseling, the number of veterinary consultations diminished and the somatic cell count of milk from the dairies decreased, thereby increasing their economic livelihood.

Farmers' choices can affect crop production as well. Producers can choose to manually or mechanically hoe weeds that compete with their crops, whether by applying herbicides that kill certain weeds and planting crops that have been genetically modified to tolerate herbicides that are supposed to kill all plants except the desired crop, sometimes by cultivating or hoeing out competing weeds, or ignoring some or all of the weeds. Depending on the approach that the farmer chooses, the outcomes are different for their crops, their farming operation, and the entire planet.

The most important context for understanding the behavior of farm people is their closeness to the land. To farmers, the land means everything. The soil, with its capacity to bear crops, is chief among what they need to enact their agrarian imperative. The agrarian imperative theory explains why people farm and why they sometimes cling to their land and resources to the point that they sacrifice themselves, which impacts the lives of others who depend on them.

The agrarian imperative theory builds on Robert Ardrey's hypothesis that a territorial drive underlies competition and conflict within—and among—most higher organisms. All species strive to acquire the most favorable territory on which to live and reproduce. The agrarian imperative theory explains much more. People farm because a powerful genetic code, acquired through selection of the fittest, impels agricultural producers to furnish essentials for life in the form of food, fibers for clothing and shelter, and fuels, as well as to instinctively protect their land and other necessary assets so they can carry out these inclinations. The agrarian imperative drive instills farmers to endure severe adversity, to cling desperately to their farmland when its loss is threatened, to undertake unusual risks in seeking solutions to threats, and to trust their own judgment more than anyone else's advice.

Our agrarian imperative drive was refined through selection of the most successful agricultural producers over many generations. The intensity of the drive varies from person to person. Successful farmers today possess the greatest propensities of any generation of humans to farm. Advantageous behaviors gradually become encoded through repetition and beneficial mutations into heritable DNA. The behaviors associated with their agrarian imperative can work against farmers' well-being when they become overwhelmed from prolonged stress, anxiety, fatigue, and depression, which sometimes results in suicidal—and, less occasionally, homicidal—urges. It's not surprising that Wendy Ringgenberg and her colleagues found that suicide occurred more commonly in the agricultural workplace than any other occupational workplace. Ringgenberg analyzed U.S. Department of Labor data collected from 1992 to 2010; their findings were reported in the May 2017 issue of the *Journal of Rural Health*.

Failure to reach out for help when needed exacerbates anxiety and fatigue, and enhances depression and suicidal thinking. Agricultural producers may also choose to avoid thinking about physical and psychological pain by relying solely on personal judgment, and sometimes by consuming alcohol or other mind-altering substances, to temporarily block psychological, physical, and monetary stressors. The outcomes of avoiding beneficial relationships with people who can give good advice and emotional support too often result in more severe anxiety, depression, and even plans for suicide. Anxiety, self-blame, and depression were identified as the most prominent factors associated with risk of suicide among farmers, according to a 2021 study of six hundred midwestern farmers by Andrea Bjornestad and her colleagues in the *International Journal of Environmental Research and Public Health*.

There is a growing body of resources for farmers and their families to manage behaviors to handle stress, like that suffered by the family mentioned earlier. One of the most beneficial resources to assist distressed farmers is the Farm and Ranch Stress Assistance Network (FRSAN), which is based on research undertaken by my colleagues and me at AgriWellness from 2000 to 2014. We worked closely with our partners in seven states (Iowa, Kansas, Minnesota, Nebraska, North Dakota, South Dakota, and Wisconsin) to determine the best programs and practices that assisted farmers during stressful times, and when they wanted more information about managing stress proactively. FRSAN is currently funded as part of the U.S. Farm Bill. These programs and practices include: (1) telephone and email hotlines in agricultural areas of the United States that respond to inquiries about how to obtain counseling and education tailored to the agricultural community; (2) community education to teach farmers and local communities about detecting distress in themselves and others, where to access professional counseling suited to farmers, and how farmers can manage their behavior to reduce their own stress and maximize optimal decision making about farming concerns; (3) follow-up counseling made available at no cost to distressed farmers and their families, and from professional counselors who have an understanding of agricultural behavioral health; (4) professional healthcare providers trained in the basic tenets of agricultural behavioral health; and (5) four regional centers created around the United States to provide technical support to state and local partners to develop culturally suitable services and to evaluate them for their effectiveness.

As new knowledge accrues, the emerging field of agricultural behavioral health is already becoming integrated into agricultural curricula, from high school vocational agriculture coursework to college and graduate degree programs in agriculture and related fields, such as agricultural medicine. It's likely that behavioral science and behavior management will be integrated into all types of business and health care education, because the principles are applicable in any discipline that entails training in business administration, human services, communication, ecology, and in realms that can't even currently be presumed. Behavioral sciences are on the cusp of much greater understanding of the processes of life. There will be a huge expansion in the applications of behavioral knowledge in the fields of agriculture, business, medicine, and more.

The media also have promoted the availability of information suited to the agricultural population about how to manage stress. Farm radio and television programs broadcast useful research finding and recommendations; farming magazines and newspapers regularly print articles about the subject geared to their readers; and social media users spread useful information among followers. The negative stigma among farmers about reaching out for help with deeply personal issues is diminishing.

According to the CDC, the suicide rate of U.S. farmers and the U.S. population in general dropped during 2019 and 2020, which were also key years for dealing with COVID-19, but data were not available from all agricultural states. Additional follow-up data are needed.

Through personal experience, I learned the shortcomings of overwork and thinking I could solve problems mostly by myself. As I wrote earlier in this book about these and additional formative events that brought me closer to what I feel is the right direction in life, I didn't clarify sufficiently how closeness to the land has always been a motivating factor in my life, and Marilyn's life as well. On December 14, 1975, during the second of my five years as an assistant professor of psychology at the University of Virginia, I began writing a private journal. I didn't remember what I wrote during our "Virginia days" and during our first couple years after moving to our farm in Iowa in 1979 until I came across my journal while we were packing to move to our next phase of life in a Pella, Iowa, flat in December 2022. I had written as my first journal entry: "The thoughts in this journal are mostly private honest feelings, longings, and urges. The compelling motive for this journal is to record the process of returning to the land after a good twelve years away from the land. I am seeking for myself and family a country life with the land as a medium for our search for heaven, with the land as a medium of our livelihood, and with the land as the inspiration for our spiritual concentration." Over forty-six years ago I had entitled my journal "The Return to the Land." Something must have been going on in my mind that was emerging from the recesses of my genetic makeup and experiences.

Can the pain that my high school classmate, her family, and our entire community felt, and still don't fully understand, be prevented? The recent, improved openness to behavioral health care is a start to more advances that may help prevent suicide and reduce the emotional pain of personal and family struggles. The advances in understanding behavior in a scientific sense complement personal formative experiences that guide the direction of our lives. For me, love of the land, agriculture, and caring for the behavioral health of farmers, as well as our environment, start from my heart, in a motivational sense. They feel right to me and closer to the purposes for which I exist. How can this imperative be transformed into future steps that benefit all agricultural producers? I know a few things about environmental health, and I have learned a few more things about human behavioral health, particularly the behavior of farmers and how its derivatives occur in all of us. My next book on the topic of agricultural behavioral health must outline this more comprehensively.

MIKE ROSMANN'S LIFE'S WORK

Mike Rosmann redefined the image of the farmer from that of a man in overalls, chewing on a grass stem, to that of a person with an immense knowledge base and the intelligence required to run a successful farming enterprise. It took a credible messenger with a real farming background, practical hands-on experience, and the necessary academic training to interpret to the nonagricultural community such matters as bushels per acre, pulling a calf, and why farmers love their land so dearly that sometimes they choose suicide rather than to surrender their farm.

Rosmann has been that unusual person who could impact both the academic understanding of farmer stress and suicide while successfully reaching out to the farmers themselves with practical solutions to alter behaviors to bring about a healthy outcome for themselves and their families. With a PhD in clinical psychology, Rosmann became a professor of psychology at the University of Virginia but chose—with his wife, a nursing professor—to move to Iowa with their two young children to operate a family farm and to help fellow farmers with serious mental health issues that they often wouldn't talk about, except to a fellow farmer who understood their travails.

Educating the people who provide assistance to the farming community has been integral to Rosmann's mission. This has included those who establish government policies, funding, and programs, as well as farm families themselves, and their communities. He was asked to join the University of Iowa Department of Occupational and Environmental Health as adjunct professor. The research and model programs that Rosmann initiated became the foundation of federal, state, and local efforts to provide behavioral health care support, such as the Farm and Ranch Stress Assistance Network. His many articles and workshops have been instrumental in the way farmers and nonfarmers now talk about their mental health, and the establishment of a new field, agricultural behavioral health. His agrarian imperative theory is the most compelling explanation for why people farm.

Rosmann's background, at one point training to become a priest, sensitized him to farmers' responsibilities as stewards of the land and the historical connection to raising food for life. His appreciation and commitment to farmers is influenced by his spiritual vision. Rosmann is almost as passionate about fly-fishing as he is about helping agricultural producers.